GROUP
DECISION
MAKING

SOME PAST VOLUMES IN THE
SAGE FOCUS EDITIONS

8. **Controversy** (Second Edition)
   Dorothy Nelkin
9. **Battered Women**
   Donna M. Moore
10. **Criminology**
    Edward Sagarin
12. **Improving Evaluations**
    Lois-ellin Datta and Robert Perloff
13. **Images of Information**
    Jon Wagner
16. **Improving Policy Analysis**
    Stuart S. Nagel
17. **Power Structure Research**
    G. William Domhoff
18. **Aging and Society**
    Edgar F. Borgatta and Neil G. McCluskey
21. **The Black Woman**
    La Frances Rodgers-Rose
22. **Making Bureaucracies Work**
    Carol H. Weiss and Allen H. Barton
23. **Radical Criminology**
    James A. Inciardi
24. **Dual-Career Couples**
    Fran Pepitone-Rockwell
25. **Policy Implementation**
    John Brigham and Don W. Brown
26. **Contemporary Black Thought**
    Molefi Kete Asante and Abdulai S. Vandi
27. **History and Crime**
    James A. Inciardi and Charles E. Faupel
28. **The Future of Education**
    Kathryn Cirincione-Coles
29. **Improving Schools**
    Rolf Lehming and Michael Kane
30. **Knowledge and Power in a Global Society**
    William M. Evan
31. **Black Men**
    Lawrence E. Gary
32. **Major Criminal Justice Systems**
    George F. Cole, Stanislaw J. Frankowski,
    and Marc G. Gertz
33. **Analyzing Electoral History**
    Jerome M. Clubb, William H. Flanigan,
    and Nancy H. Zingale
34. **Assessing Marriage**
    Erik E. Filsinger and Robert A. Lewis
35. **The Knowledge Cycle**
    Robert F. Rich
36. **Impacts of Racism on White Americans**
    Benjamin P. Bowser and Raymond G. Hunt
39. **Environmental Criminology**
    Paul J. Brantingham and
    Patricia L. Brantingham
40. **Governing Through Courts**
    Richard A. L. Gambitta, Marlynn L. May, and
    James C. Foster
41. **Black Families**
    Harriette Pipes McAdoo

43. **Aging and Retirement**
    Neil G. McCluskey and Edgar F. Borgatta
44. **Modern Industrial Cities**
    Bruce M. Stave
45. **Lives in Stress**
    Deborah Belle
46. **Family Relationships**
    F. Ivan Nye
47. **Mexico's Political Economy**
    Jorge I. Dominguez
48. **Strategies of Political Inquiry**
    Elinor Ostrom
49. **Reforming Social Regulation**
    LeRoy Graymer and Frederick Thompson
50. **Cuba**
    Jorge I. Dominguez
51. **Social Control**
    Jack P. Gibbs
52. **Energy and Transport**
    George H. Daniels, Jr., and Mark H. Rose
53. **Global Policy Studies**
    Gary K. Bertsch
54. **Job Stress and Burnout**
    Whiton Stewart Paine
55. **Missing Elements in Political Inquiry**
    Judith A. Gillespie and Dina A. Zinnes
56. **Two Paychecks**
    Joan Aldous
57. **Social Structure and Network Analysis**
    Peter V. Marsden and Nan Lin
58. **Socialist States in the World-System**
    Christopher K. Chase-Dunn
59. **Age or Need?**
    Bernice L. Neugarten
60. **The Costs of Evaluation**
    Marvin C. Alkin and Lewis C. Solmon
61. **Aging in Minority Groups**
    R. L. McNeely and John N. Colen
62. **Contending Approaches to World System
    Analysis**
    William R. Thompson
63. **Organization Theory and Public Policy**
    Richard H. Hall and Robert E. Quinn
64. **Family Relationships in Later Life**
    Timothy H. Brubaker
65. **Communication and Organizations**
    Linda L. Putnam and Michael E. Pacanowsky
66. **Competence in Communication**
    Robert N. Bostrom
67. **Avoiding Communication**
    John Daly and James C. McCroskey
68. **Ethnography in Educational Evaluation**
    David M. Fetterman
69. **Group Decision Making**
    Walter C. Swap and Associates

edited
by
Walter C. Swap
and
Associates

Hugo Bedau	**Percy H. Hill**
Richard A. Chechile	**Sheldon Krimsky**
John A. Dunn, Jr.	**Jeffrey Z. Rubin**
John S. Gibson	**Bradbury Seasholes**

GROUP DECISION MAKING

HM
73
.G76
1984

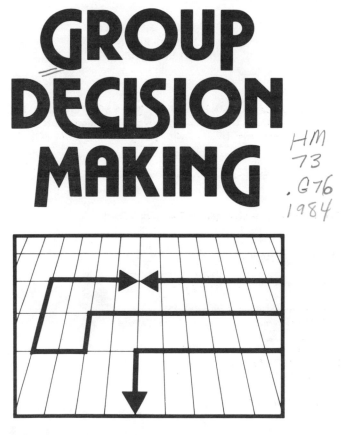

 SAGE PUBLICATIONS Beverly Hills London New Delhi

Copyright © 1984 by The Center for the Study of Decision Making,
Tufts University

For information address:

SAGE Publications, Inc.
275 South Beverly Drive
Beverly Hills, California 90212

SAGE Publications India Pvt. Ltd.
C-236 Defence Colony
New Delhi 110 024, India

SAGE Publications Ltd
28 Banner Street
London EC1Y 8QE, England

Printed in the United States of America

Library of Congress Cataloging in Publication Data

Main entry under title:

Group decision making.

(Sage library of social research ; 155)
1. Decision-making, Group. I. Swap, Walter C.
II. Series.
HM73.G76   1984   302.3   83-24763
ISBN 0-8039-2137-3
ISBN 0-8039-2138-1 (pbk.)

FIRST PRINTING

LK 12-21-84

CONTENTS

Foreword
       Jean Mayer   7

Preface
       Walter C. Swap   9

1. *Introduction*
       Jeffrey Z. Rubin   15

2. *How Groups Make Decisions:*
   A Social Psychological Perpective
       Walter C. Swap   45

3. *Destructive Effects of Groups on Individuals*
       Walter C. Swap   69

4. *Logical Foundations*
   for a Fair and Rational Method of Voting
       Richard A. Chechile   97

5. *Ethical Aspects of Group Decision Making*
       Hugo Bedau   115

6. *Social Risk Assessment and Group Process*
       Sheldon Krimsky   151

7. *Choosing Presidential Nominees:*
   Decision Making on a Large Scale
       Bradbury Seasholes   181

8. *Group Decisions and Foreign Policy*
   John S. Gibson   215

9. *Decisions Involving the Corporate Environment*
   Percy H. Hill   251

10. *Organizational Decision Making*
    John A. Dunn, Jr.   280

Index   311

About the Authors   315

GROUP DECISION MAKING

FOREWORD

This is the second text to come from Tufts University's multidisciplinary Center for the Study of Decision Making. The first text was an introduction to the techniques and goals of this very new discipline. In this volume, the focus is on group decision making—not, in many minds, a particularly useful or successful activity. After all, the most popular definition of a camel is a "horse designed by a committee."

It need not be this way. Indeed, for the future of our society and the world at large it had better not. However, both as individuals and as citizens we are thus far not very good at analyzing complex situations and arriving at reasonable decisions on action. It was this perception that motivated us at Tufts to set up a general course on decision making for undergraduates and to establish the Center for the Study of Decision Making.

The United States is only just beginning to merge from a single-issue period, following what is known as the Vietnam era. Indeed, at present the most intense pressures on our local and national legislators come from a multiplicity of small organizations that are totally immersed in one issue, which they see as of overriding importance, to the exclusion of all other considerations. At colleges and universities, students and in particular some faculty members who were 1960s activists tend to seize upon an issue and attempt to deal with it in isolation, as if there were no offsetting conditions, costs, interests, or principles that ought to be looked at rather carefully before actions are advocated.

This is not a single-issue world. Even when we are faced with one problem—for example, the Vietnam war or nuclear proliferation—that seems to fill the horizon, it is still well to remember the caution of H. L. Mencken: "For every complex problem there is one simple, obvious solution—and it is wrong."

Whether the problems to be addressed are local or international, we live in interdependent, interwoven communities. It has been truly said that modern technology and communications have made the earth itself a small, global village. If we are to continue to live together in peace, if not in harmony—if (one can hope) we are to improve the conditions under which we all live—then we must learn to deliberate and work together. Wise group decisions are as crucial to community life as wise individual decisions are to personal welfare.

In Tufts's courses on decision making, we are attempting to restore a sense of the complexity of life as well as to give students (and faculty members) tools to arrive at more rational, if more complex, decisions. They should be aware that an objective is not the same thing as a policy, and that the group decision-making process should consider the context in which policies are enunciated, but does not have to dictate every single action that should go to their implementation.

The three major things we hope that we learn in these courses, and that the reader will learn in this and our first book, are

- First, that every decision has its price, and that any decision ought to take into account a great many variables.

- Second, that there are a number of alternative solutions to every problem, and that some decisions, which at first glance seem the most desirable, are precluded because of the prohibitive cost of other factors.

- Third, that it is usually necessary to arrive at *some* course of action. Decisions have to take place, despite the fact that information is never as good or as complete as you would like it to be. One can only estimate as far as possible what costs might be incurred, what situations might develop as the result of carrying out one decision or another. Assessment and reassessment are essential components of the continuing process of decision making.

More particularly, it is our hope that this volume will leave the reader with a clearer understanding of the ways in which group decision making can avoid designing a camel for Grand Prix jumping, and a thoroughbred horse for long desert travel.

—*Jean Mayer, President*
Tufts University

PREFACE

In the fall of 1977, an interdisciplinary team of Tufts University professors began offering an innovative undergraduate course in individual decision making. To facilitate the teaching of that course, and to provide a model for similar courses at other universities, a text was developed by the teaching staff (Hill et al., *Making Decisions: A Multidisciplinary Introduction*). In his Foreword to that text, Jean Mayer, President of Tufts, wrote:

> I firmly believe that the future of our civilization and of the human race will depend on whether we, citizens of the greatest democracy on earth, members of the most highly developed technological society in the world, have the wisdom and the courage to make and to carry out the right decisions. Individual achievements and the successful pursuit of happiness will continue to be dependent, obviously, on individuals making the right decisions for themselves.

The need for understanding the decision-making process and developing individual decision-making skills is no less vital today. However, the decisions that affect the future of our civilization and of the human race are, increasingly, made in a *group* context. Similarly, in our daily lives many of the decisions that we make or that affect us are not the products of individual deliberations, but rather emerge from family caucuses, advisory boards, judicial panels, legislative bodies, government agencies, and other kinds of groups. The study of individual decision making has limited utility in understanding how these groups make decisions. Group processes are not simply extensions and elaborations of the processes that characterize individuals; when people convene in groups, a new entity is created, with its own dynamics and complexities, and "its" decisions cannot be predicted even from a thorough knowledge of its constituent members.

9

With these issues in mind, a second group of Tufts professors (partially overlapping the membership of the first group) began meeting during the summer of 1981 to plan an undergraduate course in group decision making and to develop an accompanying text. The new course had two basic goals: first, to provide an undergraduate audience with a multidisciplinary perspective on group decision making—to highlight not only the different points of view brought to bear by such fields as psychology, management, and political science, but also to demonstrate their fundamental similarities. Second, the course was designed to integrate theoretical and applied orientations; in order to accomplish this, the course instructors (book chapter authors) provided not only experimental research and theories of group process, but, wherever possible, case studies of groups wrestling with difficult decisions, coupled with practical suggestions for improving the process of making group decisions—and, by extension, the decisions themselves.

By the spring of 1982 semester, the course was ready to roll. Typed chapters were photo offset and shamelessly presented to students as a textbook. And while the group suffered many of the pathologies documented in the text itself, the course was a success, as measured by student feedback. Thus encouraged, the course and book went into a "second edition" in the spring of 1983. For, despite the best efforts of the first "group decision-making group," a course taught or a book written by nine people may suffer the fate of the proverbial spoiled broth. Based on our first semester's experiences, the suggestions of students, the observations of one another, and the astute comments of the course coordinator, Susan Carlisle, appropriate revisions were made. Chapters were rewritten and placed into a more natural sequence. Four "clusters" of chapters were organized. The authors of chapters within each cluster discussed their material with one another, and made special efforts to accentuate the natural connections. The result, we believe, is greater structure and continuity in the book as a whole.

Finally, it should be noted that the book is self-contained, and does not require an accompanying troupe of nine Tufts professors to produce an effective course in group decision making. The multidisciplinary approach is designed to highlight similarities and commonalities in all group decision-making settings, rather than to argue for the uniqueness of our particular points of view. The structure by which we believe this is accomplished is as follows:

The first cluster is comprised of three chapters written by social psychologists. Chapter 1 is an Introduction, written by Jeffrey

Rubin, Director of the Tufts Center for the Study of Decision Making. A conceptual framework is developed, basic terms are defined, and the question of how to assess the quality of both group decisions and the process resulting in decisions is addressed. Those factors that promote quality—group composition, leadership, nature of the task, and decision rules and processes—are discussed. As with many of the book's chapters, Chapter 1 concludes with specific prescriptions to improve the quality of group decision making, in this case a sequence of six steps that groups should take to improve their decisions.

Chapters 2 and 3, by a social psychologist and the book's editor, Walter Swap, provide a social psychological orientation to the study of group decision making. Chapter 2, "How Groups Make Decisions," discusses those factors that influence group decisions: member characteristics, nature of the task, group cohesiveness, size, channels of communication, and leadership. Prescriptions for improving group decision making, based on each of these factors, are discussed. Chapter 3, "Destructive Effects of Groups on Individuals," examines three pathologies inherent in many groups: the tendency to loaf or shunt responsibility onto others; the possibility of "losing oneself in the group," or ceasing to act as a thinking individual; and pressures in many groups to arrive at a consensus before alternatives are adequately considered—the "groupthink" phenomenon. The chapter concludes with a consideration of how groups react to "deviants" or members with minority opinions, and conversely, how minorities can influence their groups.

Cluster 2 includes three chapters with a common focus on the fairness and rationality of group decisions. Chapter 4, "Logical Foundations for a Fair and Rational Method of Voting," by mathematical psychologist Richard Chechile, considers those groups that reach formal decisions by some voting procedure. Some of our familiar voting schemes (e.g., plurality voting) are shown to include flaws that can lead to irrational or unfair decisions. The chapter includes an extended treatment of how voting procedures in groups should be conducted in order to make them more rational and fair, although it is acknowledged that these twin goals may never be perfectly achieved.

Chapter 5, "Ethical Aspects of Group Decision Making," is by a moral philosopher, Hugo Bedau. Just as group decisions differ qualitatively from those made by individuals, so too do different ethical issues arise when groups convene from those that arise when individuals engage in private deliberations. The chapter includes an extensive analysis of the ethical issues involved in the group decision of whether to divest an institution's stock holdings in corporations doing business in South Africa. There is also further discussion of several voting schemes, emphasizing their ethical aspects. The ethical perspective is important in both group process and the group decisions themselves, and the chapter concludes with specific rules-of-thumb for making group process and decisions more ethically sound.

Chapter 6, "Social Risk Assessment and Group Process," by urban and environmental analyst Sheldon Krimsky, is a detailed examination of a specific type of group process: that in which scientists and ordinary citizens convene to assess the risks inherent in new technologies, and to recommend policy regarding these risks. Using the recent recombinant-DNA (gene splicing) controversy as a case study, the chapter examines issues of rationality (can groups arrive at logical decisions in the complex area of risk assessment?) and ethics (how may such groups ensure a fair process? e.g., by avoiding conflicts of interest in their members). While the focus is clearly on groups assessing technical risks, the chapter provides solid advice for any group in which experts and nonexperts must reach joint decisions.

In the third cluster, Chapters 7 and 8 examine the influence of groups in national politics and international relations, respectively. In Chapter 7, "Choosing Presidential Nominees," political scientist Bradbury Seasholes analyzes those group processes that result in the nomination of presidential candidates: primaries (including hypothetical national primaries) and conventions. The practical and ethical merits of these processes are examined in detail. The nominating convention is discussed at length as an example of the unique types of group dynamics that occur in groups characterized by large size, complexity, importance, and violent passions.

Political scientist John Gibson (Chapter 8: "Group Decisions and Foreign Policy") focuses on the extraordinarily complex arena of group inputs to foreign policy and specific foreign policy decisions. While it is made clear that the president usually makes the final decisions, literally thousands of groups have been created to aid or influence those decisions. Furthermore, the extent of group influences on presidential decisions depends on how routine, protracted, or critical the situation is. These issues are illustrated with a recent series of foreign policy decisions involving the construction of a natural gas pipeline from the Soviet Union to Western Europe.

In the final cluster, Chapters 9 and 10 continue this focus on the individual who is responsible for making decisions, but who calls upon groups to aid in the process. In Chapter 9, "Decisions Involving the Corporate Environment," Percy Hill, an engineer and management consultant, analyzes the uses of groups in business organizations. Groups aid corporate executives in developing ideas, creating new products, and marketing those products. Several decision-making aids, including decision matrices and PERT networks, are discussed in detail.

In Chapter 10, "Organizational Decision Making," Tufts University Vice President John Dunn focuses even more sharply on the person within an organization who is responsible for making decisions. A detailed case study of a fictitious group of college administrators, convened to assist the Executive Vice President in making a decision about construction of a new library, is used as a springboard for analysis of the group process in organizations. In common with Chapters 8 and 9, administrative decisions tend to be made by individuals, but in close collaboration with groups. The chapter discusses when groups should be convened, what they can and cannot do, and how the skillful administrator can use groups to improve the quality of decisions in an organization.

This, then, is the general structure of our book, proceeding from a presentation of general principles and assumptions about the nature of group decision making to the analysis of group decision making in settings that are highly varied and complex. The wise application of both general principles and more specific prescriptions should go far in aiding readers in their own group decisions.

Finally, this book has benefited from the assistance of many people. Several authors received grants from the Center for the Study of Decision Making at Tufts; these funds are gratefully acknowledged. Our colleagues, Susan Carlisle, who coordinated the group decision-making course, and Seymour Bellin, who guest-lectured in the course and attended many of our planning meetings, have made major contributions to both the course and this book. Skilled secretarial assistance was provided by the Center's secretary, Gail Shulman, and Psychology Department secretaries Eileen Howard and Madeline Amico. To all these people, we extend a grateful "thank you."

CHAPTER 1

INTRODUCTION

Jeffrey Z. Rubin

   The time has come for the twenty members of the XYZ Society's Executive Council to vote on the proposed budget for the coming year. The Society's Treasurer has carefully drafted a proposed budget along with several voting options: total approval, total disapproval, or partial approval (support for certain specified line items, but not others). One week after the proposed budget has been mailed out, the Society's executive secretary places phone calls throughout the country to each of the twenty board members. Each member is asked to indicate his or her vote by phone, the results are tallied, and the Society's President eventually announces that the budget has been approved.

*   *   *

   The jurors are led into a room, seated around a large table; the door is locked behind them, and their deliberations begin. At the request of the bailiff, the jurors' first decision is the selection of a single person (the foreman) as their spokesman. Once this decision has been made, the jury proceeds to weigh the evidence in the case before them, and to move toward a verdict. After some discussion, the foreman requests that a written straw vote be taken in order to see the direction in which the jurors are leaning. After several hours of additional discussion, a unanimous decision is reached.

*   *   *

   The corporate executives of a major automobile manufacturing company have a problem on their hands. Within the last year, a major foreign corporate rival has introduced a car with a radically different design that is threatening to erode further an already badly deteriorating sales picture. After calling the meeting to order, the corporation's chief executive officer proposes that the partici-

pants begin their work by brainstorming—generating as many alternative responses, designs, and plans as possible, without any effort to support or criticize the ideas proposed. At a subsequent meeting, the CEO suggests a plan for wading through the alternatives that were brainstormed previously, deciding among them, and proceeding to develop a plan for the implementation of the chosen course of action.

* * *

Ten young men and women have been invited to a weekend retreat in order to take part in a T-group: a "training group" designed to teach participants about the nature of group process and leadership. Although there is ostensibly someone in charge—the so-called trainer—this person sits silently throughout the T-group's initial three-hour meeting without uttering a word. After adjusting to the shock of the leader's unusual behavior, the total absence of a structured agenda to guide them, and the long silences between individual comments and questions, the participants begin to talk with one another a bit more easily. Even as people begin to find out about one another, a little bit at a time, the collective attention of the participants continues to be directed to a single major issue: What should the group do? By the end of the first three-hour session, no clear answer to this query has yet been obtained.

Each of the four preceding illustrations describes an instance of a group whose work involves some form of decision making. Groups come in all shapes, sizes, compositions, and functions. Group decisions, similarly, differ enormously in their nature, antecedents, consequences, and overall quality. The goal of this book is to describe, as systematically as possible, the nature of the group decision-making process and to formulate prescriptions for increasing the quality of these decisions.

Some Preliminary Distinctions

Although we regard definitions more as demarcation signposts than rigid conceptual straitjackets, it may be useful to begin our analysis of group decisions by indicating what we mean by a group, a decision, and finally a group decision.

A *group* may be thought of as two or more people, existing in an arrangement that permits some degree of interaction, and sharing some sense of identity as members. Such a working definition leaves open the matter of how large an aggregate can be and still be denoted as a group. Similarly, the requirement of interaction is meant to subsume arrangements such as a jury, T-group, or corporate executive meeting—but also social arrangements such as the XYZ Society's Executive Council, where face-to-face contact is absent and interaction among group members is minimal. Finally, the requirement of some shared sense of identity is broad enough to include collectives whose individual members regard themselves as minimally part of some group—even if the nature of that group, its functions, and purposes are entirely unclear (to wit, the T-group example)—but also those social arrangements whose participants have a clear sense of collective mission.

In short, our working definition of a group is broad enough to encompass the following social arrangements: a trial jury, a platoon of soldiers, the members of a country club, the Supreme Court, the Congress, the National Security Council, a therapy group, a mountain climbing expedition, the Ku Klux Klan, the local Rotary Club, a tenant's organization, a youth gang, a family, a political party, an institutional review board, a board of trustees, a team of foreign policy advisors, a risk assessment board, a citizen advisory panel, a college fraternity, and a New England town meeting.

A *decision* may be defined most simply as the choice between two or more alternatives. In practice more than two alternatives are often involved, but all the typical problems of decision making arise when at least two alternatives exist. Similarly, although the choice between alternatives typically leads to some form of behavior that is consistent with that choice (for example, pulling the polling booth lever for the candidate one prefers), a decision does not require such consistency. Finally, the choice between alternatives need not be based on any rational process of assessment and evaluation, even though there is much to be said in favor of such rational processes.

A *group decision*, then, is naturally defined by means of the preceding definitions as a choice between two or more alternatives made by group members, or by a group's leader in consultation with the membership. If neither of these conditions is satisfied, then even though a group exists and a decision has been made, we will not characterize such a choice among alternatives as a group decision.

There are several implications of this definition that we hasten to point out. For one thing, if an individual group member makes a decision in such a way that the fact of membership is taken into account in making this decision, then this does not suffice to make the decision a group decision; if it did, then the decision by a member of a country club to postpone a vacation in order not to miss the club's next meeting would count as a group decision! Similarly, if an individual group member makes a decision that affects the interests of the rest of the group, that decision does not count as a group decision; if it did, then an individual's decision to resign from a Board of Trustees would be a group decision! No, a group decision requires choice among alternatives either by the group as a whole, a subset of the group, or an individual who, in interaction with the membership, serves as the group's agent.

But how can a group, as a whole, be said to make a decision—let alone be held responsible for its consequences? As the philosopher among us likes to point out, no group has two of the distinctive features of an individual: "organic embodiment" and self-consciousness. A group of persons, no matter how intimate the association among them, cannot ever do what most of its members can easily do—give birth or smile or feel insulted. Even so, groups clearly can act (witness the behavior of a lynch mob) and can be thought of for many purposes as persons who are responsible for their actions; for example, they can be sued, go bankrupt, or be held liable for injuries. Moreover, groups can even do some things that no individuals can do—such as merge with another group. It is plausible, therefore, to analyze and evaluate a group's decisions as those of a unitary—if highly complex and often conflicted—actor.

The Quality of Group Decision Making

Our objective in this book is to describe the ways in which group decisions are made and, whenever possible, to prescribe techniques that may enhance the quality of these decisions. But what, exactly, is meant by "quality"? How does one know high quality group decision making when one sees it? To anticipate our answers to these questions, quality means lots of things, and the quality of group decision making will therefore be evaluated in relation to the particular yardstick that is applied.

It is clearly possible to characterize some group decision making as inferior in quality. Groups whose members continually bicker among themselves, who take forever to make what turns out (by some external standard) to be a poorly conceived decision, and who then lack the collective capacity to implement this decision, can be said to have made a group decision of undoubtedly poor quality. Conversely, when the several barometers of quality point consistently in a positive direction, we may have relatively little difficulty characterizing such group decision making as high in quality. Unfortunately, it is rare that the indices of quality provide uniformly consistent information. Moreover, a gain in quality of one sort can often be obtained only at the expense of some other indicator. Several of these indicators are listed below, with the understanding that no order of importance among them is intended.

Efficiency. The less time it takes a group to reach a decision, the better. A group that requires less time than another in order to generate the same number of alternatives from which to choose, to evaluate them with the same degree of care, and so forth, has engaged in a decision-making process of higher quality—even though this may not be reflected in a better decision. Similarly, the fewer the number of group members required to reach the same decision in the same time (that is, the fewer the number of person-hours required), the greater the efficiency.

Careful development and analysis of alternatives. Unfortunately, although this need not be the case, it often happens that efficiency occurs at the expense of patient deliberation. The faster a group moves toward a decision, the less likely its members are to give the problem before them the attention that it warrants. Clearly, to require in the interests of efficiency that all trial juries reach a verdict within a fixed period (for example two hours), would be to risk injustice by preventing the thoroughness required in the deliberative process.

Fairness. As we shall see in Chapter 5, the ethical aspects of group decision making arise whenever the interests of other people are affected by a particular decision. Clearly, this is a condition that is likely to obtain under most group circumstances, and when it does, the issue of fairness is likely to come to the fore. A group decision is of high quality, then, to the extent that it is fair both to the interests of the group members involved in the decision, and to the interests of those others, external to the group, for whom the group decision has consequences. Fairness in the T-group example might be understood in terms of the degree to which each group member is open-minded and constructive in listening and responding to the comments of other group members. Similarly, fairness in the jury illustration refers both to the internal process by which the panel comes to a verdict and also to the consequences of this decision for people who are external to the group—the plaintiff, the defendant, and so on.

Member satisfaction and morale. Yet another criterion of group decision-making quality, quite apart from the merits of the particular decision itself, is the degree to which group members feel that they are fully involved in the process along the way. Group members who believe that the process of reaching a decision was a fair one, that individual views were taken into account, are likely to be more satisfied with the way in which the decision was reached and are apt to have higher morale. If the group will be called upon to make repeated decisions, this issue of satisfaction and morale is particularly important—since it has a direct bearing on the members' likely willingness to participate in future decisions with equal commitment, energy, and enthusiasm. Note, however, the inherent conflict between the tendency toward group efficiency and the importance of satisfaction and morale. The more time a group of auto corporation executives requires to generate a panel of alternatives and then choose among them, the lower the group's efficiency—but the higher the sense of member satisfaction and morale—is likely to be.

Leadership effectiveness. Since leaders are instrumentally involved in many (although not all) group decisions, it stands to reason that the quality of group decision making will be closely related to the quality of its leadership. As we shall see in Chapters 2 and 3 in particular, but also throughout the book, an effective leader knows when to sit back and encourage group discussion prior to moving toward some decision, and when to propel the group into action with a firm guiding hand. In this regard, one can almost accept as an operational definition of a leader the ability of a group to get along in its leader's absence. The higher the quality of decision making, the better able the group will be to continue functioning at full tilt without the "divine guidance" of the leader's hand.

Growth over time. If the process by which a group moves toward a decision is of high quality, then it stands to reason that the group's collective ability to function effectively should grow over time.

Decision-making groups that are functioning well should be able to learn from their earlier experiences, including their mistakes, and should be able to make group decisions of higher quality on subsequent occasions. Consider the T-group in this regard: to the extent that the group's members have learned how to listen to one another in an open and constructive way, to contribute suggestions and criticisms as needed in an effort to upgrade the quality of the group's process, then to that extent we might expect the quality of this process to improve over time. Subsequent meetings of this particular group of individuals should be far less frustrating and difficult for the members since they would now know not only each other, but also how an effectively functioning group actually performs.

In summary, then, the quality of group decisions must be evaluated simultaneously by reference to a complex set of multiple criteria. Although group decisions may occasionally satisfy all criteria to the same degree, trade-offs are usually involved in practice—so that high quality in relation to one factor (for example, efficiency) occurs at the expense of another (such as satisfaction and morale of group members). In the chapters ahead, you will see the quality of group decision making evaluated in relation to one, or many, of these several indicators of quality.

How Two Heads Are Different From One

But why devote an entire book to the nature of group decision making in the first place? Can't group decision making be understood as the additive, combined effect of the series of individual decisions rendered by the group's members? The answer to this latter question is an unequivocal no. As the following examples help make clear, two heads may be better than one and occasionally worse than one, but they are always very different from one. Consider the following two problems:

My dungeon did not lie beneath the moat, but was in one of the most high parts of the castle. So stout was the door, and so well secured withal, that escape that way was not to be found. By hard work I did remove one of the bars from the narrow window, and was able to crush my body through the opening; but the distance to the courtyard below was so exceedingly great that it was certain death to drop thereto. I did find in the corner of the cell a rope that had been left there and lay hid in the darkness. But this rope had not length enough, and to drop in safety from the end was nowise possible. So I made haste to divide the rope in half and to tie the two parts thereof together again. It was then full long and did reach the ground, and I went down in safety. How could this have been? [Davis & Restle, 1963]

A man bought a horse for $60 and sold it for $70. Then he bought it back for $80 and sold it again for $90. How much money did he make in the horse business? [Maier & Solem, 1952]

Given a few minutes to think about these problems, about 75% of individuals solve the rope problem (realizing that the rope could be unbraided—divided lengthwise), but fewer than half arrive at the correct answer (it's $20, incidentally) for the horsetrading problem. But what happens when groups of 5 or 6 people are formed and asked to arrive at the correct answer? Almost 96% of the groups correctly solve the rope problem, while the number solving the horsetrading problem still hovers around 50%.

Why should groups differ so much in their accuracy of solving two apparently similar problems? For the rope problem, if you wished to be reasonably certain to arrive at the correct solution, forming a group would usually be superior to polling any individual member. But groups working on the horsetrading problem seem not to benefit from discussion. There is actually one important difference between the two problems that seems to be responsible for the differences in group effectiveness. The rope problem is what is known as a "eureka" ("I have found it") problem. Once somebody solves it, it is immediately clear to all concerned that there could be no other answer. ("Oh of course! How could I have been so stupid as to miss that?") Therefore, all a group needs in order to solve the problem is at least *one* group member who knows the correct solution. On the other hand, the horsetrading problem must be worked through by logic, and in this case logic can take several turns. For instance, many people argue that the correct answer is $10, since the trader "lost" $10 when be bought back the horse, and this must offset the $20 profit he earned from selling the horse twice. A persuasive speaker could probably convince quite a few group members of the wrong answer using this approach. The point is that a problem lacking a "eureka" quality is rather ambiguous, and therefore a correct group decision may require other things besides one correct member. In fact, research has demonstrated that groups working on the horsetrading problem tend to arrive at the decision shared by the *majority* of the members.

Why should this be? Wouldn't a person who knows the right answer be able to convince the others? Wouldn't the "truth win out"? Apparently not for this type of problem. The very fact that the solution to the horsetrading problem does not elicit an immediate "of course" reaction makes it much more similar to real-life group decisions. (Can you imagine a judge and jury simultaneously slapping their palms to their foreheads in response to the defense attorney's compelling "solution" to a complex legal dispute?) Because the problem admits of more than one plausible solution, other factors besides "truth" help determine the ultimate group decision.

For example, suppose you had worked on the problem for a minute or two and had decided that $20 was the correct answer. You are now placed in a group with four other people: three co-workers and your boss. All four argue that the horsetrader netted $10. In fact, when this experiment was actually performed, using members of bombing crews (Torrance, 1954), the high status pilots were much more successful in persuading their groups than were navigators or gunners. It appears that, in addition to truth, some status, leadership, and prevailing opinion are important determinants of group decisions.

Now consider another "problem":

What is the current temperature in the room in which you are sitting? This is rather different from the previous two problems. While all three have objectively "correct" answers, this one involves a subjective judgment. Without using a thermometer, how could we best examine the correct temperature? Selecting any given individual would be pretty risky, since we would have no idea whether she or he is a good or a bad estimator. We could convene a group, and require it to arrive at a unanimous group judgment. But we know that such judgments are subject to distortions due to initial biases, status of members, and so forth. We can also confidently predict that the group would spend considerable time getting organized, setting up rules, smoothing out conflicts, and appointing leaders. Finally, we could elect to ask a large number of people to indicate their estimates, then to simply *average* these estimates to arrive at a "group decision." Such "pseudo-groups" are often superior to individuals or true groups when problems like this are to be solved. In one early study where the correct temperature was 72°, individual estimates ranged from 60° to 80°, but the average was 72.4°, a figure that was more accurate than the vast majority of individual judgments.

The question, "Are groups superior to individuals?" turns out to be impossible to answer simply. There are certainly instances in which a clearly skillful individual would be well advised to steer clear of groups and rely on his or her own resources in arriving at a decision. On certain matters of subjective judgment, a statistical averaging of individuals' judgments results in a highly accurate answer without the necessity of convening a group that will almost certainly need time to get organized. However, the fact remains that many of the most important decisions that affect our lives are made in groups of varying sizes. Sometimes these decisions seem to have profited from group discussions, while others have resulted in monumental fiascos. To understand better the conditions under which groups make effective, inadequate, or harmful decisions we need to analyze those forces that influence group decisions.

Factors That Influence the Quality
of Group Decision Making

In order to describe the ways in which group decisions of high and low quality are made, and in order to prescribe ways in which quality may be enhanced, it is necessary to delineate further the broad contours of the terrain ahead in this book. It may be useful, therefore, to indicate some of the major factors that are likely to influence the quality of group decision making with the understanding that each of these factors will be explored in greater detail in one or more of the following chapters. Just as trade-offs exist among the several barometers of group decision quality, so too do they exist among many of the factors that influence such quality.

Four major kinds of factors combine to influence the quality of a group's decisions. First, there are the several characteristics of the group's composition, per se: who the members are, how many there are, what their membership and power relations happen to be, and so forth. Second, and very much related to the matter of group composition, is the group's leadership: for example, who this person is, how he or she emerged as a leader, and leadership style. Third, quite apart from the group's composition and the attributes of its leadership, the quality of group decisions is affected by the nature of the particular work in which the group is engaged: the number and kind of issues with which the group must deal, whether these issues exist in the short-term or in the long-run, and so forth. Finally, and most directly related to the focus of this book, the quality of group decisions is affected by the particular decision-making rules and arrangements that are in place, such as requirements of unanimity versus majority or plurality rule, and decisions with consequences that are reversible rather than irreversible.

Group Composition

Just as the quality of a theatrical production is influenced by the acoustical properties of the theatre, the talent and compatibility of its cast, so too is the quality of a group decision shaped by a number of factors that are related to the group's composition. Let us now consider these factors in turn.

SIZE

Perhaps the simplest distinction that can be made about groups concerns their size. In this book, we will be touching on decision making in small groups (see Chapters 9 and 10 on corporate and administrative decision making, for example) as well as in groups that are large enough to caucus in the selection of political candidates (see Chapter 7). As simple and obvious as the matter of group size may be, it nevertheless is a potentially important factor in determining the quality of the decisions that result. Thus, the smaller the group, the fewer the number of moving parts; as a result, a small group should generally be able to come to a decision more readily than a larger aggregate. On the other hand, the smaller the group in question, the greater the likelihood that divergent, often enriching points of view will be lacking. In short, one trade-off arising from the factor of group size is enhanced efficiency at the cost of full input and exploration of alternatives.

As groups grow in size, a point is eventually reached where it is simply not convenient, or even possible, to render a group decision through face-to-face interaction. Under these circumstances, a number of things are likely to happen: First, different groupings may form (or be formed) based on differing areas of expertise; these groups might then serve as advisory groups to the leader, much as the Executive Office, Cabinet, and National Security Council do for the President of the United States (see Chapter 8). Second, subgroupings may form based not so much on differential expertise as they are on differing interests and power relations. Such subgroupings are often described as coalitions within the group as a whole; as we shall see in Chapter 7, on political decision making, such coalitions have an important effect on group decision-making quality.

MEMBER PERSONALITY CHARACTERISTICS

As we shall see in Chapter 2, although some research has been conducted in an effort to determine the sorts of personality types or traits that are associated with effective participation in group decision making, surprisingly little is really known about this important area. To be sure, some kinds of people are predisposed to be tolerant of ambiguity, and patient in their dealings with others, and such people are therefore likely to avoid moving a group to decision prematurely. Similarly, there clearly are people who are disposed to look for and listen to the advice of whoever happens to be in a position of authority as the group's leader; such people, if not good leaders, are apt to be first-rate followers. In short, what we do know for certain is that the quality of group decision making is affected by the personalities of the individual group members. Less obvious is the *way* in which quality is determined by such personality considerations. A jury composed of good followers may reach a verdict quickly, when guided by an active foreman, but will the verdict be a wise one? Similarly, a jury composed of twelve creative, free-wheeling minds may do a fine job of exploring the issues and alternatives available, but will they be able to reach the unanimous verdict required of them?

MEMBER SIMILARITY

Groups differs widely in the degree to which their members are similar or different regarding a large number of attributes, including personality, age, socioeconomic status, race, and sex. Groups whose members are quite homogeneous in background, outlook, values, and so on, are like peas in a pod, and their decision making is apt to reflect this fact. Thus, where the decision making problem at hand requires the concerted effort of group members functioning in unison, like the fingers of a single hand, groups whose members are homogeneous are likely to function effectively. When pressures exist to make decisions with extreme rapidity (for example, an executive council required to make a budgetary decision under considerable time pressure, or a group of fire fighters deciding whether and how to combat a flash fire), one might expect homogeneous groups to move toward a collective decision more quickly than their more heterogeneous counterparts.

Similarly , homogeneous groups are likely to be characterized by high esprit de corps among the members, resulting from the sense that one is with people like oneself (fine, upstanding, virtuous, and fiercely intelligent—naturally!). The high group cohesiveness that ensues is likely to make the group highly efficient in its decision making, although—as we shall see in Chapters 2 and 3—such cohesiveness is also likely to bring with it the dangers of premature closure on a group decision, as well as the exclusion of points of view and of individuals that differ from those of the majority.

Groups that are more heterogeneous in their composition—again, in terms of race, sex, or whatever may happen to be the attribute or set of attributes in question—will tend to make decisions of high quality when confronted with problems that require access to conflicting, differentiated points of view. Groups such as the advisory panels that are charged with assessing social risk (see Chapter 6), as well as the administrative and foreign policy decision making bodies described in Chapters 10 and 8, respectively, are each instances in which decision quality can only be achieved through access to groups whose members are relatively heterogenous.

Like homogeneity, member heterogenity has its trade-offs too. Extreme heterogeneity is likely to encourage so much difference of opinion that the group is simply incapable of making a concerted judgment or decision. Perhaps, as in the example of a T-group, a concerted judgment is unnecessary; but at least as often, it seems, groups are required to come to some decision, and excessive heterogeneity may get in the way of accomplishing this objective. As we will see in Chapter 2, the cohesiveness afforded by member homogeneity and the availability of divergent viewpoints afforded by heterogeneity are each valuable assets—up to a point. Beyond this point, however, decision-making quality is likely to suffer.

MEMBERSHIP OPENNESS

Some groups—such as blue ribbon panels, the rosters of restricted country clubs, jury panels, and even the group of corporate executives of our earlier illustration—are closed, or are of limited access, to new members. Membership in such groups may be a matter of law or regulation, selection by some elite or some other appointment procedure over which members have little control. Many of these relatively closed groups are closed, not only to new additions, but, interestingly, to subtractions; indeed, there may be instances in which the only way membership in a closed group comes to an end is through death. In contrast, most groups are far more open to the entry and exit of group members. Membership in such groups (witness the T-group example or the many civic associations) is typically voluntary or self-selected, a matter of individuals wishing to belong to the group and behaving in the ways that make their membership possible.

The effects of membership openness on group decision-making quality are likely to parallel our observations regarding homogeneity and heterogeneity. It often happens that relatively closed groups tend to contain members who are homogeneous in a variety of respects; consider the "white folks only" clubs of a few years back, whose members tended to think and vote alike. Closed groups may be able to move to a decision more readily than their more open counterparts, and may be highly cohesive (indeed, members may have a distorted sense of their collective worth), but such closed arrangements also run the risks of unfairness and narrowness of vision. In contrast, the members of more open groups are less likely to have an elitist sense of specialness and distinctiveness, but are also more likely to have access to the differing points of view and expertise that are necessary for many decision-making problems (such as those concerning social risk assessment, described in Chapter 6).

MEMBERSHIP POWER

For a variety of reasons—ranging from the personalities of the people involved to degree of membership openness and homogeneity of composition—it is clear that group members may differ in their relative ability to exercise power or influence in their dealings with other group members. Such differences, in turn, are likely to have a bearing on the quality of the decisions that result.

Groups whose members are of comparable power are homogeneous with regard to this most important attribute, and hence are likely to function like the members of other homogeneous arrangements—at least for a while. Consider, in this regard, such examples as juries, members of the U.S. Supreme Court, a City Council, the U.S. Senate or House of Representatives, and even a T-group. After a while, in such relatively equal power arrangements, one or more of the group's members may attempt to exercise greater influence than others upon the decisions made, and in so doing may move into a position of greater relative power. Unless or until this happens, however, groups characterized by equality of member power will tend to be high in member satisfaction and morale, insofar as these derive from equality of access to the group's decision-making process. Hence, according to these important barometers of decision-making quality, equal power arrangements will breed a sense of full participation and cohesiveness—along with the several "pathologies" of such cohesiveness, discussed in the next two chapters.

In contrast, consider groups such as the United Nations Security Council, the Electoral College, or the administrative and foreign policy decision-making bodies described in Chapters 10 and 8, respectively. Such groups contain clear differences in the relative power among their members, and these groups are likely to function like heterogeneous arrangements in which one or more persons appear to have more of the desirable benefits than the others. Members who are high in power relative to the others are likely to exercise undue influence over the group decision-making process, and are likely to be the focus of many communications and requests for information or guidance. In short, as will be seen in our exploration of this issue in Chapter 2, groups whose members have unequal power are likely to be differentially influenced by those with greater clout—and the group is likely to sink or swim accordingly. Thus, in the hands of a more powerful individual who is highly competent and effective, we might expect the resulting group decision to be of high quality. However, in the hands of a "nerd," the resulting group decision might well prove to be of far poorer quality than might have resulted through the efforts of a "leaderless" group of members with relatively equal power. In short, power inequality increases the potential risks and the potential benefits of group decision making.

ACCESS TO FACE-TO-FACE CONTACT

Most groups that we commonly think of are social arrangements in which all members meet together in a single place at one time, can look and talk with one another as they wish, and move collectively toward some decision. In contrast—as in the example of the Executive Council that votes by phone on next year's budget, or in the instance of the voting decisions that are described in Chapters 4 and 7—there are also occasions in which the members of a group are far flung, rarely, if ever, meet at one time at a single location, and yet are clearly group members embarked on some decision-making task. What differences in the quality of group decision making, if any, might we expect as a function of such access to face-to-face contact?

Although we know of no research to guide our analysis, we speculate that the risks of both success and failure are likely to be higher in the face-to-face arrangements. Thus, when such a group is able to get untracked, to listen carefully to the views of its members, to acknowledge both the verbal and nonverbal signals conveyed by each person, to have the benefit of all participants addressing precisely the same issue at precisely the same moment—under these favorable conditions, we would expect a group characterized by the possibility of face-to-face contact to make decisions of far higher quality than could possibly result in the absence of such contact. On the other hand, if the group decision process is troubled in some way (perhaps because multiple conflicts exist among the group's members), face-to-face contact may lead to decisions of poorer quality than would occur were members to have more limited interaction.

Group Leadership

Earlier, we indicated that one of the variables in the quality of a group's decision making is the quality of its leadership. However, in addition to serving as a measure or barometer of decision-making quality, group leadership—its emergence, centralization, and style— is also an important determinant of group-decision quality. Let us now consider these aspects of group leadership in turn.

LEADERSHIP EMERGENCE

Leaders obtain their positions of power and influence in groups in two fundamentally different ways, each of which has an important bearing on the quality of the decision making that results. One extremely important route to leadership is from *within*: the leader works his or her way up through the group ranks and is appointed to a leadership position by the membership. On the other hand, there are also many occasions in which leadership emerges from *without*, typically as a result of the appointment of a group leader by some individual or aggregate with superior power; consider here the example of a corporate executive who has been brought in from another corporation and given a top mangement post.

When leadership emerges from within, one would generally expect the leader to have considerable legitimacy among the membership. After all, this person has shown through his or her resourcefulness and competence to be worthy of assuming the mantle of leadership. When such a leader speaks, the members are likely to listen. When requests are made, they are likely to be honored. Moreover, group decisions are likely to be made not only relatively quickly and easily, but also with considerable satisfaction and high morale among the members; since the members have most likely been involved in the leader's emergence, they are apt to feel like full participants in the group process, people whose views are likely to be taken into account by the leader. On the other hand, relatively little legitimacy is likely to obtain when the group's leader has been appointed from without. This person has been imposed upon the group by some individual or collective superior, and the group members may well harbor resentment toward the leader who has "ridden into town uninvited." For this reason, it is probably a good idea for leaders who are appointed from without (as well as the people who much such appointments) to go out of their way to show group members that these leaders deserve their appointed position—a bit like the new regimental commander who convinces his troops that he can lead them on the field of battle even though he was transferred into authority over them from a wholly different unit. Typically, leaders in corporate and administrative group contexts (as described in Chapters 9 and 10, respectively) attain their positions through external appointment by one or more superiors; clearly, the way in which such leaders come to occupy their positions is an important consideration—as we shall see in those two chapters.

If it appears that group decisions of high quality are more likely to be made when leadership has emerged from within, then at least one important trade-off must be acknowledged. If leadership emerges from within the membership ranks, not as a result of mutual accommodation and acceptance by the members, but as the outgrowth of a fierce competitive struggle, then such leadership may in fact generate greater resentment and distrust among the membership than leadership that is externally imposed. In this regard, consider the leadership struggles within such governments as the Soviet Union and China, struggles that are likely to leave great upheaval, rather than harmony, in their wake. Similarly, when groups are rife with struggle and discord, it may be more sensible for the welfare of the group for leadership to be imposed externally rather than be the product of intensified dissension within the group. In summary, then, although a leader who emerges from within the group's membership is likely to promote group decisions of high quality, one must also take into account the group atmosphere within which this process occurs.

LEADERSHIP CENTRALITY

Although we typically think of leadership as being personified by a single individual who serves as a central fount of influence or expertise, leadership is often far less centralized. Groups sometimes have multiple leaders, differing in expertise and function, who serve the group in a variety of ways; merely consider the many advisory groups whose members differ in their respective talents and understanding of some overall problem, each of whom is able to provide leadership in different areas and at different times.

Should we expect decision-making quality to be higher under conditions of centralized or decentralized leadership? As before, there is no clear, unambiguous answer to this question. Thus, a good case can be made for the superior quality of group decisions that occur under conditions of centralized leadership. Assuming that this leader is well informed, judicious, and able to extract the best from the membership, the centralized leader should be able to move the group to decisions with greater efficiency than would occur in a more decentralized arrangement. This is the essence of the argument for "enlightened dictatorship." On the other hand, dictators are rarely enlightened; moreover, even if they were enlightened to begin with, their power is likely to corrupt their judgment. Likewise, an incompetent, bungling individual, placed in a position of centralized leadership, is capable of imposing extremely poor-quality decisions upon the group. Centralized leadership arrangements are thus far more vulnerable to incompetency than decentralized arrangements—a point that will be documented in the discussion of communication and leadership in Chapter 2.

One other problem associated with centralized leadership is worthy of mention, and this is the matter of succession. Should it happen that the sole occupant of a centralized leadership structure is forced to leave office through expulsion, death, or some other eventuality, finding a suitable replacement often becomes a critical problem. A departing centralized leader typically leaves behind a leadership vacuum that is far less likely to occur under more decentralized arrangements.

LEADERSHIP STYLE

As we shall see in Chapter 2, leaders differ not only in their origin and centrality, but also in the style they habitually manifest. If leadership emergence and centrality are determined by the structure of arrangements within the group, then leadership style in turn is clearly a function of the kind of individual who occupies the group's most important position. At least two very different leadership styles have been analyzed in some detail over the years, and no doubt there are other styles as yet unexamined. The "authoritarian" leadership style is characterized by efforts to seize and retain clear control over virtually all aspects of group life; autocratic leaders originate almost all of the decisions made by the group, and as such they are the epitome of a centralized leadership arrangement. In contrast, the "democratic" leadership style is characterized by an interest not in preserving one's own special niche as a boss with absolute control, but in sharing decision-making responsibility and encouraging fairness. Democratic leaders are leaders to be sure, but they tend to lead by example and through the active participation of the membership. The democratic style is thus analogous to a more decentralized leadership structure.

Research has been conducted by social psychologists, to be discussed in Chapter 2, indicating that an autocratic style generates more efficient group decision making on relatively simple group tasks, exactly where one might expect a centralized leadership structure to work well. In turn, the democratic leadership style seems to lead to better group decisions when the decision-making task is more complex—requiring extensive utilization of the members' areas of differential expertise. In summary, a delicate balance exists between leadership style and the nature of the tasks confronting the group in which this style prevails. In Chapter 2, we describe in more detail the general, conceptual nature of this interaction between leadership style and group tasks. Subsequently, in our Chapter 6 discussion of group decision making in the context of social risk assessment, we provide a more concrete analysis of the way in which such a blending of leadership style and group need occurs in the service of making high quality decisions.

Group Tasks

So far, we have seen that the quality of group decision making is affected by the composition of a group, as well as its leadership. Moreover, as our brief discussion of leadership makes evident, the impact of leadership must be understood in relation to what it is, exactly, that a group is required or expected to do. Let us therefore consider more explicitly the matter of the group's "work"—where this work typically consists of a set of tasks and task arrangements within which the members operate.

ORIENTATION

Some groups, such as the T-group described earlier, are primarily oriented inward, toward their own process. Typically, the focus of such groups is on the way in which communication occurs among the members, and on the way in which group decisions are made, rather than on what the group decides—the decision itself. These process-oriented groups are distinguishable from other groups whose members are oriented toward carrying out some specific behavioral agenda that involves reaching and implementing particular decisions. A jury and a budgetary advisory group are groups whose orientation is directed not to the way in which each works as a group (although such considerations may prove relevant to the quality of the decision that results), but to the act of rendering a particular decision.

Group decisions of high quality are likely to require both orientation toward group process and orientation toward specific tasks. Thus, a group whose focus is directed exclusively to the completion of specific behavioral objectives (voting a budget up or down, rendering a guilty or innocent verdict, etc.) runs the risk of giving short shrift to the individual views and concerns of its members; some account of these individual opinions must be taken if a fair and sensible group decision is to be made. Similarly, a group that focuses on the way in which it operates—in the absence of any specific set of objectives that it is to complete—runs the risk of becoming excessively preoccupied with its collective navel, thereby losing necessary contact with the reality imposed by an external world.

TASK STRUCTURE

Group decision-making tasks are structured in a wide variety of ways, and these different structures are likely to have varying impact on the quality of decisions that result. Since these considerations are explored in greater detail in Chapter 2, we will comment here only briefly on a few of the features that comprise task structure.

Some group tasks, like a vote on the proposed annual operating budget for the XYZ Society or the vote to select a particular candidate in a primary (see Chapter 7), are typically treated as a single unit: either the group votes for Candidate A or for Candidate B; either it approves the proposed budget or it does not. In contrast are those group tasks that may be structured so as to be divisible into smaller, more manageable parts; a jury, for example, first decides who will serve as foreman, then decides how to discuss the case before them, and finally decides upon a verdict. Similarly, foreign policy decision-making groups of the sort discussed in Chapter 8 typically address tasks that are divisible into component parts—as when one subgroup considers the intelligence ramifications of a possible course of action, another looks at political implications, while a third considers the economic feasibility of the proposed plan, and so forth. As the preceding would suggest, tasks that are divisible—in contrast to their more monolithic counterparts—lend themselves far better to the utilization of the multiple talents and areas of expertise that may exist among a group's members.

In addition to distinguishing tasks on the basis of their divisibility, it is also useful to consider whether a high quality task performance requires some behavior to be maximized or optimized (Steiner, 1972). Tasks that are maximizing, like the task confronting the corporate brainstorming group in our example, require group members to do as much of something as possible—in this case, generating design ideas that will offset inroads by a corporate competitor. Maximizing tasks require group members to place a premium on the speed and efficiency with which decisions are made; in a brainstorming group it is fair to say that the greater the number of alternatives generated in a given period, the higher the quality of the process. In contrast, an optimizing task requires group members not to do as much as possible, but to do the right or optimum amount; since a jury must decide how long to continue open discussion among the members before coming to a preliminary vote, it would be well advised to spend an optimal amount hearing the dissenting views and concerns of the jurors before moving on.

TASK INTERDEPENDENCE

As we observed earlier, in characterizing the defining features of a group decision, it is plausible to evaluate a group's decisions as though they were the acts of a highly complex but unitary actor. Regardless of the precise manner in which the group arrived at its decision, this decision has consequences for which the group as a whole is—at least partially—responsible. The nature, and perhaps the degree, of this collective responsibility, however, is influenced by the implications of the group's particular task for the interdependence arrangements that exist among the group's members.

Although these interdependence arrangements will be described in greater detail and in the context of empirical research in Chapter 2, it may be useful to comment briefly on some of the more important patterns. First, there are some group decision-making tasks that place members in a fundamentally competitive arrangement; to the extent that one person's preferred alternative is chosen as the group's decision, the individual preferences of the other group members are denied. Such a task arrangement would exist among the members of a family of four trying to decide where to spend a two-week vacation. Assuming that each person has a different vacation preference, and that compromises or integrative solutons are not possible, a group decision in favor of one preference automatically rules out each of the others.

A second task interdependence arrangement occurs when group members are bound together in such a way that they "sink or swim" together. Like a jury whose verdict must be unanimous, thereby requiring the development of consensus, this fundamentally cooperative form of task interdependence places pressure on group members to listen carefully to each other's preferences and inclinations; only by all agreeing can a group decision be reached.

A third task arrangement that often occurs in decision-making groups requires simply that group members reach a decision by pooling their preferences in some additive fashion; the national council voting on the XYZ Society's annual budget, for example, makes its decision by simply tallying the votes cast. Notice that additive arrangements, in contrast to their more competitive and cooperative cousins, really imply little interdependence among group members. Whereas competitive tasks are defined such that one person's decision preference precludes another's, while cooperative tasks require that there be complete agreement among the membership before a decision can be reached, an additive task simply requires that each person's decision preference be combined with those of others.

In which kind of task is the quality of the group decision reached likely to be highest? A good case can be made for the cooperative arrangement. When group members are confronted with a task that requires them to incorporate the views of the most reluctant, slowest, or concerned of its members, then a process is likely to be generated that encourages fairness, careful attention to divergent points of view, and the incorporation of whatever expertise is available. On the other hand, although a process that takes member input into careful account may produce a decision that is of high quality in relation to some criteria, there are trade-offs in terms of the time and efficiency in reaching this decision. Moreover, as we shall see in Chapters 2 and 3, it is precisely when group members have a task that requires cooperation that pressures toward consensus are likely to arise—leading the majority to exercise considerable, even undue, influence on deviant members in an effort to bring them around to their point of view. In summary, although a cooperative task arrangement may well lead to decisions that are the highest in quality, there are several offsetting risks that must be taken into account.

TIMING OF TASK DEVELOPMENT

Some groups come into being in response to a situation that requires someone to make a decision, as in the case mentioned earlier of the corporate executives meeting to respond to a deteriorating market position. Such decision-making groups are fundamentally reactive to developments; often they exist as a group only so long as it is necessary to reach and implement a decision. In contrast are those groups whose decision-making tasks develop not in reaction to some external circumstance, but on a more proactive basis. Like the XYZ Society's national council, such groups are typically required or expected to make decisions continually in order to carry out the aims, projects, or purposes of an ongoing organization. Often these decisions involve the establishment of contingency plans prior to the occurrence of some anticipated event.

Our discussion in Chapter 8 of decision making in the international arena highlights some of the several important differences between groups whose decision-making tasks are developed proactively versus reactively. The central thesis to be argued in that chapter, a point that may be applied more generally to decision making in any number of contexts, is that proactive group decision making typically leads to decisions of higher quality than occur when—like volunteer firefighters springing to extinguish an unanticipated blaze—decisions are made reactively. It has been said of United States foreign policy makers that they lack a clear and consistent foreign policy, and instead respond reactively to each most recent crisis as it arises. A more effective system is needed for anticipating the decisions that are likely to require attention in the future, and for beginning the necessary analytic work before these decisions are actually made.

Decision Rules and Processes

We have already seen that the quality of group decision making may be affected by the group's composition, the nature of its leadership, and the particular work that the members are required or expected to do. Finally, and of greatest direct relevance to this book, are those factors that relate to the decision rules and processes within the group. These factors include the particular arrangements that dictate when a group decision will have been reached, the decision's reversibility, and the social/cultural context within which a decision has been made.

EXTENT OF AGREEMENT REQUIRED

Some groups, like most juries, require consensus among their members before a decision can be made. Such an arrangement demands the persuasion or arm-twisting of each and every group member, and is hard work. In exchange, a group decision that is reached through a rule of consensus—although inefficient—is likely to have been developed with excruciating care and with attention to the necessary considerations. These trade-offs, as well as their ethical implications, are treated in some detail in Chapter 5.

If unanimity is the most strenuous, difficult, and potentially rewarding decision requirement, then it stands to reason that other, less taxing arrangements are both more efficient and also more superficial in their treatment of member opinion and expertise. An arrangement that requires agreement among a majority of the members, for example, is clearly a more efficient procedure for reaching a decision, but is also an arrangement that runs the risk of overlooking some minority perspective that, if incorporated properly, might well contribute to a group decision of higher quality. Similarly, a decision arrangement that requires no more than a plurality of the members to agree promises to be even more efficient as well as more vulnerable to the potential deficiency of a majority-rule arrangement.

Subsequent chapters of our book will be devoted to a close analysis of the implications of these various decision rule arrangements. In Chapter 4, we consider most generally the consequences of adopting one voting arrangement over another. In Chapter 7, we examine the process of jockeying for position in the determination of decision rules for selecting political candidates. And in Chapter 8, we focus on the effects of decision-making rules and processes on foreign policy group decisions.

DECISION REVERSIBILITY

Like individual decisions, group decisions differ in the extent to which they are reversible. Most group decisions that involve voting, whether decisions of a jury (Chapter 3) or a political entity (Chapters 4 and 7), are either irreversible or reversible only through rather unusual arrangements (appeal, recall, and so forth). Not unreasonably, such group decisions are likely to be made, or at least ought to be made, with considerable care and caution. It is not only the gravity of the consequences of a jury's decision that stimulates careful deliberation; it is also the irreversibility of the verdict that is reached.

In contrast, many group decisions—such as those by risk assessment groups (Chapter 6), corporate groups (Chapter 9), administrative groups (Chapter 10), and foreign policy groups (Chapter 8)—are far more reversible. Sometimes reversibility can be achieved only at considerable cost (as when a corporation decides to abandon a previously adopted plan for expansion), but such reversibility is possible. Clearly, it is a lot easier to render a group decision under conditions of reversibility. Such decisions may not be better conceived, but at least they can be reached with less collective effort and with fewer of the trappings of commitment that accompany irreversible decisions. The virtues of a straw poll, in this regard, are evident: it is possible to "try out" a decision on a tentative basis, without commitment, and thereby ascertain group members' inclinations before these are rendered irrevocable through a formal vote.

DECISION CRITERIA

Some of the more complex group decisions lend themselves to division into what has been described as "objective" and "subjective" components. Thus, in groups such as those constituted to serve as foreign policy advisors (Chapter 8), and most clearly in the groups of citizens and experts who are called upon to render decisions based on risk assessment (Chapter 6), it is often possible to distinguish objective from more subjective considerations. For example, whereas risk assessment groups may be relatively objective in their decisions on primarily technical or scientific questions, their decisions concerning the use of this information in the development of policy are more subjective. As we point out in Chapter 6, the distinction between objective and subjective decision criteria is often more illusory than real; rather, the distinction allows those with greater decision-making power—or those who wish to attain such power—to describe their own decisions as objective (and therefore less open to criticism) in contrast to what they describe as the more subjective appraisals of their less powerful colleagues.

THE SOCIAL AND CULTURAL DECISION CONTEXT

Group decisions are not made in a vacuum. Rather, they occur in a particular social context comprised of the personal attitudes of the group members who have rendered these decisions. As we will see in Chapter 2, the fact that people differ widely in their opinions and prejudices has made it possible, through social science research, to handpick those jurors who are most likely to render a particular verdict. Such decisions, moreover, are more than a simple matter of the individual personalities of the members involved; these decisions are influenced by the chemistry that results when people with differing predispositions are required or allowed to mix together in the process of making a collective decision.

But the context of group decision making transcends even these important social considerations. A society's culture, including the norms and mores that it advocates, as well as the structural constraints that it imposes, make it possible for certain group decisions to occur in one cultural environment with little prospect of occurring equally often or equally well in another environment. It is comforting to imagine, for example, that as a result of some careful corporate brainstorming and systematic decision making, an American automobile manufacturer may be able to find a way of emulating the enormously impressive Japanese pattern of industrial production (see Chapter 9, where we discuss this example in the context of corporate decision making). The quality of group decision making is thus affected by the mesh of individual groups members with the norms of their group as a whole. It is also influenced by the interaction between the group's identity and the larger societal context within which this group is situated.

Factors Influencing Group Decision Quality: Summary Comment

In the preceding pages, we have been able to do little more than highlight some of the many factors that influence the quality of group decisions. Our intention in reviewing these factors has been to provide the reader with a preliminary set of guidelines to the chapters ahead. We will be addressing a great many issues related to group decision making in the pages to come, and it may be useful to know in advance what some of the major themes are likely to be.

Our interest in writing this book stems ultimately from the belief that careful description must precede rational prescription. By carefully describing the many ways in which group decision quality is affected by various factors operating in multiple settings, we believe it becomes possible to move from how group decisions *are* made to assertions about the ways in which they *ought* to be made. It is only fitting, therefore, that we close this introductory chapter with a preliminary indication of a general prescriptive plan for facilitating more effective, higher quality group decision making. Our suggestions take the form of six steps in the group decision process.

STEP 1: DEFINE THE PROBLEM

Before a group can make a decision, it must first decide whether any problem or circumstance exists in the first place that necessitates a decision. Moreover, it is essential that the problem be defined appropriately and correctly; it hardly makes sense for a group of urban policy makers to devise a plan for combatting "white flight" to the suburbs if the cause of such migration is not racism (as the policymakers believe), but the economic advantages of suburban living.

The key to proper definition of the group's problem is access to information. Such information may be obtained by talking to other people, searching some body of literature, devising some plan for gathering hitherto unavailable data, and so on. Once the problem has been defined by the group, an attempt should be made to ascertain whether the available background information corroborates or contradicts this definition.

STEP 2: IDENTIFY ALTERNATIVES

A group decision is only as good as the alternatives from which it has been chosen. As we have seen in this chapter, a group's ability to do a good job of developing alternatives will be a function of many factors: member heterogeneity, leadership style, the nature of task interdependence, and so forth. The importance of this second step in the decision process cannot be stated too strongly. Without good alternatives—whether these are generated within the group or by access to others external to the group—the best decision analysis in the world will do little to produce a quality result. At some point, of course, the process of generating alternatives must come to an end. A group that does nothing but brainstorm alternatives, in the absence of any effort to act eventually upon these alternatives in the pursuit of a decision, is utterly ineffectual. Thus, an additional concern that must be addressed at Step 2 is the matter of how long to work at the job of generating alternatives before moving on to the next step in the process.

STEP 3: QUANTIFY ALTERNATIVES

Once a list of alternatives has been generated, the group must next turn to the matter of discriminating and distinguishing among them. In an effort to weed out those alternatives that are improbable or unsatisfactory, while beginning to narrow the list of "finalists" to a chosen few, it is desirable for the group members to quantity the relative merits of the alternatives. The risks, if any, associated with particular alternatives must be identified, along with their potential benefits. These risks and benefits must be evaluated in relation to a temporal perspective of short-term and long-term considerations; decisions that work well in the short run may turn out to have long-range consequences that are far less favorable, while decisions that involve short-term sacrifice may prove to be worth their weight in gold in the long run.

Step 3 requires the group to assign *utilities* to the various alternatives available. By utility we simply mean the well-being or satisfaction that an individual or group derives from a particular situation or event. Included in the calculation of utilities are all things, real or imagined, that the actor perceives to affect his or her welfare; the net utility is simply the negative factors (dissatisfactions) subtracted from their positive counterparts (satisfactions). Utility is thus an entirely subjective concept; it has nothing to do with the objective value or worth of an alternative, but is entirely a matter of its perceived likelihood of providing satisfaction; and such perceptions can vary from person to person. Group assignment of utilities to available alternatives thus makes it possible for the members to ascertain—individually and/or collectively—the group's collective preference.

STEP 4: APPLY DECISION AIDS

If a group decision is only as good as the alternatives that have been generated, then the alternatives themselves are only as good as the group's collective ability to evaluate them. As an aid in the quantification and relative appraisal of the decision alternatives, it may be possible on occasion to utilize various decision tools and techniques. These include game theory, linear regression, linear programming, decision matrix, mathematical modeling, and forecasting. A number of these decision aids are discussed in our earlier book, *Making Decisions: A Multidisciplinary Introduction* (1979).

STEP 5: MAKE A DECISION

When the group has gathered all the necessary information, defined the problem, generated alternatives, and subjected them to critical, quantitative appraisal—when all this has transpired, the time comes at last for the group to make its decision. More often than not, this decision is not a matter of selecting the single correct alternative or avoiding all incorrect choices; rather, the group decision will be the best guess about the best choice under the present circumstances. If the preceding stepwise process has been followed thoughtfully and with care, there is every reason to hope that the decision itself will be a sound one. Errors do occur, however, and it is important that the group acknowledge this possibility and attempt to protect itself from the tendency to stick with a decision at all costs— even it it happens to be the wrong decision. It is essential, therefore, that the actual consequences of the group's decision be observed with care. Should these consequences diverge from those anticipated, or provide unmistakable evidence that a wrong decision was made, it is often still possible to reverse course before becoming irrationally overcommitted to a poor decision.

STEP 6: IMPLEMENTATION

Once a group decision has been rendered, appropriate action must be taken in order to make certain that the decision is carried out as planned. It too often occurs that individuals and groups devote their energies so extensively and entirely to the first five steps in the decision process that they ignore the important last step of implementation. The wisest group decision will come to naught in the absence of the resources that are necessary in order to transform this decision into action.

In conclusion, the preceding six steps can serve as a rough guide to the sequential process of high quality group decision making. We hasten to add that although the process typically begins with problem definition and concludes with implementation, the six steps along the way provide multiple possibilities for feedback looping. In the process of quantifying alternatives, new alternatives may surface that were unknown or ignored before. Similarly, in the process of decision implementation, the group may come to the realization that insufficient attention was directed to the basic issue of problem definition, and that more work is needed before an appropriate decision can be made and implemented. The general point, then, is that the stepwise decision process described here both invites and requires further investigation and analysis at each point along the way.

References

Davis, J. H., & Restle, F. The analysis of problems and prediction of group problem solving. *Journal of Abnormal and Social Psychology,* 1963, 66, 103-116.
Maier, N.R.F., & Solem, A. R. The contribution of a discussion leader to the quality of group thinking. *Human Relations,* 1952, 5, 277-288.
Steiner, I. D. *Group process and productivity.* New York: Academic Press, 1972.
Torrance, E. P. The behavior of small groups under stress conditions of survival. *American Sociological Review,* 1954, 19, 751-755.

CHAPTER 2

HOW GROUPS MAKE DECISIONS
A Social Psychological Perspective

Walter C. Swap

Social psychology is concerned with how people are influenced by their social environments. A social psychologist would therefore be interested in how individuals interact with, and are affected by, friends, lovers, strangers, associates, supervisors, recreational groups, societies, and cultures to which they belong. In short, our beliefs, attitudes, and behaviors are shaped in large degree by these *group* interactions.

This chapter, and the one following, present the social psychological perspective on group decision making. In the present chapter, we examine those factors that have proven to be important in determining *how* groups make decisions. The composition of the group, the nature of its task, the degree of group spirit or cohesiveness, the number of group members and how they communicate with one another, and group leadership are all important factors in understanding the group decision-making process. We conclude with a section on the implications of these findings for improving the effectiveness of group decisions.

Studying Groups Experimentally

By and large, those who study group behavior must make a fundamental choice between investigating already existing groups (such as juries, families, or industrial organizations) or constructing ad hoc groups in an experimental laboratory. The advantage of the former approach is that one is more confident of capturing something of the processes of real, functioning groups. Unfortunately, one pays a heavy price for this luxury. What is gained in realism is often lost in experimental *control*. For example, an analysis of the deliberations of a real jury seldom leads to unambiguous conclusions about what specific factors led to the verdict. Was it the weight of the evidence? The instructions by the judge? The sex composition of the jury? The attractiveness of the defendant? The smoothness of the defense lawyers? Or some combination of these factors? Further, many real-life groups (such as, in fact, impaneled juries) are not accessible to direct observation, or only with great difficulty. (The monumental study of juries by Kalven & Zeisel [1966] is a notable exception.)

As a result of these factors, most (but by no means all) social psychological investigations of group behavior have utilized an *experimental* rather than a naturalistic approach. Laboratory groups are formed from high school or college populations, management training seminars, or armed forces personnel, and are assigned a task of the experimenter's choosing. The investigator is free to impose as much control over the situation as is deemed desirable. For example, to mention some of the factors discussed in Chapter 1, he or she can vary the size of the group, to see whether large groups are better able to reach good decisions; the degree of similiarity among group members can be controlled; leaders can be assigned or allowed to emerge spontaneously; and so on. When these experimental manipulations have been accomplished, and the results of the experiment have been analyzed, the investigators hope that they bear some resemblance to real-world phenomena. If laboratory groups reach more risky decisions than individuals, or if experimental groups of self-centered members have more difficulty reaching good decisions than do groups with members possessing smaller egos, then these are findings the social psychologist hopes to generalize to decision-making groups outside the confines of the lab.

Factors That Influence Group Decisions

Social psychologists have investigated a number of factors that seem to be important in shaping the decisions groups make. The personalities, attitudes, and skills that members bring to the group, and how their individual characteristics mesh with the needs of the group, the group's cohesiveness or esprit de corps, group size, how members communicate with one another, and the exercise of leadership are all important in determining the nature of group interaction and the quality of group decisions.

CHARACTERISTICS OF GROUP MEMBERS

It is late 1971 as the Government builds its case against radical Catholic priest Philip Berrigan. Accusing him and six associates of conspiring to explode bombs in Washington, D.C. heating tunnels, and to kidnap Henry Kissinger, the Attorney General's office wants to take no chances that the anti-Vietnam activists will be acquitted. Two million dollars are poured into the effort and the venue for the trial is set for Harrisburg, Pennsylvania—one of the more politically conservative regions in the country, with an active Ku Klux Klan, military installations, war industries, and very few Catholics. From registered voters of this area, a group of 12 people will meet to reach a decision about the guilt or innocence of the defendants.

Suppose an attorney has the unenviable task of confronting these odds by defending the Berrigans. The attorney would best proceed by developing the strongest defense possible, assailing the credibility of government witnesses, establishing the high moral character of the clients, and so on. And this is exactly what happened. What made the trial of the "Harrisburg Seven" so extraordinary, however, is that volunteer social scientists aided the defense attorneys in *selecting a jury* that would be as initially sympathetic to the defendants as the accumulated knowledge of social psychology could assure.

Basically, what was done was to develop a profile or a *recipe* for an "ideal" (that is, prodefense) juror. Volunteers traveled throughout Harrisburg interviewing registered voters to determine which personal characteristics were most strongly associated with prodefense attitudes. It was found that women were more likely to be sympathetic than men; Democrats more than Republicans; those with no religious preference more that Episcopalians, Presbyterians, Methodists, and fundamentalists; white-collar or skilled blue-collar workers more than professionals or laborers. Favorable attitudes toward opposition to the war and toward civil disobedience were also good signs.

This list of personal characteristics was to guide the defense lawyers during the selection of the actual jury. The defense team would attempt to impanel as many people as possible fitting the recipe, while using challenges to eliminate potential jurors with - "unfavorable" personal attributes. The results of this "scientific jury selection" were almost totally successful. The defense team approached the trial with the hope that they could get one or two jurors who would hold out against an otherwise unanimous guilty verdict. As it was, fully *ten* of the twelve jurors favored acquittal, the jury was hopelessly hung, and the government elected not to retry the case. Similar procedures have been followed in numerous other political trials throughout the country, invariably with the same result: acquittal or a hung jury.

Scientific jury selection illustrates an important point in group decision making: *Sometimes the most powerful determinant of a particular group decision is the composition of the group—the values, attitudes, and backgrounds of the group members.* The United States Congress is a prime example of this principle. Every two years millions of dollars are spent in campaigns to determine the majority political party and ideological composition of the Congress. Many of the group decisions reached by the Senate and the House of Representatives can be confidently predicted, given the relative preponderance of Democrats over Republicans, or of conservatives over liberals. Similarly, each time a president nominates a Supreme Court justice, debates rage over whether the Court has swung to the right or to the left. Knowing that five or more of the justices are "strict constructionists," for example, will enable an observer to predict many decisions of the Court with great confidence. Presidents who make these appointments are doing essentially the same thing as the social scientists at the trial of the Harrisburg Seven—attempting to ensure group decisions that support their own values (and biases) by forming the "right" kind of group.

The results of the Harrisburg Seven trial give us some confidence that group decisions can be largely determined by the characteristics that people bring to their groups. Indeed, these results have been confirmed in several experimental studies, one of which we now describe in more detail.

Authoritarianism, guilt, and punishment in mock juries. Perhaps the most widely studied personality variable in all of psychology is authoritarianism—the tendency to idealize powerful authority figures, to reject members of outgroups, to adopt conventional life-styles, and to value discipline and tough-mindedness—in short, an "Archie Bunker" type of personality. Bray and Noble (1978) measured authoritarianism in a large group of undergraduates, exposed them to a tape of a murder trial, then formed them into high- or low-authoritarian juries. Not one of the juries composed of low authoritarians found the defendants guilty, while 35% of the high-authoritarian juries reached guilty verdicts. Jurors were also asked to recommend a sentence, *assuming* the defendants had been found guilty. Before discussing the case in a jury, low authoritarians recommended an average sentence of about 38 years in prison; this figure dropped to about 28.5 years after jury deliberations. But the high-authoritarian subjects were far more punitive, recommending over 56 years in prison before deliberations and almost 68 years after meeting in juries.

The results raise some interesting issues of both a theoretical and a practical nature. Initial predispositions or biases can have an important effect on group decisions, although this time the "bias" was at the level of basic personality. The findings also have potential applications to our criminal justice system. In certain states where the death penalty is legal, jurors who indicate they are opposed to capital punishment are typically excused from jury duty in trials involving a capital offense. The resulting jury is then called "death-qualified." Since high authoritarians tend to favor the death penalty more than do low authoritarians, it is quite likely that a death-qualified jury will be above average in authoritarianism. On the basis of Bray and Noble's experiment, we might expect such a jury to be predisposed to a guilty verdict and, once having made that decision, to recommend harsher punishment. A defendant could, with some cause, object to the rather subtle biasing against him which these findings imply.

Concluding remarks on group composition. The variables we have examined in this section—background characteristics, attitudes, biases and authoritarianism—should be viewed as illustrative rather than exhaustive. There are many other characteristics of group members that have been linked to the outcomes of group decisions. For example, groups comprised of self-centered people tend to function poorly, as they often place their own interests above those of the group. But group composition is only a part—in many instances a minor part—of what determines a particular group decision. If this were not true, lawyers would soon begin to divert all their energies away from building a strong case to selecting the most sympathetic jury. And lobbyists, pressure groups, and ordinary citizens would soon stop communicating with their lawmakers, since all legislative decisions would be predetermined by the composition of the legislature. Fortunately, group decisions are influenced by a great many other factors, some of which we turn to now.

THE NATURE OF THE GROUP'S TASK

Decision-making groups do not always maximize their effectiveness by choosing members who are uniformly brilliant, highly skilled, or even talented individual decision makers. A president, for example, often chooses to surround himself with various combinations of the most capable people possible, the hardest working and the ideologically "pure." Experts differ as to whether the Supreme Court should be composed of the nine smartest judges in the land, the fairest, or even, to paraphrase the words of former U.S. Senator Roman Hruska, to include a mediocre man to represent all the average Americans.

The combination of individual talents most likely to result in effective group decision making depends in part on the type of task facing the group. Four different group tasks may be differentiated: These may be *additive* in nature (members' contributions are simply summed, as in tug-of-war); *conjunctive* (the group proceeds at the pace of the least proficient); *disjunctive* (the group depends on the ability of the most skilled member) or *discretionary* (also called divisible—the group must integrate the various contributions of its members). Groups facing additive tasks wish to have as many capable members as possible; those with conjunctive tasks wish to avoid clunkers; while disjunctive tasks require at least one member who can be depended upon to provide the correct answer or make the right decision. But most important, group decisions are made in groups with discretionary tasks, and here, simple generalizations about group composition elude us.

Consider the following simple experimental situation, devised by Smelser (1961). Two students are shown a circular, toy railroad track. Two trains, a passenger train and a freight, are to circle the track in opposite directions. The task is to circle the track as many times as possible in a short interval of time. Credit is given only when *both* trains complete a circle. To successfully complete the task, it is necessary to run one train off to a side track periodically to enable the other to get by. Furthermore, subjects are told, the passenger train always has priority over the freight, so the person running the passenger train can issue orders to the other person. Finally, each student has previously taken a personality test measuring *dominance*, and each pair consists of one person scoring high on the test and the other scoring low. Smelser found that the teams that scored best were those in which the more dominant member was assigned the more dominant role (running the passenger train). The least efficient groups were those involving a mismatch (dominant person operating the freight, submissive person running the passenger train). Efficiency in this simple group thus cannot be predicted on the basis of a knowledge of the features of the task or the personalities of the members. Rather, the *match* between the two must be considered. Similarly, when powerful people, used to exercising their authority, are appointed to, say, a cabinet position where they must bend their wills to that of the president, conflict may result and resignations are common.

We may conclude that, for discretionary, divisible tasks, decisions to appoint particular members should depend on how well those skills or inclinations match the demands of the task. As Ivan Steiner (1976) has remarked about the happy coordinated decision reached by Jack Sprat (who could eat no fat) and his wife (who could eat no lean), "Jack Sprat and his wife would have eaten little meat had each been matched with the portion of the task that he could not, or would not, perform."

THE MEMBER-GROUP RELATIONSHIP: COHESIVENESS

"Team spirit." "Esprit de corps." "Close-knit group." All these terms refer to the strength of the ties that bind group members together. When people like each other, find their relationship to the group rewarding, and wish to remain members, we consider that group highly *cohesive*.

President Kennedy's advisors formed a highly cohesive group in early 1961 as they planned the abortive invasion of Cuba that has become known as the "Bay of Pigs fiasco." Does this mean that cohesiveness leads to poor group decision making? Later, in Kennedy's brief administration, what has often been called the greatest crisis in the nation's history, the 13 days of the Cuban missile crisis, was successfully resolved by the same president, aided by virtually the same group of advisors. Does this mean that cohesive groups make bad decisions only half the time? Or that they learn from their mistakes? Or that there is no relationship between cohesiveness and the adequacy of group decisions? In this section, and in the following chapter, we shall analyze the important variable of cohesiveness and relate it to the effectiveness of group decisions.

Sources of Cohesiveness

Perhaps the most common source of group cohesiveness is initial member attraction to the group. A college student visits several fraternities, likes the men in one, and becomes a pledge. A group of friends form a monthly poker club. Or sometimes cohesive groups form on the basis of perceived *similarity* of attitudes, skills, or interests. A racist joins the Ku Klux Klan. A Rotarian moves to a new town and joins the local Rotary Club. The former star of the local high school debate team joins her college debate club. Granting certain assumptions (e.g., the group members are basically compatible), such groups foster cohesiveness and group membership becomes valued.

Fostering cooperation and interdependence within a group may increase cohesiveness. Elliot Aronson (1980) and his colleagues have recently developed the "jigsaw technique" for reducing competitiveness and prejudice in school classrooms. The technique consists of simply dividing up a learning task into pieces, giving each of the pieces to different children, and requiring them to "teach" the other group members their piece of the "puzzle" in order to successfully pass a test on the full material. (This is a good example, incidentally of a *conjunctive* task.) For example, five children, each holding different sets of six German words and their translations, must all teach each other their words so they can all translate a paragraph containing the 30 words. According to Aronson, the usual competitiveness and see-how-smart-I-am orthodoxy of many schools becomes maladaptive. To do well, children must respond to the new *interdependent* relationship with each other. The result is increased liking for one another and for school—that is, group cohesiveness.

In addition to initial liking, similarity, and intragroup cooperation, external threats can increase cohesiveness. During periods of national crisis, referring to a foreign enemy as a "Satan," as the United States was labeled by Iranian leaders during the hostage crisis, can result in a unity of purpose, high morale, and active participation in large demonstrations. The high level of group cohesiveness among Northern Irish Catholics in response to the British presence, and the high morale and "we-feelings" shown by Londoners during the blitz, are other clear examples. Furthermore, cohesiveness increases even more when the group is *winning* (or comes to *believe* it is victorious) against the outside threat. In sports teams, for example, a long winning streak finds players feeling good about their team and about one another; losing can be a source of depression, alienation, and "I-want-to-be-traded" talk. Similarly, the leaders of countries in conflict with one another have learned the importance of calling each small victory (or even a defeat that can be construed as a victory) a source of national celebration.

Finally, groups may feel threatened when cohesiveness is jeopardized by *internal* threats—a deviant group member. Cohesiveness may increase as the group members unite to either reform or cast out the deviate. The dynamics of group reactions to deviates will be more fully discussed in the following chapter.

To summarize, cohesiveness should be at a maximum when a group of like-minded mutually attractive people are cooperating successfully against a powerful threat.

The Advantages of Cohesiveness

The major advantage of high group cohesiveness is the positive feelings generated in group members. Individuals feel better about themselves and their relationship to the group. Research has indicated that cohesive group members have high self-esteem and are less anxious than people in low-cohesive groups. Industrial workers report being less "jumpy" on the job when their work groups are cohesive.

Cartwright and Zander (1968) have neatly summarized the positive effects of group cohesiveness at the personal level:

> (T)he improved interpersonal relations involved in an increase in cohesiveness lead to more acceptance, trust, and confidence among members and . . . each member consequently develops a sense of security and personal worth [p. 104].

Besides these personal consequences, cohesiveness increases the *power* of the group over its members. Obviously, this can be either a positive feature or a disadvantage, as we shall seee in the next section, and in Chapter 3. But since the group is highly attractive to its members (perhaps in part because of these personal benefits it bestows on them), they wish to maintain their membership. Cohesive work groups, in fact, have lower job turnover rates than less cohesive groups. The cohesive group is also able to enforce greater participation and loyalty in its members, and to generally exert greater influence on them, including conformity to group standards.

Disadvantages of Cohesiveness

The greater power of cohesive groups over group members can be viewed both positively and negatively. A football team approaching the Superbowl without the benefit of cohesiveness would be at a severe disadvantage. Intragroup conflict, an inability of the coaching staff to enforce training rules, and absenteeism could be disastrous for the team. But what about those millions of demonstrating, American-flag-burning Iranians? Or the perfect columns of goose-stepping Nazi stormtroopers? Clearly, cohesiveness can create a singleness of purpose that signals power and unity to other groups (see Chapter 3 for a further discussion of this point). But can a group suffer from too much cohesiveness? Can the inevitable pressures to maintain close intragroup relations propel the group toward foolhardy, irrational, or immoral decisions? The answer to each of these questions is yes. High group cohesiveness can be a serious threat to effective group decision making. In Chapter 3, we shall deal extensively with the dangers of too high a level of cohesiveness, and will propose specific ways of minimizing these dangers.

GROUP SIZE

Earlier in this chapter, we discussed the relative merits of individual and group decision making. Once we move to the group level of analysis, however, the issue of group size arises. What are the advantages and disadvantages of large versus small groups? There is tremendous variability in the size of decision-making groups, from the two-person husband-wife dyad to the 435 member House of Representatives or even the millions of shareholders in AT&T. In between are groups such as the U.S. Supreme Court (9 justices), the familiar 12-person jury, university boards of trustees, and corporate boards.

There are few ready generalizations to make about group size, since the type of task the group is engaged in is of such importance. For example, for disjunctive tasks (i.e., those in which there is one correct answer), all that is needed is *one* person who knows the correct answer. Suppose you wished to know how many people were in the U.S. House of Representatives, and could choose a group of any size to advise you of the correct answer. You would stand a better chance if you had a large group, since the chances would increase of having at least one person who knew the answer. Similarly, if the task were additive (e.g., a tug-of-war, a scavenger hunt), large groups should outperform small. But with the more usual and interesting discretionary tasks (e.g., deciding how to handle the Cuban missile crisis), there may be no clear relationship between quality of decision making or problem solving and group size. Furthermore, increasing group size will usually decrease efficiency (i.e., amount of time or number of solutions *per member*).

Despite these precautions, a number of tentative generalizations may be gleaned from the experimental work on group size in laboratory groups (Thomas & Fink, 1963). First, larger groups tend to be more productive and to develop higher quality products than do smaller groups. For example, Ziller (1957) found that quality of military decision making was superior in larger groups of Air Force officers than in smaller groups. Second, as group size increases, members feel freer to express disagreement and dissatisfaction. Such tendencies are more likely to be inhibited with groups of only two or three members, as people feel reluctant to anger or alienate one another. Groupthink would therefore be less likely to occur in larger groups. Third, smaller groups allow greater opportunities for members to exhibit leadership. Fourth, as group size increases, there is a tendency for subgroups or cliques to form, and for the cohesiveness of the group as a whole to decrease. Finally, perhaps because of the preceding three factors, plus the obvious fact that people have less opportunity to actively participate as group size increases, most studies have shown that member satisfaction declines with increasing group size. For example, both students and instructors of college-level discussion groups express more satis-faction with smaller classes.

The effects on group decision making of varying the size of the group parallel fairly closely the effects of cohesiveness. Smaller groups, like cohesive groups, provide greater rewards to individual members. However, these rewards (satisfaction, feelings or belong-ingness, opportunities to be leaders) are often obtained at the price of groupthink and inferior group decisions.

CHANNELS OF COMMUNICATION

An important determinant of a group's decision-making effec-tiveness is the communication structure of the group—who is allowed to communicate with whom. For example, Chapter 10 discusses different organizational reporting structures (e.g., corporate and military) that represent types of communication networks. We might want to know the answers to a number of questions relating to a network: How *satisfied* will each of the group members be? How *efficiently* will they be able to accomplish a task or make a decision? Will any one member come to be viewed as a *leader*? To answer these questions, let us return to the social psychologist's laboratory.

You are one of five subjects in an experiment. Each of you is given a card with five symbols taken from a group of six (circle, triangle, and so on). Only *one* of the symbols appears on *each* subject's card. The task of the group is to determine the identity of that common symbol as quickly as possible. The five subjects sit around a table divided by partitions. In each partition is a slot through which subjects can exchange written messages. Which slots are open or closed determines the nature of the communication network. You may be in a position where you communicate with only one other subject, or two, or perhaps all four corresponding to the patterns shown in Figure 2.1. These are just four of the many possible networks. The double arrows indicate that all communication links are two way; that is, slots permit both sending and receiving messages. (While some networks include one-way channels—such as putting a message in a suggestion box—they are relatively rare, and will not be considered here.)

Perhaps the most important characteristic of communication networks is their centrality, and the degree of centrality of a given member within the network. Centrality may be viewed as the degree of *connectedness* among the people in the network. In Fig. 2.1, the wheel is highly centralized, with C maintaining communications with all other group members. The circle is less centralized, as each member maintains but two communication links.

Let us now summarize the major findings that have emerged from research on communication networks (Cartwright & Zander, 1968). First, a given member's centrality is strongly related to his or her satisfaction with the group experience. This relationship is particularly strong among people with relatively dominant personalities. Second, people who are placed in central positions in the network come to be viewed as *leaders* by the other group members. Virtually all group members agree that C is the leader in the wheel, but there is no consensus about leadership in the circle. Third, the performance of the group (measured by such factors as speed, accuracy, rate of learning) is strongly affected by its structure. For simple tasks, such

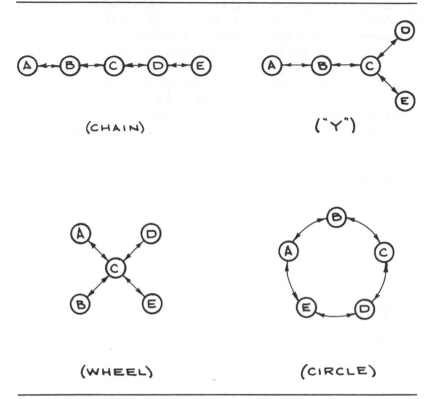

Figure 2.1   Four Different Communications Networks

as the information-gathering one described above, the more centralized networks perform better. For more complex activities such as
those requiring somebody (i.e., the central person) to operate on the
information after it is collected, centralized groups perform more
poorly. We might speculate that this result will be particularly
pronounced when the central person is basically incompetent. But a
further explanation comes from the fourth general finding: Decentralized groups as a whole are more satisfied with their group
experience than are centralized groups. While the wheel may have
one satisfied person (the "leader"), there are four peripheral,
unhappy members. Participants in a circle network, on the other
hand, are all equally central or peripheral, and share equally in the

group responsibilities. This higher degree of group satisfaction might contribute to the finding that such decentralized (democratic?) groups outperform others on more challenging tasks.

The effectiveness of group decision making should clearly vary with the complexity and nature of the group task, and with the type of communication structure. A highly centralized structure should be most effective with simpler decisions, and when a competent leader holds the central position. For more complex, discretionary tasks, a more decentralized communication structure should produce both better decisions and greater member satisfaction.

LEADERSHIP

In any group, one person (and sometimes more than one) is viewed as influential in directing the group's activities and moving the group toward a decision, solving a problem, or accomplishing some other goal. Sometimes the group leader actually *makes* the decision, perhaps with the advice of group members; other groups make decisions more democratically, but the leader's opinons remain of great importance. In either case, if we are to understand how groups make decisions, we must pay special attention to group leaders.

While most people probably think they have a pretty good idea of what leadership is, the concept turns out to be highly complex. For example, we think of the American presidency as a high *position* of leadership, yet we speak of certain American presidents (e.g., Harding, Coolidge) as being weak leaders. In a particular group there may be a formal leader (appointed by somebody "higher up") and another person to whom members more often look for guidance. Or a group may start out with no leader at all, yet rather quickly, *types* of leadership roles begin to differentiate. These are just a few examples of problems that social psycholgists face when attempting to study scientifically the importance of leadership in influencing group decisions. In this section, we shall approach the topic of leadership from several perspectives. First, different approaches to the determinants of leadership will be examined—are leaders born, made, or what? How does leadership emerge and differentiate in small groups, and how does it influence group decisions once established? Finally, some of the pitfalls of leadership will be mentioned, along with suggestions for improving the effectiveness of leaders.

Determinants of Leadership

Folk wisdom offers confusing guidance to answering the question of what makes a leader. "Leaders are born, not made." "The clothes make the man." "She was the right person in the right place at the right time." These three aphorisms neatly summarize the three different approaches to understanding the emergence of leadership: namely, an approach based on the importance of "traits," of the "situation," or an interaction of traits and situational factors.

(1) Are certain people born to lead? Of course; generally they are first-born sons of monarchs. But how about the more usual cases of leadership—presidents of coporations, legislators, scoutmasters? Are there certain personality traits, background characteristics, or skills that mark one for leadership roles? The search for such factors has generally been disappointing. A number of such traits (e.g., height, need for power, intelligence, attractiveness) have been isolated, but the relationships are not strong and exceptions can invariably be found. The trait approach to leadership has generally lost favor with social psychologists, in favor of the other two approaches.

(2) If, indeed, "the clothes make the man," then doesn't this imply that anyone (or just about anyone) can become a leader? At least in certain specific situations, the answer to this question is "yes." For example, in our discussion of communication networks, it was reported that when individuals are assigned a central position in the network (e.g, the hub of the wheel), they are almost universally perceived as the group's leader. People who sit at the *head* of a table are more likely to be perceived as leaders than when seated at the side. And people who talk a lot (regardless of the quality of their remarks) are likely to be perceived as leaders. These findings, derived from laboratory studies, find an interesting application in a rather unlikely place: the communication network of the baseball diamond. People familiar with the game of baseball can readily see that certain positions are more central than others. Outfielders, who handle the ball infrequently and have their attention focused primarily on the opponent batters, are distinctly "peripheral." Catchers, on the other hand, handle the ball on almost every pitch, often receive signals from the manager, and have their attention focused outward. The position of catcher is therefore highly central. Infielders tend to be intermediate in centrality, handling the ball less

frequently than the catcher but more often than the outfielders. They tend to "communicate" more with the other players than do their teammates in the outfield. The pitcher is somewhat anomalous: He handles the ball frequently, but is in communication primarily with one other player (the catcher). Furthermore, he appears in only a small fraction of his team's games. Grusky (1963) has studied this communication network and related it to the recruitment of team managers. Catchers are most likely to manage teams when their playing careers are over, followed by infielders and outfielders.

Creating a structure that is conducive to leadership does indeed tend to promote the emergence of leaders. However, one is seldom in a position to choose such arrangements as part of a conscious plan to become a leader. Another situational approach that has somewhat more promise is based on the premise that leadership skills can be *learned*; one need not possess leadership traits to profit from leadership training. Latham and Saari (1979) developed films showing supervisors how to be more effective in their relationships with employees. Not only did the training program produce improvement in leadership skills, but the gains were maintained a year after the training. Other studies have found that simply placing a person in a position of leadership, or convincing subordinates to *treat* the person as a leader (e.g., by encouraging him or her to talk more), can consolidate the leader's position. On the other hand, it is extremely difficult for a person who has a long history of being a follower in a particular group to suddenly be accepted as a leader. This was born out rather dramatically in World War II when enlisted men in the infantry were sometimes given field commissions after decimation of the officers' ranks. These men were not able to effectively lead the people they had formerly served with, but were able to lead adequately in different units.

(3) A recent, more sophisticated approach to the development of leadership is the *interactionist* position. Not all people who fit some ideal personality "profile" of a leader actually attain positions of influence. Not all people who are treated as leaders or who are trained as leaders fulfill their roles successfully. However, consider the possibility that *everybody* (well, almost everybody) is a "born leader," but in order for a person to function effectively, he or she must find the kind of situation that capitalizes on his or her particular kinds of leadership talents.

Constantini and Craik (1980) studied personality characteristics of political party leaders in California. There were a number of traits which generally distinguished the leaders from a group of nonleaders. For example, the leaders were more self-confident and had higher dominance and achievement needs. Of more interest to us here, however, was the finding that there were differences in personalities of leaders of different political parties, and these differences tended to reflect "party lines." For example, Republican leaders scored high on the "conservative" needs for order and self-control, while Democrats tended to be higher in the "liberal" needs for change and nurturance. Thus, a Republican leader's personality would ill equip him or her to lead the Democrats, and vice versa.

LEADERSHIP STYLES

The interactionist position suggests that a leader with a particular personality, values, and style of interacting with others could be highly effective in guiding one group's decision making, but might be a disaster with some other group. What are the general "styles" of leadership that most commonly emerge in groups? How do these styles interact with the characteristics of the group and the group task? How may we maximize the effectiveness of a decision-making group through an understanding of this interaction? It is to these questions that we now turn.

Kurt Lewin, often called the father of experimental social psychology, was part of the pre-World War II "brain drain" from Nazi Germany. Establishing himself in the United States, Lewin had a keen social conscience, and used his substantial intellect to tackle a number of social problems—in the experimental laboratory. In one of his earliest investigations (Lewin, Lippitt, & White, 1939), groups of 10-year old boys participated in "clubs" that met once a week for several months. Three adults, trained to represent three different leadership styles, took turns in directing the activities of the groups. *Democratic* leaders were trained to work with the boys in arriving at group decisions, to be friendly, helpful participants who would clearly indicate how group members would be rewarded or criticized. *Authoritarian* leaders were to act like dictators— to praise or criticize indiscriminantly, to give orders without explanations, and to distance themselves from the group. *Laissez-faire* leaders were to be friendly, but to offer little by way of guidance to the group.

The clubs behaved quite differently with the different leaders. Those with democratic leaders were highly cohesive, quite productive, and coped well with "crises" (e.g., what to do when the leader was absent). Authoritarian-led groups were also highly productive, but only when the leader was physically present. Group morale was low and hostility high. Laissez-faire groups were nonproductive, even though good relations were maintained with the leader.

Lewin's pioneering work deals with *ascribed* leadership—the leaders were appointed by the experimenter. In other kinds of group situations, however, leaders emerge from the ranks of the group members.[1] Sometimes these *emergent* leaders do not hold formal power (as through an election), but are tacitly acknowledged by the members as the leader. A few years after Lewin et al.'s experiment, R. Freed Bales began his study of group interaction processes and leadership emergence at the Social Relations Laboratory at Harvard. Bales developed a technique to study the ongoing process of laboratory decision-making groups. Every verbal or nonverbal behavior by each group member is coded by an observer in terms of various categories (e.g., "gives suggestion," "asks for opinion," "shows tension"). At the end of each session, each member is asked a number of questions, including how much he or she likes each member and who has the best ideas. Bales' work indicates that not one but *two* leaders typically emerge: a task-leader, who gets things done, but is not particularly well liked; and a socioemotional leader, who eases tensions, relates well to the other members, but is not highly productive.[2] It is ironic that the person most responsible for the group accomplishing its task may so threaten the feelings of competence of the other members that he or she must look elsewhere for popularity. Only rarely are the two leadership roles combined in one person, and the "Great Leader" emerges.

Lewin's and Bales's work deal with different kinds of groups, and different sources of leadership (ascribed and emergent). But they have in common the *differentiation* of leadership into two roles: a democratic, socioemotional, cohesion-producing leader; and an autocratic, task-oriented, less friendly leader. Lewin's work clearly suggests that the democratic leader is "better"; Bales' research indicates that he or she is certainly more popular. But mightn't there be situations where the autocratic or task leader would be preferable?

The essence of Fred Fiedler's (1973) approach to leadership is captured in his assertion that "it makes no sense to speak of a good leader or a poor leader. There are only leaders who perform well in one situation but not well in another" (1973, p. 26). Using the contingency model (literally, the effectiveness of the leader is *contingent* on the match between personal and situational factors), one must assess two things: First, is the potential leader "task-oriented" or "relationship-oriented"? (This dichotomy corresponds roughly to the task leader-socioemotional leader distinction of Bales.) Second, what is the degree of *situational control* to be faced by the leader? This factor is defined by three components, listed in order of decreasing importance: (a) leader-member relations (how cohesive is the group, how much does the group support the leader); (b) task structure (how clearly defined is the group task in terms of goals and procedures); and (c) position power (to what extent can the leader reward and punish group members). When all three of these components are high, situational control is defined as high; when all three are low, situational control is low.

Fiedler's research has generally demonstrated that task-oriented leaders excel when situational control is either high or low; relationship-oriented leaders are most effective when situational control is moderate. What rationale would support these "contingencies"? Consider three different group situations varying in degree of situational control:

In Group 1, situational control is low. The group members are squabbling, nobody knows what to do, and there is no reward structure built in. A relationship-oriented leader might come in and try to "relate" to the members, but might be reluctant to impose much structure or institute a reward-punishment system. The group would continue to flounder. The task-oriented leader comes in and attempts to get the group working. At least the group will have the satisfaction of accomplishing something.

In Group 2, situational control is high. The group is without serious conflict, people know what is expected of them, and incentives for good task performance are built in. Clearly, this will be a productive group regardless of the leader. But the task-oriented leader is in a position to fully mobilize the talents of the group members by sharply focusing them on their jobs. The relationship-oriented leader might direct more of the group's energies toward interpersonal behaviors, and group productivity would suffer.

In Group 3, situational control is moderate. Perhaps the members get along well, but it is not clear what they should be doing. Or there is a clear reward structure and the task is highly structured, but cohesiveness is low. It is this kind of situation (probably forming the majority of decision-making groups) where the relationship-oriented leader shines. He or she might increase group productivity by either making the group more cohesive, or by nudging an already cohesive group toward a goal.

Fiedler has recently developed a technique for translating the contingency model into a practical method for improving leader effectiveness. Based on the principle that it is easier to change situations than to change personalities, the Leader Match training program (Fiedler & Mahler, 1979) trains leaders to alter the level of situational control in their groups to match their leadership styles. The program consists of a self-paced workbook requiring about five hours to complete. The trainee first determines whether he or she is task- or relationship-oriented, then learns how to determine the degree of situational control in his or her group. Finally, the prospective leader is taught how to *change* the situational control to match up with his or her leadership style. Results of this procedure indicate that both performance and ratings by group members improve after training.

Leadership and Risk-Taking in Groups

An important aspect of a group's decisions is how risky they are. We place no particular value judgment on risk-taking per se. Indeed, we may safely label certain decisions as foolhardy. But in other instances, a conservative decision (e.g., American automobile manufacturers' decision to continue producing almost exclusively large, gas-guzzling cars, ignoring the impending fuel crisis and success of small imports) may be disastrous, while a high-risk decision (e.g., almost any decision that in retrospect we consider "visionary"—the Marshall Plan, Columbus, Henry Ford, etc.) may turn out very well indeed. Perhaps a safe generalization is that *significant* decisions (either desirable or unfortunate) are frequently those involving a high degree of risk.

Strong leadership is clearly associated with the riskiness of group decisions. Leaders are particularly likely to adopt strong, high-risk policies when they have strong social support. Lyndon Johnson, fresh from an 18-million vote landslide victory over Barry Goldwater in 1964, was largely responsible for pouring billions of dollars and hundreds of thousand of men into Vietnam. Ronald Reagan, after a landslide victory of comparable proportions, succeeded in reversing spending and taxation policies—policies that had been dubbed "voodoo economics" by the man who was to become his vice president, George Bush. The tendency to adopt strong, high-risk policies under conditions of wide popular support has been dubbed the "mandate phenomenon" (Clark & Sechrest, 1976). In a laboratory analog of the phenomenon, group members were led to believe they had been chosen group leader by *all* their fellow members, by a bare *majority*, or else *assigned* the role of leader by an experimenter. Leaders were then asked to commit the group to a future action (enduring a number of unpleasant odors), which might have aversive consequences (nausea, sinus pain), but could result in a high payoff (the more unpleasant the odor endured, the more money the group would be paid). Leaders elected unanimously made substantially *riskier* decisions than the other leaders. Clark and Sechrest conclude that a leader with a mandate "will endorse a more extreme course of action, even when he does not know the others' preferences and when the consequences may be unpleasant" (p. 1060).

Related to the mandate phenomenon is Edwin Hollander's concept of *idiosyncracy credit*. A leader who performs important services for his or her group gradually builds up an "account," from which the leader may draw in the future. During the two years preceding the 1968 presidential election, Richard Nixon traveled hundreds of thousands of miles speaking on behalf of Republican candidates for office. He accumulated a considerable store of credits that he was able to translate into support for his own successful campaign. A leader who has a large account may draw from it until the "debt" is repaid. Sometimes, the leader's behavior deviates from the expected—for example, asking one's group for support in voting for some unpopular legislation—in which case we speak of using idiosyncracy credit. Because supporting the leader in a high-risk endeavor exposes the group to censure should the venture fail, the leader is limited in the amount of risky behavior he or she may engage in before the debt is repaid.

Leadership and Improving Decisions in Groups.

Our analysis of leadership suggests several ways in which decision-making groups can be made more effective. First, it is important to understand that people possess different kinds of leadership skills. A person who seems like a "natural-born" leader in one context could flounder in another.

Fiedler's interactive approach emphasizes the importance of matching individual characteristics with those of the situation.

Second, besides simply matching the right person with the right group, it is possible for people already in leadership situations to alter their behavior and the structure of the group to effect a better match. Third, groups should be aware of the fact that a strong, charismatic leader increases the chances of a highly risky decision. In certain situations, where there is much to gain and little to lose from high-risk decisions, this tendency does not present problems. Groups and their leaders should be vigilant, however, of those tasks where a poorly thought-through, risky decision might spell disaster. In Chapter 3, we shall return to the issue of strong leadership in decision-making groups, and shall present specific ways for leaders to avoid premature decisions.

Making Groups More Effective Decision Makers

What are some of the lessons of social psychology for decision-making groups? First, we now realize the importance of group composition in influencing a final decision. The individual members' personalities and biases have been measured and found to strongly influence jury decisions. It therefore becomes important, if a "fair" or unbiased decision based on the available evidence is desirable, to carefully select group members who either do not evidence the important biases, or whose biases cancel each other out. Research also indicates that groups comprised largely of self-centered members tend to perform poorly. Selecting members whose concern for the group overrides needs for self-assertion may help promote the kind of healthy group interactions that result in good decisions. Finally, it is important to match individual characteristics with those of the task. Dominant members are likely to be unhappy and unproductive in peripheral positions, while a recluse may not excel in a directive role.

The second class of implications deals with the important dimension of group cohesiveness. The effects of cohesiveness on group morale and interpersonal relations is almost always positive; but highly cohesive groups often make disastrous decisions. (Janis suggests that groups of moderate cohesiveness may be optimal for good decision making.) This does not mean that efforts should be made to deliberately decrease a group's cohesiveness, but it suggests that it is crucial for highly cohesive groups to avoid the premature consensus-seeking that can preclude a critical appraisal of alternatives and lead to poor decisions. Cohesive groups should be sure to establish explicit group norms that counter tendencies toward groupthink.

Third, it is crucial to assess accurately the nature and structure of the decision-making group and its task. For example, How shall the group's effectiveness be measured? By its productivity (in which case member satisfaction may be secondary)? By intragroup harmony? (A group of friends may value this over any tangible product they may produce.) By the quality of its decisions? And what kind of task is being performed? Is it an additive task, in which large numbers may be welcome? Or a discretionary task, in which group size (not too large, not too small) and complementary skills become important issues? And what is the degree of "situational control"? Are member relations positive? Is the task structured? Can the leader reward and punish members? Answers to questions such as these will direct such important activities as choosing the group membership and assigning members to tasks within the group.

Fourth, group leaders are in a uniquely powerful position to influence group decisions. This position can be used most advantageously when the leader adapts his or her behavior to match the characteristics of the group and its tasks. Then, by implementing appropriate group norms supporting effective decision-making, the pitfalls of groupthink can be minimized.

In this chapter, we have focused primarily on the *group* and its most influential member: the leader. The flow of influence has been from the group member and the leader to the group and its decisions. In the next chapter, we shall examine carefully the converse of the relationship: How do groups influence individuals, and what are the consequences of this influence for group decisions?

Notes

1. One of the characteristics of a bureaucracy is that group leaders are appointed. An ambassador or cabinet member, for example, is appointed by the president, and may have no particular leadership qualities. In fact, as James MacGregor Burns (1979) has pointed out, they possess authority, rather than leadership.

2. Interestingly, when groups interact via a video "teleconferencing" set-up, each member viewing all other members on television monitors, leadership roles do not tend to emerge (Strickland, Guild, Barefoot, & Paterson, 1978).

References

Arsonson ,E. *The social animal* (3rd ed.) San Francisco: Freeman, 1980.

Bray, R. M., & Noble, A. M. Authoritarianism and decisions of mock juries: Evidence of jury bias and group polarization. *Journal of Personality & Social Psychology,* 1978, 36, 1424-1430.

Burns, J. M. *Leadership.* New York: Harper Colophon, 1979.

Cartwright, D., & Zander, A. *Group dynamics* (3rd ed.) New York: Harper & Row, 1968.

Clark, R. D., & Sechrest, L. B. The mandate phenomenon. *Journal of Personality & Social Psychology,* 1976, 34, 1057-1061.

Constantini, E., & Craik, K. H. Personality and politicians: California party leaders, 1960-1976. *Journal of Personality & Social Psychology,* 1980, 38, 641-661.

Fiedler, F. E. The trouble with leadership is that it doesn't train leaders. *Psychology Today,* 1973, 92, 23-29.

Fiedler, F. E., & Maher, L. A field experiment validating contingency model leadership training. *Journal of Applied Psychology,* 1979, 64, 247-254.

Grusky, O. The effect of formal structure on managerial recruitment: A study of baseball organization. *Sociometry,* 1963, 26, 345-353.

Kalven, H., & Zeisel, H. *The American jury.* Boston: Little, Brown, 1966.

Latham, G. P., & Saari, L. M. Application of social-learning theory to training supervisors through behavioral modeling. *Journal of Applied Psychology,* 1979, 64, 239-246.

Lewin, K., Lippitt, R., & White, R. K. Patterns of aggressive behavior in experimentally created "social climates." *Journal of Social Psychology,* 1939, 10, 271-299.

Smelser, W. T. Personality influences in social situations. *Journal of Abnormal & Social Psychology,* 1961, 62, 535-542.

Steiner, I. D. Task-performing groups. In J. W. Thibaut, J. T. Spence, & R. C. Carson (Eds.). *Contempoary topics in social psychology.* Morristown, NJ: General Learning Press, 1976.

Strickland, L. H., Guild, P. D., Barefoot, J. C., & Paterson, B. A. Teleconferencing and leadership emergence. *Human Relations,* 1978, 31, 583-596.

Thomas, E. J., & Fink, C. Effects of group size. *Psychological Bulletin,* 1963, 60, 371-384.

Ziller, R. C. Group size: A determinant of the quality and stability of group decisions. *Sociometry,* 1957, 20, 165-173.

CHAPTER 3

DESTRUCTIVE EFFECTS OF GROUPS ON INDIVIDUALS

Walter C. Swap

In the previous chapter, some of the determinants of group decisions were analyzed. Individual group members were considered primarily as they influenced their group's decisions. For example, juries may reach different verdicts when composed of people with certain biases or background characteristics; and different qualities in leaders may propel groups in quite different directions.

Another way to view things, however, is to consider how groups affect their members and, ultimately, how these effects can influence the group's decisions. This seemingly circular relationship between group and individual influence may be clarified with a simple example. If one characteristic of a group is that pressures develop to reach agreements on important issues, then members will experience these pressures whenever they deviate from the prevailing group sentiment. The result may be a premature decision that, though unanimous, may not be the best, most considered decision available to the group.

In fact, groups can and do exert powerful influences on their members. These influences are often destructive, and must be understood and overcome in order to promote effective decision making. In this chapter, we consider three such group influences. First, members of groups often exert less effort than do individuals, a phenomenon known as social loafing or diffusion of responsibility. Second, certain groups have a dehumanizing or, more accurately, a deindividuating effect on group members, so they behave in irrational and immoral ways. Third, as our example suggests, groups do exert pressures on individuals to conform or arrive at a consensual decision that may be premature and even harmful. These three group influences will be considered in turn. We shall analyze the nature of these influences and what determines them. We shall consider if there are positive aspects to each, but will focus more on their destructive effects on group decision making. Finally, we shall discuss what can be done—especially by individuals—to resist these influences and improve the quality of decision making.

Diffusion of Responsibility and Social Loafing

One determinant of group decision-making effectiveness (although by no means a guarantee) is how hard the group members work at the task before them. A highly motivated, hard-working member is more likely to make a contribution than is a slothful counterpart. In a variety of situations, groups seem to inhibit the best efforts of individuals. For example, the more bystanders in an emergency situation (e.g, a mugging), the less likely it is that any given bystander will come to the victim's aid. Somehow being one of ten nonresponsive bystanders is less guilt inducing than being the *only* nonhelper. Factory workers in large groups tend to be less productive per person that those in smaller groups. Many teachers have noted the inherent difficulties of "group" projects where individual contributions are combined in one final report. The more active members of the group often complain of "free-loaders," who do little work but benefit from the group evaluation. Others argue that they would have received a better grade had they done the work on their own; instead, some shirker has "contaminated" the group product by his inferior contribution.

Bibb Latané and his colleagues have extended these findings to the area of group performance. Imagine a psychologist organizing a tug-of-war in a laboratory. First the subject is induced to pull on a rope as hard as he can; then he is placed in teams of three or eight and again urged to tug mightily. Meanwhile, the force exerted by the subject on the rope is carefully measured. What is found is that as subjects move from individual to group conditions, the average individual force exerted on the rope *diminishes*. In a further demonstration, subjects yell and clap with less vigor (even though repeatedly told to do so as loudly as possible) as group size increases. This phenomenon has been dubbed "social loafing" and seems to occur most often when group members are not motivated by the group's activities, either because the task is too easy or boring, or because everybody is doing the same thing. Lacking a sense of engagement and uniqueness, people will "slack off," particularly when detection of malingering is difficult or impossible (Harkins & Petty, 1982). To return to our tug-of-war example, subjects pulled on an anchored rope (thus the normal competitive aspect of the sport was absent), and were probably not terribly engaged by the task. In the yelling and clapping study, subjects were undoubtedly self-conscious and at least somewhat reluctant to do the experimenter's bidding. Acting alone, the subject could not shirk, and in order to fulfill his obligation, probably tugged, screamed, or applauded with as much vigor as he could muster. In a group, however, individuals probably felt relatively safe in easing up a bit.

These results translate readily to the context of group decision making. To prevent the diffusion of responsibility for reduced effort, group leaders should ensure that either members be selected who demonstrate interest in the group's function, or else attempt to increase motivation among the existing members. Wherever possible, members should be made to feel that their contributions are valuable to the group. If, however, the group's task is inescapably boring or easy, individuals should be made accountable for their contributions to the group to prevent social loafing. In Soviet boarding schools, for example, the desk *row* is the group unit by which performance is evaluated. Since a single shirker can destroy the row's performance evaluation, tremendous peer pressure can be exerted to bring the student back into line.

Latané, Williams, and Harkins (1979) have made two very interesting observations. First, when not toiling on collective farms, Russians are allowed to tend private gardens of up to one acre. Even though such plots constitute less than 1% of total Soviet farm acreage, they produce 27% of the total agricultural produce. Second, communal farming efforts in Israeli *kubbutzim* have yielded *more* milk and eggs than those produced noncommunally. Thus, social loafing need not result from collective efforts; but lowered productivity, efficiency, and we might speculate, quality of decisions, could well result in groups where individual motivation is low, as are the risks for loafing.

Deindividuation

Increasing individual motivation and involvement with the group's activities may spur members on to work harder, but it is no guarantee that more effective group decisions will be made. Indeed, certain groups may be composed of members whose very fanaticism for reaching some goal may result in tragic, inept, or disastrous decisions. Consider the following examples:

The scene is a familiar one to movie fans. The mob arrives at the jailhouse carrying torches while the sheriff bravely tries to bar their way to the (of course) innocent prisoner. Or a group of "respectable" whites, some covered with sheets and hoods, lynch a black man and then return to their homes and stores. The black man stands almost no chance against his anonymous executioners. In the first scenario, the prisoner is sometimes saved by a show of force; at other times the smooth-talking sheriff singles out the touch-bearers: "You, Charlie, what are you doin' mixed up in this? Go back home to Martha and the kids." In so doing, the sheriff reestablishes Charlie's identity as an individual, and he and the others begin shuffling off, heads down.

Under certain conditions, loose collections of individuals can coalesce into mobs, and the decisions these mobs make are rarely admirable. The transformation from a planful, aware individual into part of a mob has been called *deindividuation*. Ed Diener (1980) has characterized this state as follows:

> People who are deindividuated have lost self-awareness and their personal identity in a group situation. Because they are prevented by the situation from awareness of themselves as individuals and from attention to their own behavior, deindividuated persons do not have the capacity for self-regulation and the ability to plan for the future. Thus ... they become more reactive to immediate stimuli and emotions and are unresponsive to norms and to the long-term consequences of their behavior (p. 210).

An important part of this description is the loss of self-awareness. To social psychologists, this has a rather technical meaning. At any given time, a person may be in a state of either "subjective" or "objective" self-awareness. Most of the time, we are subjectively self-aware—that is, our attention is directed outwards, toward our social environments. When we are absorbed in activities, or performing familiar or habitual behaviors, we do not tend to focus on ourselves as objects; rather we are the "subject" of our actions. When a novel situation arises, requiring a conscious decision, thought, or planning—or when our attention is directed inward, for example by seeing ourselves in a mirror or on a television screen, or by having people stare at us or call us by name—then we may become, literally, "self-conscious," or objectively self-aware.

In the context of this discussion, the important research finding is that when people are in this state of objective self-awareness, they are more likely to strive for consistency with personal values and social standards of appropriate behavior. A mundane example is of the man who can't pass by a mirror without straightening his tie. More dramatic are research findings that people are far less likely to cheat on a test when they can see themselves in a mirror. And in a clever experiment, trick-or-treaters asked to take only one candy from a bowl were more likely to comply when a mirror had been placed behind the bowl. When the mirror was absent, children tended to take more than one.

As Diener's description indicates, deindividuation is characterized by a loss of objective self-awareness. The deindividuated person is free from the normal restraints that personal and societal norms impose upon his or her behavior. On the other hand, "individuation" involves objective self-awareness, and a heightened sensitivity to personal values and societal norms.

With this theoretical background, we may now examine the effects of groups on deindividuation. One factor that has been shown to be particularly important in fostering deindividuation is the *cohesiveness* of the group (see Chapter 2). That is, groups where members are highly similar to one another, where mutual attraction is high, and where members respond to the group as a whole rather than to the individual members, tend to create states of intensified *subjective* self-awareness, and a consequent increase in behavior uninhibited by personal values and social norms. Individuals in such groups often report unconcern about what other people might think of their behavior, show a lack of future orientation and planning, a loss of personal identity, and drug-like altered states of awareness.

What seems to distinguish such groups from those in which people are in their normal subjectively self-aware state is that highly cohesive groups insulate their members from those interventions that normally create an objective self-awareness. Consider a decision-making group of moderate cohesiveness. Unhappy with the decision the group seems to be steamrolling toward, one of the members says, "Hey Joe, Mary, Ed. Listen to yourselves. You're all saying we should drop the bomb. Let's think about the consequences of that decision. Let's think about our own values. Let's try out some other alternatives." This intervention includes several techniques for increasing objective self-awareness, including addressing people by name and reminding them of their capacity for making conscious choices. In a moderately cohesive group, the intervention should be effective. However, in a group whose level of cohesiveness has led to a state of deindividuation, such an intervention is likely to have little impact. Having already attained a "group identity," members simply do not respond as self-aware *individuals*, and, with the group's support, can readily dismiss efforts to refocus their attention on themselves.

All this is not to say that people should—or even could—maintain a state of continuous objective self-awareness. Where important decisions are not involved, the experience of deindividuation may be quite pleasant, or even personally beneficial. Therapy groups or religious experiences may produce a feeling of "losing oneself in the group," opening oneself to a feeling of deep community with others or with some entity. Even in such groups, however, people may pay a price for losing their unique identities, as countless experiences in cults have revealed, most dramatically and tragically in the mass suicides at Jonestown.

But deindividuation can be death to making considered, intelligent decisions in groups. Not only do deindividuated groups not carefully weigh alternatives, seek outside opinions, or otherwise critically assess decision alternatives, but they seem immune to influences that might "individuate" their members, and thereby make them sentitive to norms of appropriate behavior.

We tend to think of deindividuation in the context of crowds, mobs, cults, and radical political groups. Yet many of the decision-making groups that have been characterized by "groupthink" may also have strong elements of deindividuation: high cohesiveness, adoption of a group identity, a reduction in critical planfulness, feelings of invulnerability, and a disregard for personal norms and values. One of the members of the "Nixon Group" that planned and subsequently covered up the Watergate break-in, Charles Colson, wrote that to help Nixon's campaign, "I would walk over my grandmother if necessary" (White, 1973). Lawyers who obviously knew intellectually that they were breaking the law nonetheless approved buggings, break-ins, cover-ups, and laundering of illegal campaign funds. Such total disregard for personal and societal standards in the service of a group goal is clearly symptomatic of deindividuation.

Deindividuation of members of highly cohesive decision-making groups may lead to disastrous decisions. While a certain level of cohesiveness is desirable, an excess of "group spirit" can result in attention being drawn away from each individual's set of moral and ethical prescriptions, and toward "the group" as a whole. If the process of deindividuation proceeds far enough, group members may be unable to return to a state of objective self-awareness that is necessary for an informed decision to be made. Group leaders must ensure that members adopt a critical, even confronting orientation, both to prevent too high a level of group spirit, and to ensure that as many individual perspectives as possible be included in the discussion.

Pressures Toward Group Consensus

When individuals convene in groups, there are frequently pressures, either implicit or explicit, to arrive at a unanimous group decision. In most voluntary groups, these pressures are aided considerably by the fact that most members will already be highly similar to one another in terms of background, attitudes, or goals. For example, a couple decides to vacation at the seashore rather than in the mountains; a group of friends decides to see movie X rather than movie PG; a college drama society decides which plays it will perform. In other, nonvoluntary groups, pressures toward uniformity may be legislated, as in a jury. Apparent exceptions to the tendency for groups to move toward a common decision incude groups organized on an adversary system, such as many legislative bodies. The exception may be more apparent than real, however. While there may be little pressure for a legislature as a whole to reach agreement on a bill, there may be considerable pressure on members to "toe the party line." In some cases, as in the jury example, unanimity is legally required to ensure that a guilty verdict not be reached without overwhelming proof. In most cases, however, groups strive for consensus for reasons that have a less logical base. Before analyzing the potentially destructive effects of group pressures toward consensus, it is important to examine *why* such pressures arise in the first place.

Functions of Group Pressures Toward Consensus

We shall consider four functions that uniformity can serve: to enable the group to move efficiently toward its goals, to help the group maintain itself and continue in existence, to present a strong front to other segments of society, and to provide social standards by which the group and its members can evaluate themselves.

MOVEMENT TOWARD GROUP GOALS

Company management has the goal of making a profit. To accomplish this goal, it may enforce rules requiring employees to arrive and leave on time, to communicate through appropriate channels, and to maintain a high rate of productivity. A group of factory workers within the company has the goal of maintaining a steady, moderate rate of productivity. To accomplish that goal, the group may pressure members to increase or slow down productivity to arrive at the desired rate. A policymaking group of executives in the company establishes certain procedural rules, such as raising hands to be recognized, limiting debate, and not interrupting, which the group believes will improve its decision-making efficiency. In each of these examples, a group has set up certain norms, or shared beliefs of acceptable and appropriate behavior, which help move the group toward its goal. If members deviate from the norms, progress toward the goal will be hampered.

MAINTAINING THE EXISTENCE OF THE GROUP

If a group holds a meeting and nobody comes, the norm of faithful attendance has been violated and the group may cease to exist. Those forms of individual deviance that antagonize other members, or that tend to destroy the cohesiveness of the group, may threaten the group's existence. Pressures toward consensus on group norms help ensure that the group will continue to maintain itself.

PRESENTING A STRONG FRONT

After the last ballot is held and the winner finally is announced, it is common practice at political conventions for the defeated candidates to unite behind the winner, and move that the victor be nominated "by acclamation." The new "unanimous" vote promotes the illusion that all areas of conflict among the candidates have been resolved, and the party can now present a united front before the electorate. The perception of the party as being united behind its candidate will presumably convince the voters that ideological differences within the party are minor, "and if candidates X, Y, and Z support the platform and the victorious candidate, surely you can too." The function of group uniformity in this case is to present a stronger position to society by suggesting that the group decision was supported by people of various ideological hues. This constituency will presumably be more persuasive to others than if the group split into factions, each faction appealing to its unique constituency.

SOCIAL REALITY

Perhaps the most important, and potentially dangerous, function of uniformity within groups is to create a social reality that the group and its members can use to judge the appropriateness of their actions. People have a need to evaluate their abilities, attitudes, and emotions. "How skilled am I?" "What should my opinion be about this issue?" "What is this feeling—could it be love?" There may be no *objective* answers to questions such as these. But groups— particularly unified, consistent groups—can provide a *social* reality to satisfy our need to clarify our abilities, attitudes, and emotions. The danger is that conformity pressures may lead the group to a decision that is socially "correct," but is so at odds with objective reality that in retrospect, we consider the decision laughable, perplexing, or deluded.

We seldom become aware of the fact that two distinct types of reality guide our judgments and behavior. As I write this, the ther- mometer hovers around 0° Fahrenheit—an objectively "cold" day for Boston. This information is further supported by the behavior and conversation of those around me: people are bundled up, red in the face, and complaining about heating bills. This *social* reality confirms what my *objective* thermometer has revealed: it is cold today. The reason why we do not normally distinguish between objective and social reality is that the two seldom disagree or, if they do, we tend to ignore one in favor of the other. For example, I am amused but not bemused by the sight of Boston's equivalent of the Polar Bears Club going for a swim in the ocean today. I ignore this piece of social information that suggests "it is warm" in favor of the more objective reality of my thermometer and my senses.

But what happens when what appears clearly to be objectively real is countered by an equally convincing social consensus? For example, I am certain I hear a buzzing sound, but nobody else hears it; what do I conclude? In an influential series of experiments, Solomon Asch (1956) set out to demonstrate that when objective reality clashes with social reality, people will go with the evidence of their senses and will discount the opinions of others. To test this, Asch devised a simple experiment. A naive subject entered the laboratory, found he was the last to arrive, and was seated in the last chair in a row. Unknown to him, all of the other "subjects" were in fact accomplices of the experimenter. The experimenter produced a large card with four lines—a standard line and three comparison lines. The task of each subject was to indicate which of the three comparison lines was the same length as the standard. On the first trial, it was obvious that line B was the same length as the standard. And, in fact, all seven of the "subjects" answered "B." The real subject also answered "B." On the second card, line "C" was clearly the correct answer, and all the participants correctly gave that as an answer. By this time, the real subject may have begun to think what a boring experiment he was in for. Not to worry! On the third trial, line A was obviously correct, but the first subject answered "B." ("Idiot!" thinks the real subject. "That line's at least 2 inches shorter than the standard.") But then subjects 2, 3, 4, 5, 6, and 7 all gave the same "obviously" wrong answer. What does the naive subject respond: the *objectively* correct A, or the *socially* correct B?

Much to Asch's surprise (and disappointment), only about 20% of the subjects resisted group pressures on all trials. On about one-third of the trials, the socially correct but objectively wrong judgment was given. And 10% of the subjects conformed with the "erroneous" judgment on virtually all the trials.

In the absence of a clear objective reality, *or even in spite of it,* group uniformity creates a social reality that defines the appropriateness of an individual's behavior. In the Asch conformity experiment, social reality takes on a rather sinister quality, forcing decent young college students to conform with the objectively incorrect judgments of others. Yet there are many situations in which social reality is all there is to go on. For example, how does a racquetball player who has practiced alone for a year determine how good she is? By playing someone at about her own level of skill. How does someone decide on the appropriateness of his attitude toward some entirely new social policy? By comparing that attitude to those of his peers. How does a person who finds herself perspiring, her heart pounding, and her palms feeling clammy determine whether she is experiencing anxiety, anger, love, or a heart attack? By affiliating with people in a similar state and observing their reactions. In each of these situations, objective standards are absent; in each case, the individuals involved must rely upon social reality to determine their abilities, attitudes, and emotions.

We are now in a position to more clearly understand how social reality is facilitated by group pressures toward uniformity. Because people have a need to evaluate their abilities, attitudes, and emotions, they often must depend on social reality. Social reality is most easily provided by *similar* others. Therefore, a group of people who are similar to one another, or a group that is *becoming* increasingly homogeneous, will provide its members with unambiguous *social* standards by which they can validate and judge the appropriateness of their abilities, attitudes, and emotions. People are therefore attracted to such groups, and pressures develop within the group to maintain or increase the homogeneity so that members can continue to compare themselves with one another, and thereby develop a clearer (but not necessarily more accurate) conception of reality.

But while the social reality function has obvious value in those cases where there is no objective truth to be found, we have seen that social reality may prevail despite the evidence of one's senses, logic, or basic values. While there may be only one objectively correct decision in a given situation, there are many socially "correct" ones, awaiting only an emerging consensus among group members. Since these alternative "realities" are products of the distortions, ideological biases, or self-serving goals to which people are prone, there is far less assurance that a group uniting behind a desire for social reality will arrive at the most effective, considered decision.

As the last section indicates, pressures toward uniformity in groups do not always signal a pathology in group process. Indeed, a group consensus can serve many important functions. However, in decision-making groups a rush to consensus before all the alternatives have been carefully considered may result in an inferior decision with corresponding negative consequences for the group. And while we might expect groups such as corporate boards, national security councils, and other decision-making groups at the highest levels to approach their tasks in a logical, open-minded way, such is not always the case. In fact, unless such groups take certain precautions, they are likely to be victims of what Irving Janis (1982) calls "groupthink." What is groupthink? When is it most likely to occur? How can it be prevented?

What Causes Groupthink?

Janis defines groupthink as "a mode of thinking that people engage in when they are deeply involved in a cohesive in-group, when the members' strivings for unanimity override their motivation to realistically appraise alternative courses of action" (1982, p. 9). Although Janis analyzes several decision-making fiascos, ranging from the failure to adequately protect Pearl Harbor to the Watergate cover-up, the most dramatic and clear-cut example is undoubtedly President Kennedy's decision to authorize the invasion of Cuba at the Bay of Pigs:

> On April 17, 1961, the brigade of about fourteen hundred Cuban exiles, aided by the United States Navy, Air Force, and the CIA, invaded the swampy coast of Cuba at the Bay of Pigs. Nothing went as planned. On the first day, not one of the four ships containing the reserve ammunition and supplies arrived; the first two were sunk by a few planes in Castro's air force, and the other two promptly fled. By the second day, the brigade was completely surrounded by twenty thousand troops of Castro's well-equipped army. By the third day, about twelve hundred members of the brigade, comprising almost all who had not been killed, were captured and ignominiously led off to prison camps [Janis, 1972, p. 15].

We shall return to this case at several points throughout the remainder of this chapter. For now it is sufficient to note that the groupthink that probably contributed to the Kennedy group's decision represents a special kind of consensus pressure, resulting from a high level of group cohesiveness, with a corresponding failure to carefully examine options. The group gets locked into a particular decision, often the one advocated by the leader, and chokes off attempts to look beyond that decision.

Why do groups fall victim to this pathological striving for consensus? Clearly, cohesiveness is a major factor and we shall examine this in more detail later. We might also expect that pressures on members to conform will be great to the extent that each of the *functions* of consensus-seeking, analyzed in the last section, is made salient or important. Consider the following illustrations:

For a major college football team moving toward the goal of a post-season bowl bid, pressures on members to conform to training rules will be greater than for a team playing at the club or intramural level.

A group whose existence is important to its members, such as a fraternity, will exert greater pressures on them than a group that has no future, such as a group of strangers conversing on an airplane. It may be more important for the democratic party to present a unified front to the electorate after its national convention than after a state caucus. And the need for social reality will be strongest when people are uncertain about *important* abilities, attitudes, and feelings. But there are other factors besides these that are important in determining the strength of group pressures toward conformity. We turn to these now.

PERSONALITY AND CULTURAL FACTORS

There is some evidence that certain kinds of people are more susceptible to conformity pressures than are others. A general personality trait of persuasibility has been isolated that may account for certain people's tendencies to believe what they are told. In addition, people in authoritarianism or low in self-esteem are often more easily influenced than are egalitarian or high self-esteem people, Women are also somewhat more easily influenced than men by a persuasive communication. Recent research suggests, however, that this may be due in part to the particular *topics* used in this research. Women tend to be more influenced than men on masculine topics, but men are more persuasible on female topics.

Stanley Milgram (1961) has found that Norwegians conform more than Frenchmen on an Asch-type judgment task. Milgram speculates that Norwegians form a more homogeneous, cohesive group than do their French counterparts, and are therefore less tolerant of differences that may threaten that cohesiveness.

But while personality and cultural factors may play a part in tendencies to conform in groups, their influence is rather small compared with the many *situational* factors.

SIZE AND UNANIMITY OF THE GROUP

Most experimental studies of conformity have demonstrated that, up to a point, increasing the size of the unanimous group leads to greater conformity. A subject in the Asch line-judgment experiment, who finds himself making judgments with just one other subject can rather easily dismiss that person's clearly erroneous judgments. ("He's just an oddball or a troublemaker.") But if 2, 3, 4, or 10 other "subjects" make unanimous but erroneous judgments, it becomes increasingly difficult for the naive subject to resist the conformity pressures. This becomes even more true when the experimental confederates deride the subject when he resists the group pressure and makes an objectively correct response.

ISOLATION

Members of a group that is closed to input from the outside are strongly dependent on the group for the social reality needed to validate opinions and feelings. Numerous examples could be given of isolated groups creating their own idiosyncratic or perverse "reality." The mass suicides at Jonestown are perhaps the most dramatic and tragic recent example of pressures toward uniformity born of a twisted social reality, allowed to fester in the remote jungles of Guyana.

In her recent book, *Secrets,* Sissela Bok (1983) argues that even military secrecy may ultimately be self-defeating. The aborted rescue mission of the American hostages in Iran in 1980 is a case in point. Because of the high level of secrecy surrounding the mission, members of the planning force were prevented from gathering outside expert advice and even from communicating fully with one another. This extreme "information isolation" may have contributed to the decision that ultimately led to the doomed mission. Finally, Kennedy's decision to invade Cuba was reached by a policymaking group that, out of concern for secrecy and national security, insulated itself against the kind of expert opinion that might have prevented the disaster.

How can isolation be reduced and, as a result, groupthink? Janis proposes that decision-making groups be opened up to include soliciting the considered opinions of trusted associates of the group members as well as bringing in experts to challenge members' opinions. Even when "national security" is a serious issue, according to Bok, the risks inherent in limiting the group to a few members and insulating it from outside experts are likely to far outweigh the dangers of "leaks."

It is instructive to examine the changes in decision-making procedures instigated by Kennedy after the Bay of Pigs. During the Cuban missile crisis, numerous outside experts were invited to meetings to offer their frank advice and to question members of the Executive Committee. Through this and other actions, isolation was minimized, groupthink was avoided, and the crisis was successfully resolved.

GROUP COHESIVENESS

In Chapter 2, the concept of cohesiveness, or esprit de corps, was analyzed. While a high level of cohesiveness confers several important benefits to group functioning, such groups are also more likely to be victimized by groupthink. For example, there is considerable evidence that highly cohesive groups exert greater pressures on their members to conform than do groups whose members do not value their membership. After all, if a member of a noncohesive group doesn't wish to go along with the majority, he or she can simply leave. Where membership is valued, such an option may not be realistic; it may be less painful in the long run to conform.

Irving Janis' analysis of groupthink implicates cohesiveness as the central cause of consensus-seeking tendencies in groups. Group members may be so concerned with maintaining positive interpersonal relations and reducing conflict that they lose the ability or willingness to critically evaluate the risks and advantages of decision alternatives. As a result, they develop characteristic behaviors and attitudes that are symptomatic of groupthink.

As groups begin to reach a high level of cohesiveness, there is a strong tendency for the members to become euphoric, to believe that the group is all powerful and all protective. Highly risky decisions can be made without seriously considering alternatives and consequences, largely because the group has boundless confidence in its luck. If the group is confronting an "enemy," the members will tend to develop stereotypic views of the opposition as weak and stupid, while maintaining their own self-image as white knights. (After all, don't the good guys always win in the end?) As Janis points out, the unrealistic illusion of invulnerability was dramatically illustrated prior to the Bay of Pigs invasion, as the invasion force of 1400 men prepared to do battle with Castro's army of 200,000.

In a highly cohesive group, particularly one in which individuals are either insecure about their membership or else wish to avoid being seen as troublemakers, members may be quite reluctant to express any misgivings about a group decision. Picture for a moment yourself as a member of such a group. As the finishing touches are put on a highly risky and dangerous decision, you wonder whether you should express your doubts. But as you look around the table, you see the members, all esteemed and brilliant experts, nodding their heads in apparent agreement with the plan. What you *don't* know is that many or most of them have the same doubts as you, but hearing no objections from *their* fellows (including you!), they continue to support the plan. The fact that the emperor is indeed wearing no clothes may not be discovered until it is too late, as in the Bay of Pigs fiasco. Thus, not only is unanimity assumed, but what doubts members do have tend to be suppressed.

Are noncohesive groups more likely to make effective decisions? Are cohesive groups doomed to make bad decisions? No and no. Low-cohesive groups are often characterized by inner wrangling, conformity to avoid punishment, and behavior in the service of personal gain rather than the attainment of group goals. Such groups avoid groupthink, but at too high a price. Members of cohesive groups, on the other hand, feel good about themselves, secure in their membership, and accepted by the others. There is evidence that as a result they feel freer to express their true feelings without fear of censure or ridicule. The problem in such high-cohesive groups is that critical judgments will simply never develop. Members will not appraise alternatives in a critical manner, and the group consensus will be preserved. The dilemma facing a highly cohesive group is therefore how to maintain the advantages of cohesiveness while avoiding the critical judgment-blunting effects of groupthink. In the next section, we see how this dilemma may be resolved.

INAPPROPRIATE GROUP NORMS

A social norm is simply a standard of appropriate behavior. Society-wide norms ("Thou shalt not kill"), group norms ("Don't make us look bad by working too hard"), or family norms ("Do as your father tells you") serve a similar function: to promote the smooth functioning of the group. Furthermore, many of society's norms are internalized and become personal norms of appropriate or desirable behavior.

Conflicts occur when a norm of one group conflicts with that of another group, or when a group norm conflicts with an individual norm. For example, the assembly-line "rate-buster," who produces far beyond the rates of his or her co-workers soon gets the message to "cool it" and slows down. Cartwright and Zander (1968) have provided the following description of the pressures exerted on a rate buster by fellow clerical workers:

First we would talk about her unfairness among ourselves. If that did not reach her, we talked about her where she could overhear us. If she still did not change, one of us would approach her in the lounge and ask her if she was trying to kill our jobs. That usually did the trick [p. 14].

Cohesive groups seem best able to enforce these artificially low rates of productivity, a result that has been supported by observations of assembly-line workers, as well as through laboratory experiments. In a related vein, Janis (1963) has analyzed the antisocial behavior of delinquent gangs. These highly cohesive groups provide norms for delinquent acts that individual members acting outside the group would be unlikely to perform.

Whether or not a cohesive group will be productive or nonproductive, benign or destructive, seems to depend largely on the norms it adopts. If a person is to remain a member of a valued, attractive group, he or she will be motivated to do as the group and its norms command. If the group norms conflict with personal standards of appropriate behavior, then the person will do the group's bidding in proportion to the level of cohesiveness, until, in the extreme case of deindividuation, personal norms are totally sacrificed to those of the group.

Consider the suppression of individual norms by those of President Kennedy's cohesive group during the planning of the Bay of Pigs invasion. Normally capable and even brilliant decision makers (one member, Robert McNamara, while president of Ford Motor Company, had developed innovative decision-making schemes!) allowed their critical powers to be blunted by their desires to maintain solidarity with the group. As Janis quotes another member of the group, Arthur Schlesinger, Jr.:

In the months after the Bay of Pigs I bitterly reproached myself for having kept so silent during those crucial discussions in the Cabinet Room, though my feelings of guilt were tempered by the knowledge that a course of objection would have accomplished little save to gain me a name as a nuisance. I can only explain my failure to do more than raise a few timid questions by reporting that one's impulse to blow the whistle on this nonsense was simply undone by the circumstances of the discussion [1982, p. 39].

Group cohesiveness thus seems to lead to defective decision making when the members place the solidarity of the group and the perceived norm of consensus above their individual norms of being thoughtful, critical decision makers. When the group norm, "Don't rock the boat, don't be a 'nuisance'" takes precedence over norms such as, "Evaluate alternatives carefully," or "Make contingency plans," then the quality of decisions is likely to suffer.

Kennedy's National Security Council was able to maintain its high morale despite the disastrous invasion of Cuba, and thus learned from its mistakes. The president instituted a number of procedural changes for the group in times of national emergency. These changes, including bringing in outside advisors and appointing "intellectual watchdogs" and devil's advocates, defined a new group norm: "striving to be thorough in their appraisals of alternatives" (Janis, 1982, p. 142). This new norm, superseding the old unspoken group maintenance norms, may have helped the "Kennedy group" respond appropriately to the Cuban missile crisis.

The imposition of new group norms to prevent premature consensus-seeking has been studied in a number of laboratory studies. As one example, Hall and Watson (1970) had groups reach decisions using the NASA Moon Survival Problem (which equipment should a marooned expedition on the moon choose to take with them to reach their distant base). Some groups were given instructions specifically intended to break down the norm of premature consensus-seeking. For example, "Avoid changing your mind *only* in order to avoid conflict and to reach agreement and harmony. Withstand pressures to yield which have no objective or logically sound foundation. . . . View differences of opinion as both natural and helpful." Other groups were given no such set of instructions. Results indicated that the instructed groups reached better decisions (as determined by NASA experts), were more creative, and reached decisions that, 75% of the time, were superior to that previously reached individually by the group's best member.

DIRECTIVE LEADERSHIP

The behavior of the group leader may be crucial in determining whether individuals are pressured into a premature consensus or will make a careful search of decision alternatives. Even a highly cohesive group, which is particularly prone to consensus pressures, may be induced to follow appropriate decision-making techniques through the skillful intervention of the leader. On the other hand, perhaps the single most important—and difficult—thing for a strong leader of a cohesive group to do is to refrain from too much strong leadership. When such a leader expresses a preferred solution to a problem, it is very difficult for group members to offer an alternative, since it may be perceived as a challenge to the authority of the leader.

A prime example of this is President Truman's outspoken advocacy of increased involvement in the war between North Korea and South Korea, culminating in the United States' entry into the war in late 1950. Failure to anticipate Communist China's entry on the side of North Korea turned an apparent victory into, at best, a costly stalemate. A more subtle form of directive leadership is Kennedy's behavior during the Bay of Pigs invasion meetings. Central Intelligence Agency representatives were allowed to control meetings and the few outsiders who were allowed in to criticize the plan were not probed or questioned (Janis, 1982). In both the Truman and Kennedy groups, the norm that was clearly communicated was "Do what the president wants—and it's clear what that is." Reluctant to jeopardize one's standing in the group by openly opposing the leader, each member joined in the unanimous chorus, thus reinforcing the feelings of total support. These feelings, in turn, may have produced what Janis calls the "illusion of invulnerability" that can lead to highly risky decisions.

Particularly when the group is under stress (due, perhaps, to time pressures or the magnitude of the decision task), the premature "suggestions" of a strong leader may lead members to feel hopeless that any other solution may be possible. The combination of stress and hopelessness leads to what Janis and Mann (1977) term "defensive avoidance." Basically, this means that when people under stress are forced to choose among imperfect alternatives, they will seize upon the least undesirable one and attempt to bolster it. Even a terrible solution proposed by a strong leader of a cohesive group may be preferable to the alternative: proposing a better solution, but placing one's group membership in jeopardy.

Therefore, if a decision-making group is to enjoy the benefits of critical appraisal of all the options, it is essential that the leader refrain from advocating a particular solution to the problem. Of course, if the leader is seeking a mandate for a decision he or she has already made, then the leader can cynically convene a group, advocate a position, and sit back until the group ratifies that position. Kennedy, although he believed at first that the Cuban missile crisis could be resolved only by military intervention, scrupulously avoided saying so. Instead, he actively sought out as many alternatives as possible, then had the group weigh the advantages and disadvantages of each possible solution. In addition, he deliberately was absent from many meetings, to allow a less inhibited flow of ideas. This new nondirective leadership style helped open up the discussion, and may have contributed to the happy resolution of the crisis.

SUMMARY COMMENT ON GROUPTHINK

Of the three pathologies we have considered, diffusion of responsibility, deindividuation, and pressures toward conformity, the latter presents the most serious obstacles to effective group decision making. The combination of high cohesiveness, isolation from alternative opinions and facts, group norms that stifle debate and the expression of minority views, and a directive leadership style that forces conformity, produce the groupthink phenomenon. As a result, the group is prone to making risky decisions. Of course, a risky decision does not promise a disaster, but the odds for such an outcome shorten when the alternatives are poorly explored and the risks are not adequately evaluated.

A group suffering from groupthink is likely to display a number of symptoms, including stereotyping the "enemy," bolstering one's own morality, developing an illusion of invulnerability, self-censorship, and the censorship of potential critics (Janis, 1982). One final symptom, exerting pressure on deviant members, is the focus of the following section.

The Individual Confronts the Group: Minority Influence

Our discussion of group pressures to conformity might suggest that deviance will never arise in a cohesive group. Of course, dissent might be relatively infrequent compared to less cohesive groups, but some controversy is still likely to occur. What is particularly interesting is what happens when a member of a cohesive group *does* dissent. What forces will determine the strength of the negative reaction by other group members toward the deviate? What are those reactions likely to be?

DETERMINANTS OF NEGATIVE REACTIONS TO DEVIATES

As might be expected, many of the same forces that propel groups toward consensus also determine the strength of pressures exerted against members who resist that consensus. Such pressures are likely to be great, for example, in highly cohesive groups entrusted with an important decision to make. However, there also exist a number of additional factors which determine how strongly the group will move against the deviate.

External threats. In an earlier section, the *functions* of group pressures toward uniformity were discussed. One of the most important of these functions has been termed "maintaining the group's existence." When the maintenance or very existence of a group is threatened, it may be expected that deviance will be decreasingly tolerated. This reasoning was tested experimentally by Pat Lauderdale (1976). Five-person groups were formed to discuss the case of a juvenile delinquent, and to make a group recommendation. In each of these groups, an experimental confederate was planted who adopted an extreme position. Halfway through the group discussion, an outside observer (a "criminal justice authority") announced to the experimenter, "This group should probably not continue," then left the room (the "threat" condition). In the other groups, no such threat was made. Lauderdale found that in the threat groups, the deviant was more strongly rejected by the other members.

Interference with goal attainment. Pressures against deviates should also increase when that person threatens another important function of group uniformity: movement toward group goals. When a deviant member is viewed as obstructing the attainment of the group's goal, that member should be strongly rejected. Numerous studies have demonstrated that when a group member is perceived to be interfering with the successful attainment of some goal (e.g., prizes, cash, social recognition), that member becomes the target of scorn, influence attempts, and eventual rejection.

Personal responsibiilty for deviance. The conclusion of the preceding paragraph should be qualified somewhat. The negative reactions of group members are reserved for those deviates whose disruption of the smooth attainment of a group goal cannot be attributed to "extenuating circumstances." A group member who makes constant interruptions because he is hard of hearing is rejected less than is one who has no such excuse. Low intelligence can also be a factor that groups sympathetically into account when assigning blame for poor group performance.

Perceived influencibility of the deviate. Consider the following situation: You are a strong supporter of the Women's Movement, and are a member of a group discussing a sex discrimination case. Two other members especially attract your attention. One is an avowed antifeminist, the other a profeminist like yourself. In the ensuing discussion, however, both these members adopt positions counter to yours and the other group members—that is, they argue *against* the woman in the case. How are you (and the group) likely to respond to these two deviates? Based upon the results of an experiment similar to this conducted in the mid-1960s (Sampson & Brandon, 1964) some clear predictions could be made. The group should react to the "deviance" of the profeminist by attempting to change her opinion ("She's one of us; she'll see the light") or, failing that, with open hostility ("Traitor!"). The other deviate is a bit of an embarrassment to everybody, and the group reacts to her primarily by ignoring and hoping she'll go away ("Where did *she* come from?") In other words, the latter type of deviate is viewed as beyond persuasion, is "deviant" in some deeper sense of the word, and is rejected by ignoring or isolating. Greater activity is directed toward the former type of deviate because the group perceives that she can be "saved."

Extremity of deviance. The effects of this variable are quite clear: The more extreme the position adopted by the deviate, the more strongly he or she is rejected.

Consistency of the deviate's position. What kind of deviate is likely to be most strongly rejected: one who deviates from majority opinion consistently over time; one who starts out in agreement with the group consensus but moves to a deviant position over time; or one who starts out a deviate but finally concurs with the group? Not surprisingly, the convert tends to be applauded by the group. He or she has seen the light, and it's never too late to be saved. While one might think that consistent deviates might earn some grudging admiration for their firm stand, such has not been the case in experimental studies. This type of deviate is most strongly rejected by the group (Levine, 1980). But while the traitorous "backslider" may be disliked by the group, he or she may exert considerable influence upon the majority opinion by adopting this strategy. ("It took a lot of courage for her to buck the group consensus—she must have some pretty sound reasons for changing her mind.") A more detailed account of minority influence on majorities will be found in the last section of this chapter.

VARIETIES OF GROUP REACTIONS TO DEVIATES

As the preceding section has demonstrated, various factors increase the probability that a group will react negatively to a member who refuses to conform to an otherwise unanimous group decision. These factors may also help determine the particular form that the negative reaction will take. A strident obnoxious person who delights in taking unpopular positions may provoke quite a different reaction than will a thoughtful member who is obviously agonizing over adopting a minority stand. Nonetheless, perhaps the single most common reaction to any deviate is *disliking* by the other members. To buck the tide of group consensus is to invite strong displeasure in others. Beyond disliking, the more specific group reaction varies with such factors as the magnitude of discrepancy between the group's and the deviate's positions and the perceived persuasibility of the deviate.

The initial reaction of most groups is to divert attention to the deviate. Increased communication, requests for clarification, and overt influence attempts mark this phase of the interaction. Basically, the group is attempting to sway the deviate with logic, various forms of social power (such as coercion), or appeals to group "unity." Along with increased communication, interactions with the deviate may take on an increasingly hostile character, particularly as initial influence attempts are beginning to appear ineffective.

When persuasion fails to alter the deviate's behavior, the group may move to a qualitatively different level. Communications directed to the deviant member may decrease radically, or even cease altogether (the "silent treatment"), as the group attempts to redefine its boundaries so as to exclude him. The person may be given unimportant or undesirable group chores (e.g., unpopular committee assignments), be deprived of privileges (such as access to the leader), or otherwise be made to feel unwelcome. If possible, the extreme or unyielding deviate may be expelled from the group. It is quite common, for example, for high civil or military officials who criticize an administration to be fired (or requested to resign). The firing of General MacArthur by President Truman is a noteworthy example. Sometimes the exclusion occurs before the group even forms, as a potentially valuable person is viewed as a "troublemaker." George Kennan was excluded from President Truman's Korean advisory group in 1950 because he had prepared statements cogently arguing against allowing MacArthur to cross the 38th parallel (Janis, 1972). Cyrus Vance, President Carter's Secretary of State, was excluded from the final decision to try to rescue the hostages in Iran, because he was known to oppose the plan. Rather than having to deal with somebody who might challenge the preexisting consensus, the groups simply decided not to invite the deviates to join.

One of the more unusual reactions to a group member who violates implicit norms of consensus is "domestication" (Janis, 1972, pp. 119-120). In certain decision-making groups (such as President Johnson's during the escalation phase of the Vietnam war), perhaps to maintain the illusion of open-mindedness, certain dissenters (notably Bill Moyers and George Ball) were allowed to express their deviant views so long as they (1) were not *too* deviant, and (2) were not expressed to outside critics of the administration. Even so, these men were constantly ridiculed with epithets like "Mr. Stop-the-Bombing." The curious result of this process of domestication was that the dissenters felt they were serving a useful function by bringing alternative views to the group, and the group could congratulate itself on being so open and tolerant of such views. Yet the narrow range of permissible deviant opinion and the thinly veiled hostile responses that greeted such opinions indicate that domestication in fact hinders any useful discussion of decision alternatives in the same way that tokenism may hinder true racial or sexual equality.

MINORITY INFLUENCES ON MAJORITIES

Thus far, our analysis would suggest that the member who resists group pressures toward uniformity is invariably the object of scorn, exclusion, and rejection. In fact, the very word "deviate" has a rather unwholesome ring to it. While these may be common reactions, they are by no means the only group responses. For example, many readers of this chapter may find themselves reacting rather sympathetically to our hypothetical deviate. The "lone wolf" who courageously battles evil conformity pressures is a popular hero in fiction. Furthermore, in certain social institutions, the input of deviates or nonconformists may be welcome (if not always without meeting resistance). For example, in the advertising, fashion, and high technology industries, innovative and unusual solutions may be actively sought out. By contrast, deviance is less likely to be tolerated in more hierarchical or authoritarian institutions, such as the church or the military.

A group member who finds him or herself disagreeing with an otherwise unanimous group decision is in a precarious situation. By arguing an unpopular position, the member courts almost certain disfavor, which may lead to rejection or even explusion from the group. And yet minorities are not without resources. As we have seen, deviates attract almost instant attention. The deviate has the floor and, if the minority position has merit and the person can skillfully argue the case, other group members might defect from the majority.

The immediate goal of a deviate confronting a cohesive majority is rarely to persuade everyone simultaneously. Rather, he or she seeks an ally. Then the two of them may prove a formidable force in attracting additional converts. Consider once again the Asch line-judgment studies discussed earlier. Naive subjects were highly conforming to an erroneous, but unanimous judgment by a group of experimental confederates. However, if the unanimity is broken by a single confederate, the conformity rate shrinks to near zero. That is, if eight confederates incorrectly state that line B is closest in length to the standards, but a ninth correctly identifies line C, the subject will breathe a great sigh of relief and answer C also. In fact, conformity pressures decrease even when the lone confederate goes against the majority by giving another *incorrect* (i.e., line A) response. Of course, in real decision-making groups, when the majority may *not* be obviously incorrect, minorities face a stiffer challenge to gain acceptance for their positions.

The work by Moscovici, Nemeth, and their colleagues (e.g., Nemeth, 1979) provides some guidelines for effective minority influence. First, to be effective a deviate must argue the minority case *consistently*. Random deviations attract little support and likely will result in the deviate being branded a crackpot. But consistency does not mean rigidity. The person must be willing to make small concessions, to see the merit in some of the majority arguments. Second, the deviate must project *confidence* in his or her position.

For example, in one study (Nemeth & Wachtler, 1974), deviates who chose to sit in the "leader" chair (at the head of a rectangular table) were more influential than those who were either assigned that chair by the experimenter, or who chose a side-chair. The influential deviate was perceived by the other group members as being both more consistent and more confident than other deviates. Third, Nemeth's research indicates the importance of *persistence*. If a dissenter can manage to hold the floor for an extended period, and is able to make more comments in support of his or her position than are the advocates of the majority position, then there is an excellent chance of the minority position being adopted (Nemeth, 1979). This means, obviously, that the deviate must be both extremely well informed about the arguments for the minority position and skilled in the *means* by which they can be communicated.

Unfortunately for those who would like to find that a successful minority influence attempt will be rewarded by the love and esteem of the group members, the unhappy fact is that influence is generally purchased at the price of being disliked. Majority members perceive the deviate as uncooperative, cold, and unreasonable (as well as independent and strong-willed), but they also report that the deviate made them *think* more than did fellow mainstreamers. This latter finding is particularly true if there are *two* deviates arguing the minority position. But rather than adopting either the minority or the majority position, the group is often stimulated to reach some other, nonobvious decision as an alternative to either of the two.

The intolerance of dissent is one of the major symptoms of groupthink: "direct pressure on any member who expresses strong arguments against any of the group's stereotypes, illusions, or commitments, making clear that this type of dissent is contrary to what is expected of all loyal members" (Janis, 1972, p. 198). President Kennedy, realizing that such pressures may have contributed to the Bay of Pigs disaster, explicitly framed a new norm to guide discussion during the Cuban missile crisis. Members were urged to thoroughly explore all decision alternatives, and Robert Kennedy and Theodore Sorenson were ordered to adopt devil's advocate roles, challenging the suggestions of the other members and attempting to ensure that no possibilities for action were overlooked. The institutionalization of the devil's advocate role is one of Janis' major recommendations for preventing groupthink. By preventing the rejection, isolation, or expulsion of the deviate (although probably not the disliking), the group ensures that a premature consensus will not be reached, and that effective, innovative decisions may be reached.

References

Asch, S. E. Studies of independence and conformity: A minority of one against a unanimous majority. *Psychological Monographs*, 1956, 70 (9 Whole No. 416).

Bok, S. *Secrets: On the ethics of concealment and revelation.* New York: Pantheon, 1983.

Cartwright, D., & Zander, A. *Group dynamics* (3rd ed.). New York: Harper & Row, 1968.

Diener, E. Deindividuation: The absence of self-awareness and and self-regulation in group members. In P. B. Paulus (Ed.), *Psychology of group influence.* Hillsdale, NJ: Erlbaum, 1980.

Hall, J., & Watson, W. H. The effects of a normative intervention on group decision-making performance. *Human Relations,* 1970, 23, 299-317.

Harkins, S. G., & Petty, R. Effects of task difficulty and task uniqueness on social loafing. *Journal of Personality & Social Psychology,* 1982, 43, 1214-1229.

Janis, I. L. *Groupthink* (2nd ed.). Boston: Houghton Mifflin, 1982.

Janis, I. L. *Victims of groupthink.* Boston: Houghton Mifflin, 1972.

Janis, I. L., & Mann, L. *Decision making: A psychological analysis of conflict, choice, and commitment.* New York: Free Press, 1977.

Latané, B., Williams, K., & Harkins, S. Many hands make light the work: The causes and consequences of social loafing. *Journal of Personality & Social Psychology,* 1979, 37, 822-832.

Lauderdale, P. Deviance and moral boundaries. *American Sociological Review,* 1976, 41, 660-676.

Levine, J. J. Reaction of opinion deviance in small groups. In P. B. Paulus, (Ed.), *Psychology of group influence.* Hillsdale, NJ: Erlbaum, 1980.

Milgram, S. Nationality and conformity. *Scientific American,* 1961, 205, 45-51.

Nemeth, C. The role of an active minority in intergroup relations. In W. Austin & S. Worchel (Eds.), *The social psychology of intergroup relations.* Monterey, CA: Brooks/Cole, 1979.

Nemeth, C., & Wachtler, J. Creating the perceptions of consistency and confidence: A necessary condition for minority influence. *Sociometry,* 1974, 37, 529-540.

Sampson, E. E., & Brandon, A. The effects of role and opinion deviation on small group behavior. *Sociometry,* 1964, 27, 261-281.

White, T. H. *The making of the president—1972.* New York: Bantam, 1973.

CHAPTER 4

LOGICAL FOUNDATIONS FOR A FAIR AND RATIONAL METHOD OF VOTING

Richard A. Chechile

A group charged with the responsibility of making a decision must eventually decide. Debate and deliberation are usually important in the decision process, but a unanimous decision does not always result. In general, the actual decision is determined by some type of vote. Clearly, it is necessary that the voting procedure be rational. For example, if an alternative that is favored by every member of the group is bypassed for another alternative under the rules of voting, then that particular voting procedure is irrational and, clearly, undesirable.

In the broadest sense of the term "voting," just about any method of achieving a decisive conclusion may be regarded as a voting method; consequently, there is a virtually limitless number of voting methods. A "benevolent dictatorship," or for that matter, any dictatorship, is method of voting, albeit only one voter determines the outcome of the election. The decision reached by the dictator might be rational, ethically sound, and in many important ways it might be the "right" decision, but in general the decision does not fairly represent the collective preference of the members of the group. The dictator's decision is not really a group decision at all. It is rather an individual decision made for the group. Consequently, fairness to the preferences of the members of the group is an essential requirement for a group's decision to be truly a *group* decision.

A goal of this chapter is to explore what properties a voting procedure should have in order to be both rational and fair. In fact, fairness and rationality will be defined in terms of a number of formal properties of a voting sytem. In terms of the desired properties developed for a rational and fair voting system, a number of the most familiar voting systems shall be evaluated. Later in the chapter, a formal analysis shall define, in general, the conditions under which any voting scheme can satisfy or not satisfy the necessary properties of rationality and fairness. Consequently, the chapter deals with a prescriptive analysis regarding how voting ought to be done.

A central concept in the prescriptive decision sciences is utility. Most simply, utility is the subjective value held by the individual regarding an objective or an outcome. Utility is regarded to have many possible dimensions. For example, a winter coat's utility might include its monetary, decorative, comfort, and functional values for being the most protective coat on the coldest of days. The weighing of these dimensions could vary from individual to individual. In the prescriptive decision sciences, the goal is usually to show how a best or an optimal decision can be achieved. The optimal decision is generally the decision that, on average, leads to the greatest utility. A prescriptive decision analysis is a rational approach to decision making: A central step in the prescriptive approach is the empirical measurement of utility through procedures like the Decision Matrix, discussed later in Chapter 9.

In terms of group decision making and voting, each member of the group can be regarded as having a utility associated with each possible decision alternative. The group's utility is, thus, a collective property of the group; a property that needs to be measured in order for the group to select the alternative that maximizes their utility. The voting procedure is the method of measuring the group's utility associated with the alternatives. If there is unfairness in the procedure of transforming individual utilities into a group utility, then the resulting group utility is not truly representative. The group preference ranking of the alternatives would in that case be an invalid assessment. Thus, while rationality and fairness are separate concepts, in prescriptive decision making, an unfair system of aggregating individual votes results in a potentially nonoptimal decision in terms of the group's utility. Hence, the goal of fairness in the assessment of the group's preference is not merely a culturally motivated goal, but it is an essential component of a rational decision analysis.

A final introductory remark is required about the possibility of achieving a fair and rational voting decision, but not satisfying higher criteria imposed by ethical considerations. An optimal decision from the point of view of maximizing utility might not be ethically correct or even legal. In the next chapter, the more general issues of ethical decision making are discussed in detail. At this point, it is only necessary to point out that an ethical analysis is potentially capable of eliminating alternatives. From the utilitarian position, an alternative rejected on ethical grounds has zero utility; the ethical component of the utility function can be regarded as overriding all of the other dimensions of subjective value. However, ethical considerations rarely narrow the alternatives to only one course of action. The result of the ethical analysis usually is either having several ethically acceptable alternatives or having no ethically acceptable alternatives. In either of these two cases, the group must make its decision, and if the decision is to be rational and truly a *group* decision, then the voting method must fairly represent its individual members.

A Case of Dues

A national professional society has, according to its bylaws, an executive committee of 15 members who have the power to determine the membership dues for the following year as well as a number of other leadership issues.

The professional society has three large subgroups. The largest subgroup consists of practicing professionals who are in business for themselves. The second biggest subgroup consists of students who are typically within a few years of completing their training. The third subgroup consists of the educators who are running the professional training programs. All society members vote for their representatives on the executive committee. As a result of those elections, the current executive committee consists of five student members, four educators, and six practicing professionals. The bylaws of the society provide virtually no guidelines on how the executive committee is to carry out its business. The executive committee is therefore free to set its own internal rules as to how to run the meetings and to vote on issues. The current executive committee decided early in the year that one of the educators who was quite well known would be their best choice for their chairperson. The chairperson's powers merely consisted of running the meeting regarding procedural matters.

A meeting to set policy in regard to society dues was called by the chairperson. In the lengthy proceedings, three quite different proposals were advanced. The practicing professionals wanted to raise the dues substantially in order for the society to open up a congressional lobby group that would seek to change the current laws on insurance payments so that the practicing professionals could receiver higher payments from their clients. The educators proposed a plan to also increase the dues nearly as much as the previous proposal, but the educators wanted the increased income for a number of national prizes that would go to the most "worthy" members for their contributions to the profession. The students had yet another proposal; no dues increase at all. The students felt that they would have some difficulties in paying either of the increases proposed by the other two groups.

For the practicing professionals, their favorite plan was the increase with the congressional lobby mandate; however, they also felt that the educator's plan had some merit since it would advance the national image of the whole society. The practicing professionals strongly objected to the students' lack of a positive plan. They regarded the students' lack of initiative as a failure of commitment.

For the educators, their second favorite plan was no increase whatsoever in the dues. As educators, they worked daily with the students and believed an increase in dues, which largely benefited the most wealthy in the society, was not reasonable. The dues increase to support their national prizes was, however, a reasonable goal since the prizes would benefit the image of the entire society.

For the students, their second favorite plan was the congressional lobby. If there were to be a dues increase, then they would see the practical gains by the changes in the insurance laws to outweigh the impractical gain of increasing the society's image. Most of the students clearly planned for a career as a practicing professional, so they were influenced by the benefits of a congressional lobby.

During the debate, the chairperson recognized that the practicing professionals' proposal would win if each member of the executive committee voted for just a single plan (plurality voting) since there were six practicing professionals on the committee. The chairperson also came to understand that the practicing professionals' proposal would also win if each member of the committee ranked all three plans, where the favored plan would then receive three points, the second favorite would receive two points and the last alternative would receive just one point. The chairperson quietly listened to the debate, and then began to speak after a delay in the debate.

"I think we debated this issue rather completely, so it is now time to vote on a policy regarding next year's dues. Since there has been considerable debate between the students' plan and the plan proposed by our practicing professionals, I want us to vote first just between those two plans. All in favor of the professionals plan, raise your hands (six hands are raised). Now all in favor of the students' plan, raise your hands (nine hands are raised). Well, the professionals' plan is defeated. Now, we need to vote between the students' plan and the educators' plan . All in favor of the students' plan raise your hands (five hands are raised). All in favor of the educators' plan raise your hands (ten hands are raised). Well, people, we have a new policy for next year. Since our business is now completed, the meeting is officially over."

A strange silence fell over the committee.

Ground Rules for an Analysis of Preferences

The case study of the professional society illustrates that odd outcomes are possible in elections, so a careful and formal analysis is necessary to understand the properties of a voting system. Historically, ideas associated with voting procedures date back to the eighteenth century with the work of Borda (1781) and Condorcet (1785). More recent work blossomed after Kenneth Arrow's (1951) important analysis of voting systems with three or more alternatives.

The first step in a formal analysis of voting is to establish several ground rules for any rational voting system. These rules have no direct bearing on the concept of fairness, but the ground rules set some minimal logical standards for a voting system.

The first ground rule is that there is the same set of alternatives for each member of the group. A voting procedure would certainly be bizarre if some members' alternatives were different from the alternatives voted on by others. No rational winner could possibly emerge when the set of alternatives is not the same for the entire group.

The second ground rule is the freedom for each member to specify all the relationships between any two alternatives. If alternative A is preferred to alternative B, then that is written as $_APB$. However, if the group member is indifferent between A and B, then it is written as $_AIB$. So if there is a set of three alternatives, A, B, and C, then a member could express the preference of $_A P_B$, $_A P_C$, $_B I_C$. If certain group members are permitted only to express a preference relationship on some alternatives but not on others, then the election result would be meaningless.

The third ground rule is the requirement that when there are three or more alternatives, each group member gives what is called a transitive ranking. The term transitive refers to the property that if A is preferred to B and B is preferred to C, then A must be preferred to C. For example, a corporate president would be intransitive if his perferences for the location of an office were such that Atlanta is preferred to Boston and Boston is preferred to Chicago, but Chicago is preferred to Atlanta. Whenever intransitivity occurs, rational decision making is impossible. To see the dilemma posed by intransitivity, let us examine further the consequences of the corporate president's preferences. Suppose the office is currently located in Chicago. Since Boston is preferred to Chicago, then he should be willing to pay some amount (say $30,000) to move to Boston. Now the office is in Boston, but since Atlanta is preferred, the president should be willing to pay some amount to relocate in Atlanta (say another $30,000). However, Chicago is preferred to Atlanta so the office should again be moved to Chicago for an additional amount (another $30,000). Consequently, the president spent $90,000 to end up at the same location from which he started. Furthermore, the circuit would continue until all of the corporation's money was exhausted. As irrational as intransitivity seems, it is important to know that psychologists have provided evidence that so-called reasonable individuals can behave so as to hold intransitive preference rankings (see Tversky, 1969). However, a voting system cannot be meaningful if it permits individuals to be intransitive.

The fourth ground rule is that the voting system must be decisive for all possible configurations of individual preference rankings. If the group is voting in order to make a decision, then the voting procedure should determine a winner. It is not enough for a voting scheme to choose a decisive alternative under some circumstances; it must work decisively for all conditions of preference. It is worth noting here that the familiar majority rule is not a proper voting scheme according to this ground rule. It cannot always select a winner when there are three or more alternatives, since no one alternative may get 50% of the vote. Plurality voting, however, does satisfy the ground rule of decisiveness.

Ranking Order

Voters	1st	2nd	3rd	4th
1	A	B	C	D
2	D	A	B	C
3	B	C	D	A

Figure 4.1   Example of a Violation of the Pareto Principle

NOTE: The letters denote the four alternatives. The Pareto principle could be violated here with pairwise voting.

Criteria for a Fair and Rational Voting Method

The four ground rules specified above only insure that the individual group members are free to express any rational ordering of their preference on the full set of alternatives. The general idea of a voting scheme, however, is the manner in which the individual preferences are aggregated to determine a preference for the group. Additional criteria are required to insure that aggregation rules do not result in either an irrational or unfair result.

PARETO PRINCIPLE

According to this principle, if an alternative, B, is less preferred than another alternative, A, by all members of the society, then alternative B should not be one of the final "winners." More technically, if $_A P_B$ for all group members, then B should be excluded from the set of chosen alternatives. This is a relatively weak requirement of a voting system, but there are several voting procedures that sometimes violate the Pareto principle. For example, the sequential pairwise election procedure used by the chairperson in the case study of the professional society can violate the Pareto principle. For the pairwise procedure, the Pareto principle is violated for the case illustrated in Figure 4.1. In this case, there are three voters and four alternatives, A, B, C, and D.

Notice that $_B P_C$ relationship holds for all voters. Suppose alternatives A and B are first paired against one another. Alternative A

Agenda	First Contestents	Second Contestants	Third Contestants	Winner
1	BD $\longrightarrow$ B^{P}D	BA $\longrightarrow$ A^{P}B	AC $\longrightarrow$ A^{P}C	A
2	AD $\longrightarrow$ D^{P}A	DB $\longrightarrow$ B^{P}D	BC $\longrightarrow$ B^{P}C	B
3	AB $\longrightarrow$ A^{P}B	AD $\longrightarrow$ D^{P}A	DC $\longrightarrow$ C^{P}D	C
4	AB $\longrightarrow$ A^{P}B	AC $\longrightarrow$ A^{P}D	AD $\longrightarrow$ D^{P}A	D

Figure 4.2   An Illustration of the Agenda Effect for Sequential Pairwise Voting

NOTE: Based upon voters' references in Figure 4.1. Depending on the particular voting agenda, any of the alternatives can win.

wins by a 2 to 1 margin and is next paired against D. Alternative D beats A, so the last contest is between D and C. Unfortunately, C beats D and we have C as the social choice despite the fact that B is preferred to C by all three voters.

The example in Figure 4.1 also illustrates another problem with the pairwise procedure. It is the problem of the agenda. In Figure 4.2, four different pairing agendas are shown. Depending on the agenda, any of the four alternatives can emerge as a winner. As a general rule, the later an alternative is brought up in the sequential pairings, the better the chances are that the alternative will win. In the case of the national professional society, any of three proposals could have won depending on the sequence of pairwise votes.

CITIZEN SOVEREIGNTY

According to this principle, it is necessary for any two alternatives, such as A and B, that there be some way for the society to prefer A. Imagine a case where the sovereignty condition were not satisfied. In such a case, B would be preferred to A regardless of how the individual members of the group rated A and B, even when A was preferred to B for all group members. Such a procedure would not be fair and the results of the election would be, at least in part, imposed since the citizens would lack the sovereignty of ranking A versus B.

GROUP TRANSITIVITY

A vital principle of rationality is that of group transitivity. Even when each member gives a transitive ordering of the alternatives, it

	Case 1				Case 2		
	Ranking Order				Ranking Order		
Voters	1st	2nd	3rd		1st	2nd	3rd
1	A	B	C		A	B	C
2	B	A	C		B	C	A
3	C	A	B		C	A	B

Figure 4.3   An Example of Group Intransitivity

NOTE: Case 1 results in a transitive ordering while Case 2 results in group intransitivity.

does not always result in group transitivity. Group intransitivity occurs in the case of the national professional society, since $_A P_B$, $_B P_C$, but $_C P_A$. Group intransitivity is not unfair, but, nevertheless, it is as unacceptable as individual intransitivity, as can be seen in the following example. Again using the pairwise procedure system, an illustration of group intransitivity is present in Figure 4.3

In Case 1, the social order is transitive and would be $_A P_B$, $_B P_C$, and $_A P_C$. However, in Case 2 the social order is intransitive since $_A P_B$ and $_B P_C$, but $_C P_A$. In Case 1, there is a clear winner, namely alternative A, but in Case 2 there is no winner. Alternative A cannot be a winner since C is preferred to A by a majority. Alternative C is not a winner because B is preferred to C by a majority. Finally, B is not a winner because A is preferred to B by a majority. Furthermore, the pairwise method can encourage false reporting of individual preference. For example, the only difference between Case 1 and Case 2 is in the second individual's preference order. Suppose that the true preference for the second individual were the one shown for Case 1. If the second individual knows that ranking A over C results in B losing to A, then there is also an incentive for false reporting. By switching to the order of A and C for the third and second position respectively, Voter 2 can produce an intransitivity and hence keep the chances of his favorite, B, alive. Consequently, a rational system of social choice must prohibit even the possibility of group intransitivity. In addition we desire a voting procedure that will not provide incentives for false reporting of individual preferences.

POSITIVE ASSOCIATION

The requirement of honest reporting has led to a formal condition that the election results should be positively associated with individual values. By positive association, it is meant that if A were preferred in the original preference profile, then A should be also preferred in a new profile whereby in each individual paired-comparison between A and the other alternatives, A's relative ranking is either unchanged or improved. To see how this condition of positive association is related to honesty, imagine a case where it is violated. Suppose that A is the winner of an election despite the fact that for some individual, X, A is the least preferred alternative. However, under the rules of the election, had that individual ranked A higher, then B would have won. Clearly, such rules have actually provided a strong incentive for individual X to rank A high and thus result in B's victory. Such a case demonstrates the difficulties that can occur if the positive association condition is violated. Without a positive association of the social welfare function with the individual rankings, then a fair and representative group utility measurement would be impossible.

THE INDEPENDENCE OF IRRELEVANT ALTERNATIVES

Before discussing the next criterion, let us first consider the weighted vote scheme of preference assessment. This method is frequently used in judging contests and in club elections. The procedure requires that the members of a society place weighting to their preference order (e.g., 5 for first choice, 4 for second, . . . and 1 vote for the fifth choice). The procedure is very old, dating back to Jean-Charles de Borda (1781). The weighting scheme for voting does have many desirable properties, such as satisfying group transitivity and positive association between individual and social choice. However, the weighted vote technique does have other problems, as will be brought out in examples in Figures 4.4 and 4.5

Suppose there are three judges in an athletic contest and four contestants. The judges give weighting scores to each contestant as shown below in Case 1 (i.e., 4 points for the top choice down to 1

Judges	Case 1				Case 2		
	Full Set of Contestants				All but D		
	A	B	C	D	A	B	C
1	2	1	4	3	2	1	3
2	2	4	1	3	2	3	1
3	4	3	2	1	3	2	1
Total Point Score	8	8	7	7	7	6	5

Figure 4.4   An Example of the Borda Voting Method

NOTE: A and B are tied for first place in Case 1, but in Case 2, after D is disqualified, A is the winner.

point for the least preferred). From the total point score, we see that contestants A and B are tied for first, followed by contestants C and D, which are also tied. However, suppose that after the judges had recorded their votes, it is disclosed that contestant D broke the rules and thereby is disqualified. There are three remaining athletes so the points must be rescaled (3 points for the top choice down to 1 point for the least preferred). The results of the rescaling are displayed in Case 2.

Unfortunately, the results of the contest are now different. Contestant A is the clear winner with B and C in the two remaining positions. Contestant B feels cheated since he lost only after a last place contestant, D, was dropped from the contest. It seems unreasonable that B loses to A only as a function of whether or not D is among the set of available alternatives. Interdependency in the relative social choice rankings can also lead to strategic manipulation. For example, suppose that contestants A and D were teammates and D deliberately violated the contest rules so that A could win. The Borda weighted-voting scheme is thus susceptible to unfair manipulations because A's strength in comparison to B's strength is not a function of just the two contestants. A-strength versus B-strength also depends on how they rank in regard to the

	Case 1				Case 2		
	Alternatives				Alternatives		
Judges	A	B	C	Judges	A	B	C
1	3	2	1	1	3	2	1
2	3	2	1	2	3	2	1
3	3	2	1	3	3	2	1
4	2	3	1	4	1	3	2
5	2	3	1	5	1	3	2
Total Vote	13	12	5	Total Vote	11	12	7

Figure 4.5   Another Example of Problems with the Borda Method

NOTE: Case 1 represents the true voter preferences, whereas in Case 2, Judges 4 and 5 form a coalition and reduce A's vote. This strategy results in B winning the contest.

other contestants. Another type of dishonest representation that is possible with the Borda method is illustrated in Figure 4.5.

Suppose that Case 1 is a true representation for each judge and according to the rules of the election A beats B. However, judges 4 and 5 realize that C is likely to be least preferred by all judges. By forming a coalition, they both report C as being preferred to A. The resulting vote is shown as Case 2. The shift to C over A now means that their favorite, B, wins the election. Notice in both cases that 3 of the 5 judges prefer A to B, but nevertheless B can still win the election. Clearly such deceptive voting confounds the assessment of group utility. When Borda was questioned about the possibility of dishonest and manipulative voting with his method, he is reputed to have stated, "My scheme is only intended for honest men." Unfortunately the weighted vote method provides, under some circumstances, incentives for dishonesty.

The criterion of the independence of irrelevant alternatives is specifically designed to eliminate problems of the type posed in Figures 4.4 and 4.5. According to this principle, the relative ordering between any two alternatives depends on only those two alternatives. The independence of irrelevant alternatives is a very strong condition; however, a voting system that satisfied the independence condition also removes the incentives for the type of difficulties encountered in the examples in Figures 4.4 and 4.5. For instance, in

Voters	Ranking Order		
	1st	2nd	3rd
1	A	B	C
2	A	B	C
3	B	A	C
4	B	A	C
5	C	A	B
6	C	A	B
7	C	A	B

Figure 4.6   An Example of a Paradox with Plurality Voting

NOTE: C is the Plurality winner, despite the fact that a majority of the votes prefer A to C and a majority prefer B to C.

the example in Figure 4.5, if the independence condition were satisfied by some other voting procedure, then it would not be posible for a minority coalition to reverse the results of the election as was done with the Borda scheme.

CONDORCET PRINCIPLE

As part of the background for considering the next criterion, let us first examine the widely used plurality voting method. Here, each individual votes for one alternative, and the alternative with the largest number of votes wins. This procedure does have attractions, such as satisfying the Pareto principle, positive association, and the independence condition. However, there are other difficulties with plurality voting that are illustrated in the example in Figure 4.6. Notice the $A P_B$, $_B P_C$, and $_A P_C$, but nevertheless with the plurality voting, scheme C wins the election, despite the fact that C is the least preferred by 4 of the 7 voters. Furthermore, the problem of the weak mandate that occurs with plurality voting is not improved when a runoff vote is coupled with a plurality vote (Straffin, 1980). Clearly such bizarre results confound meaningful group utility measurement.

The criterion that prevents the problems of the example in Figure 4.6 was first advanced by the Marquis de Condorcet (1785). According to the Condorcet principle, if an alternative obtains a majority in all pairwise contests, then that alternative should be selected as the social choice. Hence, alternative A should have been the winner in the example since $_AP_B$ and $_AP_C$, rather than alternative C, which is the winner with the Plurality procedure. The Condorcet principle does not apply if no alternative wins all pairwise contests. However, if there is a winner of all contests, then it should be the societal choice.

NONDICTATORSHIP

The last criterion for a social choice voting system is quite simple: There should not be a dictator. A dictator capable of determining all orderings of the alternatives completely violates the concept of an assessment of group utility. It is merely an individual preference measure for one of the group members. One might wonder why it is necessary even to be concerned about dictatorship in light of all the previously mentioned criteria. The answer is that the prior criteria are not so strong as to eliminate dictatorship as a method of social choice. A dictator does not violate the Pareto principle, nor the principles of citizen sovereignty, group transitivity, positive association, and independency of irrelevant alternatives. The Condorcet principle need not apply if there is no clear winner of all pairwise contests. Nevertheless, there is no doubt that a dictator is unfair, and to prohibit that eventuality, the nondictatorship criterion is included.

The Impossibility of a Generally Satisfactory Voting System

One of the more remarkable discoveries made in the social sciences was the demonstration by Kenneth Arrow (1951) that a satisfactory voting system is impossible when there are three or more alternatives. In the case where there are only two alternatives, then majority rule is a satisfactory procedure. One of the extraordinary aspects of Arrow's impossibility theorem is that there are an infinite number of possible voting systems. Plurality and Borda-voting schemes are but a few possible methods of social choice. Without specifically analyzing any particular voting method, Arrow proved that no such method can meet all of the criteria of rationality and fairness. Arrow's achievement has not gone unrecognized. In 1972, the Swedish Academy of Science named Arrow as a co-winner of the 1972 Nobel Prize in Economics. In assessing Arrow's contribution, economist Paul Samuelson, who is also a Nobel Laureate, wrote,

> What Kenneth Arrow proved once and for all is that there cannot possibly be found such an ideal voting scheme. The search of the great minds of recorded history for the perfect democracy, it turns out, is the search for a chimera, for a logical self-contradiction . . . Aristotle must be turning over in his grave. The theory of democracy can never be the same [Samuelson, 1972].

Essentially, what Arrow (1951) proved was that a voting system that meets the criteria of positive associationism, citizen sovereignty, and the independence of irrelevant alternatives, in the case where there are three or more alternatives, also implies the existence of a dictator. Blau (1957) discovered a flaw in Arrow's original proof, but he was able to show that the principles of Pareto, positive association, and independence of irrelevant alternatives did imply a dictator. Blau wrote "the intellectual impact of Arrow's result is undiminished . . . and it seems appropriate to refer to the theorem . . . as Arrow's Theorem." In fact, Blau's proof is very close to Arrow's original argument. The proofs are subtle and can be skipped by those willing to accept the conclusions of the formal analysis. For the interested reader, a more informal variation of Arrow's proof is discussed in the appendix at the end of this chapter.

Conclusions

In this chapter, formal criteria have been described for a fair and rational voting system. The criteria discussed were: the Pareto principle, citizen sovereignty, group transitivity, positive association, independence of irrelevant alternatives, the Condorcet principle, and nondictatorship. Unfortunately, Arrow's Impossibility Theorem demonstrates that all the criteria cannot be satisfied when there are three or more alternatives. In light of Arrow's Impossibility Theorem, how can we assess group utility? One possible answer is to make sure the group is never confronted with more than two alternatives. Yet what possible mechanisms could be invented to restrict the alternatives to only two choices? Is the restriction itself unfair? It seems both hopeless and unwise to pursue the approach of only permitting two alternatives. Decisions do not frequently lend themselves to only two possible sources of action. Consequently, to restrict the alternatives to only two choices is to trivialize many complex decisions and therefore is an unacceptable general solution to the Arrow Paradox. Nevertheless, while we do not desire to enforce procedures that restrict the number of reasonable alternatives, we need not encourage a proliferation of alternatives. Group pressure to limit the serious proposals to only two would be wise.

Another possible response to the Arrow Paradox is to abandon the search for a method of assessing group utility. This possibility is totally unacceptable. While it is impossible to meet all criteria of fairness, not to measure group utility is both arbitrary and unfair. Various voting schemes differ in regard to how many criteria they can satisfy. Much of the recent theorizing (i.e., Richelson 1975, 1978a, 1978b) on social welfare has been directed toward determining how many criteria a voting method can satisfy. A method that violates fewer criteria might yield fewer elections with an unfair and misrepresentative group utility. It is too early to recommend a best bet for a voting system, although a few of the more promising new procedures will be described briefly. All of the procedures can be unfair to some degree. Thus, a voting method can be regarded as having a graded susceptibility toward unfairness. Consequently, not to measure group utility is an arbitrary and totally unfair method of social choice—a dictatorship—merely because perfection cannot be achieved by representative voting schemes.

One of the more promising voting methods discussed today by social welfare theorists is approval voting (viz. Brams & Fishburn, 1978). With the approval scheme, individuals can vote for as many alternatives as they wish. Such a voting scheme has been shown to reduce dishonest voting. For example, if three alternatives are all above a voter's threshold for acceptability out of a set of 5 alternatives, then the individual is permitted to cast one vote for each. The alternative with the most votes wins. This voting method is easy to implement and it is promising as a method with a reduced susceptibility toward misrepresentation. For example, suppose that the voter's most preferred alternative is not perceived as likely to win; the voter would not be disadvantaged by still voting for the top choice along with the other acceptable choices.

Another promising voting scheme is the one proposed by Duncan Black (1958). According to this method, the preference rankings are examined to construct all pairwise contests. If there is a Condorcet winner (i.e., a winner of all pairwise contests) then that alternative is selected as the social choice. However, if there is not a Condorcet winner, then the choice procedure reverts to a Borda weighted vote scheme. One advantage of the Black procedure is that it is easily implemented, but nevertheless is complex enough that a voter cannot be sure how to misrepresent his views for strategic advantage, thereby encouraging honest voting. For most group decisions, the Black voting scheme works quite satisfactorily. However, the procedure is not perfect. For instance, in the example in Figure 4.4, the Black method would also have problems with the independence of irrelevant alternatives. However, the susceptibility for unfairness is less likely with the Black scheme. Other methods may be invented that reduce the susceptibility of misrepresentation even further. Arrow's Impossibility Theorem has ended the search for an ideal democracy, but social scientists can still pursue the search for a better democracy.

Appendix

Theorem: A social welfare function that satisfies positive association, group transitivity, and the independence of irrelevant alternatives implies the existence of a dictator if there are three or more alternatives.

Proof: Following Arrow (1951) we well assume a social welfar function that is decisive for all possible individual rankings. Suppose the social ordering for all three alternatives are A^PB, B^PC, and A^PC. Thus, society collectively is decisive for the issue of A versus B. Now let us construct a minimally decisive set V_{AB}. Such a set must exist since the combined society is decisive so we can omit individuals one at a time until we obtain a set V_{AB}. If we omit further individuals, then V_{AB} is no longer decisive. Furthermore, the individuals excluded from V_{AB} are irrelevant for the social choice between A and B. In fact, we can assume that all individuals outside of V_{AB} prefer B to A, but still society prefers A to B. The general representation is

$$V_{AB} = V_1 \ U \ V_2 \ U \ V_3$$

where V_1, V_2, and V_3 are subsets of V_{AB}, where individuals $i \ni V_1 \Rrightarrow A^PB$, B^PC, A^PC, and $i \ni V_2 \Rightarrow A^PB$, C^PB, A^PC, and $i \ni V_3 \Rrightarrow A^PB$, C^PB, C^PA. In a similar fashion, there exist minimally decisive sets V_{AC}

and V_{BC} on the issues of A versus C and B versus C. In order to maintain group gransitivity it follows that

$$V_{BC} \subset V_{AC} \subset V_{AB}$$
$$V_{AC} = V_1 \cup V_2$$
$$V_{BC} = V_1$$

For V_{BC} and V_{AC} to be decisive implies that $\jmath \ni V_3$ are irrelevant in regard to the choice between B and C and the choice between A and C. So, V_3 could be the set where C^{PB}, B^{PA}, and C^{PA}. If it were, however, then V_{AB} would not be minimally decisive. The solution to that dilemma is to conclude that V_3 is empty. Similarly, V_2 is irrelevant in regard to the B versus C choice, which similarly results in the conclusion that V_2 is empty. Thus

$$V_{AB} = V_{BC} = V_{AC} = V_1$$

However, how can we construct a social choice rule that guarantees a priori that individual 2 within V_1 will vote the same as individual 1? We cannot; therefore, V_1 is a set of a single individual and thereby is a dictator.

References

Arrow, K. *Social choice and individual values.* Cowles Commission Monograph, 12, New York: John Wiley, 1951.

Black, D. *The theory of committees and elections.* London: Cambridge University Press, 1958.

Blau, J. H. The existence of social welfare functions. *Econometrica,* 1957, 25, 302-313.

Borda, J. C. Memoire sur les Elections au Scrutin, *Historie de l'Academie Royale des Sciences,* 1781.

Brams, S. J., & Fishburn, P. Approval voting. *American Political Science Review,* 1978, 72, 831-847.

Condorcet, M. *Essai sur l'application de l'analyse a la Probabilite des Decisions Rendues a la Pluraliste des voix.* Paris: 1785.

Hill, P. H., Bedau, H. A., Chechile, R. A., Crochetiere, W. J., Kellerman, B. L., Ounjian, D., Pauker, S. G., Pauker, S. P., & Rubin, J. Z. *Making decisions: A multidisciplinary introduction.* Reading, MA: Addison-Wesley, 1979.

Richelson, J. T. A comparative analysis of social choice functions. *Behavioral Science,* 1975, 20, 331-337.

Richelson, J. T. A comparative analysis of social choice functions, II, *Behavioral Science,* 1978, 23, 38-44. (a)

Richelson, J. T. A comparative analysis of social choice functions, III, *Behavioral Science,* 1978, 23, 169-176. (b)

Samuelson, P. A. The 1972 Nobel Prize for Economic Science, *Science,* 1972, 178, 487-489.

Straffin, P. D., Jr. *Topics in the theory of voting.* Boston: Birkhouser, 1980.

Tversky, A. The intransitivity of preferences. *Psychological Review,* 1969, 76, 31-48.

CHAPTER 5

ETHICAL ASPECTS OF GROUP DECISION MAKING

Hugo Bedau

In order to focus precisely on our topic, the ethical aspects of group decision making, it will prove useful to contrast it with the two major distinct topics adjacent to it. As other chapters of this book have made clear, there are *nonethical* aspects of group decision making, such as how a group should make prompt and effective decisions. There are also ethical aspects of *nongroup* (individual) decision making (Bedau, 1979) an important topic but one omitted from this book along with all the other features of individual decision making (except where they overlap with or are usefully contrasted to group decision making). In this chapter, however, some of the discussion will concern how the ethical aspects of group decision making are related to each of these allied topics. In real life, situations requiring decision making do not present themselves neatly labeled and separated into rigid categories called "group" and "individual," or "ethical" and "nonethical." Rather, actual situations blur and overlap these boundaries, and our discussion will have to take this into account.

By the *ethical* aspects of a group's decisions is meant those aspects that are based upon, conform to, or violate some ethical norm, whether or not the decision maker accepts that norm or even recognized that the decision conforms with or violates it. An ethical norm (as will be explained later in greater detail) is, typically, any general rule of conduct designed to govern those who accept it insofar as their behavior affects the interests and welfare of others. (It should also be mentioned that, throughout this chapter, the terms "ethical" and "moral" will be used interchangeably, even though for some purposes it is useful to keep them distinct.)

The ethical aspects of group decision making divide naturally into two sets of subtopics. As discussion elsewhere in this book makes clear, sometimes our attention needs to focus on the *process* by means of which a decision is reached, whereas at other times we are interested only in the *result* of that process, the decision itself. As we shall shortly see, the process and the decision each have their ethical aspects, and the issues raised in each context are not the same. Distinctions among the kinds of goals or objects of the decision-making process will also prove relevant to our task. In some cases, the decision-making group is trying to reach what its members regard as the ethically correct decision, the decision that is the best one from the moral point of view; later in this chapter, we will examine such a real-life case in detail. In other instances, however, the group conceives of its goal as ethically neutral or indifferent, or (more likely) as a case where the ethical aspects of the goal are recognized but are treated as subordinate to one or more nonethical aspects. These differences are worth closer inspection; we turn to this task first.

Preliminary Distinctions

Just as it is possible for an individual to do the morally right thing for the wrong reason (e.g., on the basis of a faulty line of reasoning), so it is possible for a group to do the thing that is right from an ethical point of view, but to reach this decision by a process that is ethically faulty or objectionable. The reverse also is possible—that is, to reach a decision that is ethically objectionable by means of a procedure that cannot be improved upon, ethically speaking. This process-product or procedure-result distinction has been used throughout this book; it is quite as relevant to the ethical aspects of decision making as it is to the nonethical aspects. Where there are clear contrasts between individual and group decision making, the most conspicuous differences emerge in the *process* of group decision. No sharp contrasts are to be found in either the *results* of decisions themselves, or in the actual *reasoning* employed in search for and support of the decision, as we shall see below.

PARTICIPATION AND RESPONSIBILITY

The process of group decision making varies both in the conditions of participation in deliberation that confront group members of different groups, and in the way individual responsibility for a group's decisions will vary according to the quality of individual participation. Deliberation is the cognitive process that culminates in decision; where a group is involved, deliberation takes the form of verbal give-and-take in discussion. To the extent that a member of the group is denied the right or the opportunity to participate in the group's deliberations, it is unreasonable to hold that member morally accountable for the group's decisions and actions.[1] Thus, two centuries ago, in those parts of the nation where slavery was practiced, it would have been unreasonable to hold *any* slave morally responsible for *any* governmental decision (local, state, or national), since no slave could participate in any political deliberations. Likewise, at the turn of this century before female suffrage, a similar reduction (or even cancellation) of moral responsibility for political decisions applied to all women, because they were disenfranchised. As recently as a generation ago, this was true of black Americans in the Jim Crow southern states: Although blacks had been citizens since 1874 they were still entirely excluded from political participation.

There is, of course, a difference between having the right to participate in a group's deliberations and exercising that right. And one can exercise the right minimally and passively (by no more than being present during the deliberations) or actively (by speaking up, running for office, etc.). One of the chronic problems of individual moral responsibility for group conduct arises at precisely the point where a group of which you are a member does something morally objectionable, and although you have the right and the opportunity to participate in the group's deliberations, you do not. Does your passivity and failure to exercise your right excuse you from all responsibility? Or does the fact that you had the right to participate impose on you full responsibility? Except in very special cases, the truth lies between these two extremes, because a person's responsibility in general varies with the degree to which he or she has the right to participate.[2] If you do not exercise your right, knowing that the group may well decide upon an immoral act, then you cannot plead your nonparticipation as a complete exoneration for any blameworthiness arising from the immoral act of the group. For it is clear that you could have done something to avert that decision, or that you could at least have protested or disassociated yourself from it, and you didn't.

POLICIES AND RULES

We need to look more precisely at what is involved in recognizing the principle that the individual moral responsibility of a group's members for its decisions is in part a function of the quality of participation in the decision-making process. Imagine yourself as a member of a certain group—not a leader or executive, but merely one member among others. The group is newly organized and must reach decisions on various agenda items. Reasonable but not extreme urgency indicates the desirability of doing so with some dispatch. You expect to play a role in deliberation with other members of the group, but the group has as yet no settled manner of conducting its deliberations. What would be a plausible set of policies and rules to govern the deliberations (the decision-making process) of the group?

Let us begin with the *policies*. Here is a partial set: (a) agree upon procedures whereby substantive decisions of the group are to be reached, and abide by those procedures and the results reached by using them; (b) seek to increase opportunity for all group members to participate in the deliberations; and (c) treat the views expressed during deliberation seriously and with respect. Three things should be noticed about such policies. First, they seem to be the sort of policies you might hope would appeal to every member of the group. They do not seem to favor any particular member or faction in the group—in other words, they seem fair to all. Second, these policies may be said to arise out of an ethical norm that decrees respect for the *equal moral worth of all members* of the group, rather than either from some exalted view of the ethical status of the *group* itself or for *efficiency* in the deliberative process (such policies may in fact be inefficient in the short run). However, these policies by themselves do not take us very far toward actually achieving the goals they prescribe. For that we need to formulate certain *rules* of procedure.

For illustration, let us focus on the problems that might arise out of a desire to implement policy (b) above. Assume that you are willing to accept the policy, and that the other members of the group are too. To give it full effect, you might well consider adopting all of the following rules of participation in deliberation: (1) due notice (including the agenda) will be provided to all members of the group in advance of any meeting; (2) no deliberation may commence or continue without a quorum of the group present; (3) anyone who speaks must limit comments to two minutes' duration; (4) no one may speak twice on a given issue until everyone else has had a chance to speak once; (5) cloture (end of a debate) requires a two-thirds vote of all present.[3]

On reflection, are these rule for deliberation acceptable? Do they enhance realization of policy (b)? Do they do so at the cost of thwarting realization of some other policies no less worthy of implementation by rules? Are additional rules needed before policy (b) is adequately implemented and protected? Above all, would *you* be willing to see these rules accepted by the group and enforced by the chairperson and parliamentarian? We cannot try here to pursue these questions further, but they are the very questions that must be answered before one can be confident that a set of ethically acceptable rules has been designed.

Notice two important things: First, these questions cannot even arise where individual decision making is concerning. They are all essentially tied to the fact that you are involved with others in a decision-making process. As soon as the others (the rest of the group, or your membership in it) disappear, so does any need to answer these questions.

Second, the rules and policies under discussion in this hypothetical example seem to be task- and topic-neutral. That is, it does not seem to matter what kind of decision the group is trying to reach or what topic is under examination (though, of course, other aspects of group composition and structure may be relevant). Groups of very different character, charged with deciding questions of totally different nature, still might find it best to subject their proceedings to the same policies and rules. We can even imagine a group of criminals, bent on some ghastly and wicked deeds—for example, Nazis in Occupied Europe in 1942, trying to decide whom to "dispose of" (Jews versus Poles versus Russians) at what rate (a thousand versus five thousand per week) and in what fashion (labor camp versus death camp), who conduct their deliberations using such rules. However much we might denounce from the ethical perspective *any* decision they reach, we might still have no reason to find fault with the internal procedures they used in reaching those decisions.

This leads to asking whether, in general, there is any connection between the ethical quality of a group's decision-making processes and the ethical quality of the group's decision itself. Could we hazard the hypothesis, for example, that the more a group's deliberative procedures are free from ethical objections, the more the decisions reached under such procedures will be free from ethical objections?[4] Such a hypothesis is attractive (if it were true, it would help to justify our concern over procedures), but it is not easily subject to verification, and one can think of apparent counter-examples in many settings. Even so, a prudent group member, given that he or she has the ethical aspects of group decision making primarily in mind, might reason as follows: Difficult as it is to be sure that the rules and policies we adopt in our group for conducting our affairs are ethically correct, it is even more difficult to determine whether the decisions themselves are the right ones; therefore I will strive, and endeavor to get other members of the group to strive, to identify acceptable procedural norms and to comply with them scrupulously. In any case, it is clear that the fascination over the years with proper parliamentary procedure, familiar to most of us through *Robert's Rule of Order* (Robert, 1970), is testimony to the generally shared concern for *fairness* in the rules of the game—the game of deliberation—quite apart from the outcome.

Doing the Right Thing

As noted earlier, the decisions that a group undertakes to reach can be usefully divided for our purposes into two main types. In some cases, a group self-consciously undertakes to reach what it regards as an ethically correct decision; that is, the group is attempting to decide what the ethically correct thing is for it to do, so that the group can then do it. In such cases, the admittedly nonethical aspects of the decision (e.g., the costs of implementing it) may be deliberately ignored. Judicial tribunals typically see their task in this fashion; their conscious purpose is to do justice to the conflicting claims of the parties before them. As another example (one we shall shortly discuss in considerable detail), consider the deliberations in recent years of various groups over whether to withdraw their investments in South African corporations, or in American or multinational corporations doing business in South Africa, because of the group's opposition to South African racial policies (apartheid). The Divestment controversy, as it has come to be called, is a primary example of just this sort, where a group (not an individual) is trying to make an ethical decision, to do the right thing, to act fairly. Thus, the main issues are to try to find out *what* is the right thing to do and why, as well as what the consequences will be of such action for all concerned, and then to get the group to adopt that policy.

In other cases, however, far more common for most groups (as well as for most individuals), a group attempts to decide something that is (or is thought to be) ethically neutral, or wholly nonethical, or where the ethical aspects of the decision are not the paramount object of concern. As an example (one discussed at length in Chapter 7), consider the deliberations of the American electorate as it decides who is to be the next president. Trying to reach a decision that is ethically correct is not the primary object of the process at all; perhaps it does not even make sense to think of electing the "ethically correct" president, and the best we can ever say is that the person elected was decided upon by a fair method or process. In such cases, the *process* is the exclusive focus of ethical attention. If the process is unfair, or seems unfair, then the result of the election will in turn be deemed unfair and will, to that extent, be viewed as not binding on the electorate (or on the losing candidates), even if the unfair process produced the "best" result.

To take another example, consider the case of a business organization attempting to decide which of several products (say, prescription drugs) to market two years hence, and where the products vary in two important respects: safety from harmful side-effects, and the population potentially benefited from the drug. Both safety and size of potential benefit are ethically relevant factors that the group will take into account in reaching its marketing decision. But neither of these is the group's primary consideration. Other factors (such as prospective market share, capacity of the company's detail men to sell the drug alongside the other products the firm already markets) will also be taken into account. All of these factors will bear on the primary objective, which is to maximize profit for the firm (the dominant objective of business corporations, as explained in Chapter 9). Now, profit-maximization is not itself an ethical goal (nor, except for certain kinds of radicals, is it an ethically objectionable goal), even if the ways this goal is pursued obviously can raise ethical questions.

The two major types of goals suggested by these two examples give rise to different ethical concerns. The main question raised by the election example is this: How should a group whose primary objective is to reach an ethically correct decision determine what that decision is? The main question raised by the drug marketing example is quite different: How much weight should be given to the ethical aspects of a decision when doing the ethically correct thing is not (perhaps for good reasons) the primary objective of the group? These two questions sometimes seem to merge into one another and in any case are not easy to answer; before we can try to do so, we need to do some direct exploration of the very idea of *ethical* decision making in general.

Practical Reasoning

Insofar as the process of group decision making is an exercise of the cognitive capacities of the members of the group, we can think of the process an an exercise in group deliberation, in much the same fashion as we think of an individual's cognitive decision-making process as an exercise in individual deliberation. A clear case of group decision making that involved group deliberation is what a trial jury does prior to rendering its verdict. In deliberation, what is under examination is a series of arguments, or fragments of arguments, one after the other (sometimes in a disorderly, overlapping, and confusing manner). Some of these arguments are simple, others complex; some are good, others are better; perhaps a few are worthless. In each instance, the proposed conclusion of the argument is the decision favored (for the moment, at least) by whatever group member is advancing that argument. This is equivalent to saying that the activity of deliberation during the process of decision making is always *practical reasoning* (rather than theoretical or abstract reasoning) because everyone is advancing and evaluating reasons for *acting* in one way rather than another. (The issue is what to *do*, not what to *believe*, except as that is a preliminary to action.) These reasons are in effect the premises of arguments, and the conclusions are actions or commitments—decisions to act (for further discussion of practical reasoning, see Gauthier, 1963; Raz, 1978). Let us take a closer look at the general structure of such reasoning.

THE GENERAL STRUCTURE

Philosophers since Aristotle, looking at human decision making (whether by groups or individuals), see in it nothing but forms of practical reasoning. (Such a view is, to be sure, not merely or primarily descriptive of actual thought and speech during group decision making; it is prescriptive and reconstructive, so to speak—it is an attempt to characterize a model that seizes on the essential features of the phenomenon under discussion and ignores as irrelevant or adventitious everything else.) But not all practical reasoning is ethical reasoning; the former concept is considerably broader. So let us look first at the general character of practical reasoning. The simplest form of such reasoning has this structure:

Major premise: Under conditions C, actor A ought to do act D.
Minor premise: Conditions C in fact apply in *this* case.
Conclusion: Actor A ought to do act D in *this* case.

(For our purposes, actor A will always be a group, or a person acting as agent or representative of some group.) The major premise is always a hypothetical or conditional proposition (of the form "if . . . then—"), whereas the minor premise is always an assertion to the effect that the antecedent of the hypothetical (the condition stated in the conditional, i.e., what follows the "if" and precedes the "then") is true. Aristotle (1925) called reasoning of this form "the practical syllogism," in contrast to theoretical reasoning. He also said that the conclusion of such a practical syllogism is an "action." Actually, this is not quite right, since practical reasoning is always *reasoning*, and the product of reasoning is always a *conclusion* (a proposition derived from other propositions); but a conclusion is not an action. However, Aristotle was not completely off the mark, because in the normal case any agent (individual or group) who accepts the premises of a bit of practical reasoning—that is, who acknowledges that the premises apply to him or her (or to his or her group) in the situation at hand (thus, I am actor A in the schema above, and I see that I am in condition C)—will draw the conclusion from these premises, and therefore will *act* in accordance with that judgment. After all, finding out what to *do* in the situation at hand was the whole point of the exercise of deliberation (i.e., constructing the practical syllogism) in the first place![5]

The examples we shall be studying below of practical reasoning that involve ethical decision making will be more complex than those found in the simple schema above, with only two premises leading straightaway to a decision for action; in actual cases, the practical reasoning used by individuals or groups who are trying to reach an ethically correct conclusion is almost always more complex than that. Nevertheless, the basic structure is (or can be reconstructed as being) *always* the same: one or more general premises of a hypothetical structure that link certain conditions with appropriate action; one or more premises stating that these conditions really do obtain in the present situation; and a conclusion—the decision itself—that serves as the directive to action.

ETHICAL REASONING

The difference between ethical reasoning and other kinds of practical reasoning generally lies entirely at one point; it is in the character of the major premise of the practical syllogism. Consider the following two examples:

Example I: If the group is going to prosper, then it must get more members soon.
The group wants to prosper.
The group must recruit more members soon.

Example II: If a company makes a promise to its customers, then it must intend to keep that promise.
The company is about to promise its customers a full money-back refund on defective merchandise returned within 90 days of purchase.
The company must intend to keep that promise.

Both these examples fit the general schema outlined in the previous section, in that each has a conclusion that is a judgment and that, in the normal case, will result in the action indicated; each has a minor premise stating that certain conditions obtain; and each has a major premise specifying what is to be done by the group in circumstances of a certain type. The major premises are also alike in that each expresses, or relies upon, a *norm*. Acceptance of a norm has the result of enabling those who accept it to eliminate from further consideration alternatives for decision and action that are incompatible with that norm. But the two norms differ in that the kind of norm embodied in the major premise of Example II is an ethical norm, whereas in Example I it is not, it is merely a norm of self-interest or prudence. In fact, it is nothing but a means-end relationship. Its nonethical character can be brought out even more clearly by considering still another example:

Example III: In order to turn on the light, the switch must be turned to the left.
I want to turn on the lights.
I must turn the switch to the left.

No one would seriously propose that the major premise in Example III is or embodies an ethical norm. Yet the purely means-end feature of the major premise here is no different in principle from that to be found in the major premise of Example I.

Exactly why the norm in Example II is different is easier to sense than to say. One obvious difference is that the existence of other people besides the actor is utterly irrelevant in Example III. While possible conflicts of interests or the rights of others are really not in question in Example I, there is essential reference to the interests and tacit reference to the rights of others in the norm that governs Example II. The rights of other people (here, innocent and well-intentioned customers of the company) must eventually be acknowledged as part of any argument for the major premise in this example. Also, the means-end relationship to be found in the other two norms is missing. Whereas those norms are of the other form "to achieve end E, one must take step S," no such connection is implied in the norm that connect an intention to keep one's work with one's promise-making act. The former is not a means to the end of making a promise; it is rather an essential condition of a sincere, genuine, or morally legitimate promise.

ETHICAL NORMS

We are now in a position to face two general questions. First, how do we tell whether we are relying on an ethical norm in our practical reasoning (as in Example II above) rather than some other kind of norm. What, in short, is the criterion for a norm being an *ethical* norm? (for further discussion, see von Wright, 1963) Second, given that we are using such a norm, how do we tell whether it is the only relevant, or the best, ethical norm for that situation? After all, it is plausible to suppose that in any given decision-making situation there is more than one possible ethical norm that the decision-maker (individual or group) might find relevant, in which case there arises a possible conflict between the decisions recommended by each norm. It is not possible in this brief space to give an adequate answer to either question, so a partial answer will have to suffice for present purposes.

First of all, it is pretty clear that a norm that omits any reference to how a decision affects persons outside the group that is making the decision is not a very plausible ethical norm (except in the special case, if there is any, where in fact the group's decision affects no one except the group's members). Hence, some philosophers have gone so far as to define ethics and ethical norms in terms of rules that take into account in a systematic and uniform way the interests of others. On this influential view, ethical norms must be formulated with explicit reference to the welfare, needs, rights, or best interests of *all* persons affected by the decision in question. By contrast, a nonethical norm will have reference either to no one's welfare, or (more typically) merely to the agent's.

In a parallel fashion, we can and do criticize norms from the ethical point of view in part by reference to how much the norms favor the interests of some rather than others or all of those affected by the decision. Thus, the maxim "My country, right or wrong" may be a perfect testament to group loyalty and to that extent morally all right. But if it means (as it often does) that the persons or groups who embrace this maxim should never under any conditions criticize their own government, or never take seriously the possibility that their government may have acted unfairly or harmfully toward people of its own or another nation, then the maxim loses its persuasiveness as a moral maxim acceptable for all occasions. Instead, it becomes nothing more than an expression of chauvinism. Likewise, the maxim "Blood is thicker than water" suggests that a moral person will show most concern for the effects of her actions on her immediate family than on her neighbors, and more concern for those effects on her neighbors than on distant fellow countrymen, and little concern by comparison with these others for any effect of her actions on persons temporally and spatially remote. If this maxim is treated as a norm, then its underlying ethnocentrism puts it at a disadvantage in competition with more universal and egalitarian norms (such as underlie the doctrine that "all persons are children under the fatherhood of one God"). Roughly, then, of any two ethical norms relevant to a given decision, the better of the two is the one that is the fairest to all, the norm that is least vulnerable to the charge of selfishness, group prejudice, and the like.

The Divestment Controversy

We have looked briefly and in the abstract at the major elements involved in the ethical aspects of group decision making. In order to see them at work, and in order to study some of the more familiar complications not so far discussed but regularly encountered in actual cases, it will be useful to examine closely from the moral point of view a typical example of a group decision. The example to be studied has become familiar on college and university campuses, as well as in the stockholders' meetings of many corporations, during the 1970s. I refer to the Divestment controversy mentioned earlier, that is, the problem that groups (as well as some wealthy individuals) face in trying to decide whether to withdraw their investments in companies that do business in or with South Africa, because of the racist policies of South Africa (see Litvak, DeGrasse, & McTigue, 1978; Schmidt, 1980; Bok, 1979, 1982, 1983). As indicated earlier, this example can be seen as one of the two major types of group decisions when those decisions are distinguished according to the object or goal of the decision (viz., that type in which the goal is to do the ethically correct thing). As we shall see, decisions defined initially so that they fall into this class have a way, even before they are actually made, of sliding over into the other category (viz., decisions in which ethical factors are merely some of the considerations that influence the decision maker).

First, let us be convinced that the Divestment controversy really presents us with a case of *group decision making*: (a) It is a matter for *decision*, because the investments in question are always a result of choices, made by identifiable persons acting on behalf of or as the agent for the group among alternative investment opportunities. Funds do not automatically invest themselves (in the way it might be said that interest "automatically" accrues on a good investment), and funds invested today in one corporation can be invested tomorrow in another corporation, provided there are buying and selling opportunities available in the marketplace and provided the investor decides to shift the investment portfolio from its current holdings. (b) It is also a matter of *group* decision making. For one thing, the ultimate investment decisions are typically made by a small group rather than by one individual, usually the finance committee of the board of trustees or their agents in the investment community. For another, it is quite possible that where Divestment is under consideration, several campus groups with different constituencies (including students, faculty, alumni, and trustees) will send representatives to sit on a committee appointed or elected precisely for the purpose of advising the ultimate decision makers.

Second, it is important to see that the parties to the decision will likely view their task as one of trying to decide what the ethically correct thing is to do. No one imagines that proposals for Divestment are ethically neutral or indifferent, or that they are intended primarily to enhance the return on investment (though if this were to result, few would complain!). Nor is any other nonethical goal uppermost in the minds of those who favor Divestment, although nonethical goals are often (even if not invariably) uppermost in the minds of those who oppose Divestment. Furthermore, those who believe that Divestment is the ethically correct policy for the group to follow, typically argue from considerations that are unquestionably ethical in nature (even if they may be vulnerable to incompatible but superior ethical reflections). First, they want to be able to view themselves as members of a group that is trying to do the right thing. Second, they want to act on the moral judgments they have reached to the effect that *apartheid is unfair,* that *apartheid is a racist practice,* and that *racism is a grave moral wrong.* Furthermore, they believe as a matter of fact that if their group has investments in the South African economy, then *they* are connected personally and collectively as a group to the unfair and immoral racist practices that they condemn.

Now, given the above depiction of the matter, the group faces two major tasks: (a) *how* to reach its decision in a manner that is ethically acceptable, and (b) *what* decision to reach so that the group can act in an ethically acceptable manner. Earlier, we discussed some general features of group decision making procedures from the ethical point of view. They now become irrelevant here, especially if the group that will decide (or decide how to advise the decision maker) is rather large, and if there is reason to believe that it encompasses sharp divergences in viewpoint and convictions relevant to the Divestment controversy. These two factors tend to encourage the adoption of more rather than less formal procedures, in order to be fair to all involved.

There is no need to elboarate further in the present context on such procedural considerations. Instead, let us concentrate on the kinds of practical arguments that will be under discussion by the group, at least one of which must be accepted by everyone who eventually votes for Divestment. (Not everyone, of course, must accept the *same* argument; it suffices if everyone who votes for Divestment accepts some argument leading to that conclusion. Similarly, it suffices to make rational a refusal to vote for Divestment that the voter cannot think of a single good argument to that conclusion.) There are many such arguments that could be formulated, and we cannot possibly explore them all here with the detail that a group deliberating the Divestment controversy ought to do. We must content ourselves with considering two major arguments, one in favor of divestment and the other against it. The former is the Clean Hands argument, the latter the Leverage argument.

THE CLEAN HANDS ARGUMENT

The Divestment controversy has been created largely by those who want to "get out" of South Africa, or more precisely, who want to get themselves out of corporations in South Africa or to get their corporations out of South Africa. The Clean Hands argument is the central kind of argument embraced by those who favor the former alternative, and it goes like this:

Assume the group believes that (1) apartheid is morally wrong, because it is a racist practice and racism is always wrong, and that (2) everyone ought to do whatever is possible, consistent with other ethical requirements, to disassociate his or her own actions from wrongdoing. Now suppose the group also believes that (3) continued investment in corporations doing business in South Africa amounts to a willingness to profit from the favorable economic climate and artificially low costs created by apartheid, and that (4) only by divestment of holdings in these corporations can one disassociate oneself from the wrongdoing that attempting to profit from apartheid represents. If the group believes these premises, then it must infer that (5) everyone ought to divest holdings in South African corporations, and in particular that (6) our college or university ought to divest its holdings.

The key ideas of this argument are to be found in premises (3) and (4); they express the idea that, quite apart from any effects from divestment that might mitigate or eliminate apartheid itself, those who disassociate themselves by selling off their investments avoid getting their hands any dirtier than they already are from involvement in apartheid, and that, morally speaking, this is what decent people ought to do. The idea seems to such whereas it may not be within the group's power to have much affect on South Africa's racist practices, it is within the group's power to put some distance between itself and those practices. In so doing, the group says in effect, "There may be moral evil in the world, which we did not create and cannot prevent or eliminate; but we do not need to support it, much less profit from it; and so we ought not to." The fundamental ethical norms here, however, are what underlie premise (2) and the judgment expressed in premise (1).

Notice that the argument has equal application to the decisions of an individual investor in South African corporations as well as to group investors. The practical conclusion of the argument—Clean your hands by divestment!—applies to all, individuals or groups, whose investment portfolio brings them within the scope of the argument. To the extent that this is typical of such arguments, it suggests that there is nothing about either the *reasoning* process itself through which a group would go, or about the *decision* reached, that is peculiar to the group in contrast to the individual. To put this another way, what constitutes good reasoning and a morally correct decision for a group may hold as well for the individual. The differences arise at two or three somewhat different points. One is getting the group to *see* the cogency of the reasoning; the others are getting the group to *make* its decision, and then persuading it to *act*. Here, there are sharp disanalogies between individual and group decision making.

THE LEVERAGE ARGUMENT

In the Divestment controversy, morality is not exclusively on the side of those who would divest. As actual events in this controversy have shown, some members of the college community who think of themselves as no less moral that those who favor divestment have argued in favor of *not* divesting. All such arguments share certain important features to be found in the Leverage argument, which goes like this:

Opponents of divestment might well begin by insisting that they, too, believe that (1) apartheid is morally wrong, and (2) everyone should do whatever is feasible, consistent with other ethical requirements, to end or avoid further wrongdoing, whether one's own or that of another. However, it is also true that (3) corporations doing business in South Africa could help to diminish and even end the wrongdoing that apartheid involves; but (4) such corporations will not resist apartheid on their own initiative. Therefore, (5) everyone with investments in corporations doing business in South Africa should bring pressure on the management of such corporations, and in particular, (6) our college or university should bring such pressure as it can.

The central ethical norms of this argument are, of course, those found in premises (1) and (2). The key features of the argument, in contrast to other possible arguments, are in the two premises (3) and (4), because they express the idea the corporations are in a position to exert leverage against apartheid. But to exert this leverage, it is crucial to exploit, not sell off, one's investments in South African corporations. To see this more clearly, consider the way in which the group might reason to justify premise (3) as above: (a) apartheid laws apply to the daily business affairs of all corporations doing business in South Africa; therefore (b) any company doing business in conformity with these laws is to that extent helping to sustain apartheid; (c) if the grip of apartheid can be weakened in the market-place then it will be weakened everywhere; (d) the South African government cannot afford to lose the business and industry represented by the multinational corporations; and therefore (e) if the South African government knows that a multinational corporation does not want to comply with apartheid, that will put pressure on the government to change its racial policies or not to enforce them insofar as they affect the corporation; therefore (f) these corporations can help to undermine apartheid (= premise (3)).

Like the Clean Hands argument, the Leverage argument applies as well to individuals as to groups, provided the individual comes within the scope of the argument (i.e., has investments in corporations of the appropriate sort). Once again, the practical imperative of this argument—Lobby your corporation to fight apartheid!—even though it differs from the conclusion of the Clean Hands argument, applies to individuals and to groups, and this reconfirms the point made above to the effect that practical reasoning as such is the same thing whether a group or an individual does it.

THE CRITICISM OF ARGUMENTS

Now let us imagine that the group, confronted with these two incompatible arguments, wants to conduct the ideal deliberation over their merits, prior to accepting either, as a necessary condition of behaving responsibly on this important matter. How might these arguments best be evaluated? Let us leave to one side the questions of social psychology discussed in Chapters 2 and 3, that bear on the capacity of the group to perform this task. It is the *logic*, not the psychology, of the group's deliberative process that concerns us here.

Critical evaluation of these arguments can (and should) in practice involve each of three major types of review, and any effort devoted to other factors is strictly irrelevant. (We assume that questions of procedure, discussed earlier, have already been settled by the group. We also ignore here any deliberation that takes the form of producing further types of arguments beyond the two under consideration. These other arguments, after all, will in their turn need evaluation, which will involve exactly the same three stages we are about to consider.)

First, there is the critical discussion of the *ethical norms and judgments* employed in the arguments. In the present instance, we may assume that everyone in the group agrees with the initial premise of our two arguments, the judgment (1) that apartheid is morally wrong. Interestingly enough, advocates of the Clean Hands argument as well as the advocates of the Leverage argument start from this premise. Disagreement over the morality of apartheid, therefore, if not what divides them; reinforcing the proposition that apartheid is wrong will not produce agreement over which argument to accept. Nevertheless, it is useful to see how this crucial moral judgment might be defended or criticized. Here is one argument for the judgment: (a) apartheid involves using the law to establish certain rights and duties, benefits, and burdens, according to the race of the person; (b) the white race gets the lion's share of the rights and the advantages, whereas the nonwhites get the duties and the disadvantages (e.g., about 85% of the national territory, including almost all the best lands, are in the hands of the white minority, about 15% of the total population); (c) this division of rights and duties became law and is sustained as law by means of a political process that excluded any participation or consent by nonwhites;[6] (d) any policy under law that is so antimajoritarian as well as antimeritocratic, so unequally beneficial and burdensome, and that is imposed without participation and consent of those who must endure the burden and disadvantages, is morally wrong and unjust. Any criticism of the judgment that apartheid is morally wrong will have to challenge one or more of these four steps, (a) through (d).

Are there other ethical norms that play a role in either the Clean Hands or Leverage arguments? Premise (2) of each argument obviously expresses a fundamental ethical norm, albeit a rather abstract and somewhat formalistic one by comparison with the norm that underlies premise (1). Although the second premise is not the same in our two basic arguments, they are obviously close relatives, and express the outlook of anyone who self-consciously takes a moral stance about something (viz., that doing the morally right thing is important). Again, because premise (2) of each argument is nearly the same, disagreement over the norm or norms involved here is not what divides supporters of the Clean Hands argument from proponents of the Leverage argument. What does divide them lies elsewhere.

The second area where critical discussion by the group is required concerns various kinds of *factual assertions and generalizations* that appear in each argument, reminiscent of the minor premises in the illustrative practical syllogisms discusses earlier. To take the simplest possible example, both arguments depend to some extent on a common factual assumption, that the college actually does have some investments in corporations doing business in South Africa. Obviously, the whole Divestment controversy is strictly irrelevant to a college community in which the college's endowments include no investments in such corporations. Once this threshold is passed, the size of these investments seems to have a differential impact on the merits of divestment, depending on the argument (Clean Hands versus Leverage) being used; below, we shall look more closely at this factor of scale. Far more controversial are the ways certain generalizations are employed in the arguments, and it is likely to be these generalizations and the beliefs behind them that are the true source of disagreement. For example, consider the crucial third premise in the Clean Hands argument (viz., (3) investment in South African business expresses a willingness to profit from the immoral practices of apartheid). It might be argued that it is unreasonable to attach much weight to this proposition in light of the following: (a) most of the companies in which our college has investments are not making a profit, but they are giving employment to many nonwhites in South Africa; (b) if and when they do make a profit, the college can use those revenues to create scholarships so that nonwhite South Africans can come to the college for undergraduate or professional studies; and (c) the companies in which the college is heavily invested are already working persistently and subtly to modify, resist, and compensate for the apartheid laws and policies under which they do business. The upshot of these facts (if that is what they are) in the overall context is to suggest, if not to prove, that selling off the college's investments in the corporations in question would not serve any important moral purpose.

Finally, it is possible to attack the argument's *validity*. This is the most sophisticated line of criticism; how to do it and how to cope with such criticisms are the subject of countless textbooks in elementary logic and ordinary reasoning. Roughly, the idea is this: Any argument is valid if and only if the conclusion cannot be false if all the premises are true. (Hence, a sound argument—one that *proves* its point—is any valid argument all of whose premises are known to be true.) Suffice it to say here that since practical reasoning purports to be valid reasoning, any concrete arguments, such as the two we have been discussing, are always open to challenges of this sort. True, so long as the arguments remain in the simple two-step form of our illustrative examples earlier, their validity or invalidity is likely to be obvious on the face of it; and if they are invalid (that is, if it is false that—were the premises all true—the conclusion could not be false), then the source of the trouble can usually be quickly spotted and repaired (for instance, by replacing a premise with another one formulated slightly differently). But when the argument gets complicated, with many premises and with several subordinate arguments needed to prop up each of the main premises, as is obviously true of the Clean Hands and Leverage arguments, then deciding on the validity or invalidity of the overall argument requires considerable patience and logical acumen.

What our discussion in this section shows is that if a group sets itself the task of properly criticizing the arguments set before it, the task is likely to be a difficult and protracted one. There is always more to say, more to learn, and more to think about, quite apart from trying to achieve consensus at a high level of factual detail and mutual understanding, and quite apart from the obstacle created by the all-too-human failings of impatience, inability to take criticism, incipient distrust of some members by others, and so forth. Yet underlying this whole process is an important ethical mandate. The *need to be mutually rational* as members of a group engaged in deliberation is itself an ethical requirement of group decision making. For example, if I favor the Leverage argument, but you are not sure that you do, then it is necessary for me to try to explain to you why that argument and my reasons for it are meritorious. It is equally necessary for you to be willing to show respect for my reasons until such time as you or someone else in the group can persuade me to set them aside, or abandon them altogether (because they were not based on all the facts, etc.). If you will not show respect for my reasons, then how can you claim to respect *me?* (Showing respect for my reasons, of course, does not require you to agree with them; it does require you to take them seriously and help me to evaluate them critically on the assumption that I am not pathologically attached to them but, rather, accept them only because they seem to be true and relevant.) And the same considerations apply to my reactions to your reasons. Ideally, everyone in the group wants to resolve the Divestment controversy by means of everyone in the group accepting all and only the best reasons, thereby tending to increase the likelihood that the decision entailed by these reasons is itself the right decision. That may prove in practice to be an impossibly high standard. Unanimity, as we noted before, may be completely out of reach, and the group may have to reconcile itself to settling this controversy by no more than majority agreement. Yet even this may require hours of intense discussion, position papers on various details about the college's investment portfolio, studies of how particular corporations in which the college holds investments actually conduct their business in South Africa, the connections between economic and political apartheid, and so on.

Additional Factors Relevant to Evaluation

The Divestment controversy is sufficiently complex, in part because it depends for its proper resolution upon a host of particular facts, that it is not possible here to explain concisely what the right decision would be for any given group that confronts the issue. It is desirable, however, to look at several additional factors in that controversy, which vary from case to case and which bear on the evaluation of alternatives. We shall look particularly at effect of scale, the role of collective action, competing responsibilities, and the unequal political status of group members. All are manifest in the Divestment controversy and are typical of group decision making.

EFFECTS OF SCALE AND COLLECTIVE ACTION

The Clean Hands and Leverage arguments differ from each other in one important respect. The Clean Hands argument does not require either that anyone else (groups or individuals) holding investments in South African corporations also divest or that the holdings divested are a substantial fraction of the total wealth invested in the corporation. A college ceases to be a passive accomplice in and willing profiteer from the immorality of apartheid as soon as its investments are disposed of; this is the chief claim of the Clean Hands argument, and its chief appeal. This argument relies on the idea that moral responsibility is largely an individual (in this case, an individual group) matter, and that the consequences of a decision are morally less important than is the principle on which the individual acts.

Not so with the Leverage argument. Unless a college has a very large fraction of the total wealth invested in a given corporation (in fact quite unlikely), or unless it can band together with other individuals and groups who share its antipathy to apartheid and who are coinvestors in South African corporations, so that collectively they hold a significant fraction of the company's wealth, there is little reason to believe that any given college is ever in a position to exert leverage on the way a corporation manages its affairs in South Africa. The Leverage argument, in short, almost certainly requires collective (intergroup) action in a way that the Clean Hands argument does not. The likelihood of such collective action thus emerges as a crucial factual contingency to be taken into account in deciding whether to act on the Leverage argument.

At the extremes of investment possibilities, however, there is a certain symmetry in the two arguments. If a college's investments in South African corporations are very slight (say, only a few hundred thousand dollars spread across several dozen such corporations), it could be argued both that its hands are not very dirty (certainly, not as dirty as they would be if millions were invested in each of those corporations) and that its possible leverage is slight to zero. At the other extreme, a similar parallel obtains, where both the acquiescence in substantial wrongdoing and the possible leverage may be considerable. It is in between these two extremes where the effects of scale have a significant impact on the Leverage argument but relatively less on the Clean Hands argument.

COMPETING RESPONSIBILITIES

In any thorough review, the Clean Hands argument is likely to be criticized for ignoring an ethically relevant factor; a factor, moreover, that if properly taken into account, undermines the argument's conclusiveness. As this counter-argument is especially likely to be advanced by those who oppose divestment, it deserves close scrutiny.

Suppose you are a member of the board of trustees of a college in which most of the proponents of divestment rely on the Clean Hands argument. While you (let us further suppose) are strongly inclined personally to object to apartheid (you certainly would never support it directly, in South Africa or elsewhere), you also believe that (a) your college's "hands" are not very dirty from its current South Africa investments, and (b) the college would not really be fighting apartheid by selling these holdings to some other investor. (Since this new investor's hands now become dirtied precisely to the extent that the college's become clean, this shows that shifting the dirt from one pair of hands to another does nothing to weaken the grip of apartheid.) Even so, reasons (a) and (b), in your judgment, merely counterbalance or challenge crucial assumptions of the Clean Hands argument; they do not refute it.

What does have the effect, in your view, is this: (c) Your chief responsibility as a member of the college's board of trustees is to support policies that advance the college's welfare, and this leads directly to favoring investment policies that bring the greatest financial return commensurate with the risk; and (d) you believe that the investments in corporations doing business in South Africa are among the most productive and risk-free in the college's entire investment portfolio. In fact, you are strongly tempted by reasons (c) and (d) to recommend shifting more of the college's investments toward, rather than away from, these corporations. Moreover, you believe that reason (c) should be recognized as appropriate for the conduct of all the other members of the board of trustees, and also for the rest of the college community (administration, faculty, staff, alumni, students, and their parents) as well. Everyone in the college community should strive to see that the college's endowment brings in the greatest possible return commensurate with risk, in order to expand or upgrade the college's program.

You believe, further, that this is your *moral* duty and the moral duty of everyone associated with you in trying to protect and advance the college's fortunes. You are even inclined to go one step further, and argue that reasons (c) and (d) are so strong that they cancel the effect of the Clean Hands argument. (Whether they also support the Leverage argument, rather than merely negate all possible arguments for divestment, is doubtful, but we need not try to settle that question here.) You have concluded that despite your moral disapproval of apartheid, and despite your agreement in principle with the aims of both the Clean Hands and Leverage arguments to implement that principle, the truth is that the college's divestment at present would be largely a *symbolic* moral attack on apartheid, whereas the *real* economic consequences for the college in the current economic climate might represent a very tangible loss on endowment of (say) $100,000 in the first year, owing to the high rate of return paid by companies doing business in or with South Africa in contrast with the much lower rate of return on all other equally safe investments. This is a direct and concrete loss to an institution to which you have made a personal commitment. The gain from divestment, on the other hand, is vague, oblique, and remote, and even on the most optimistic scenario would do little or nothing to dismantle apartheid—recall reason (b) above—or wipe out the strain on all who live complacently in a world where apartheid survives.

We need not resolve here the question whether the above reasoning really does undermine the conclusion defended by the Clean Hands argument. What we do need to determine is whether the above analysis, in which reason (c) appears to rely on a norm that is incompatible in the circumstances with a norm crucial to the Clean Hands argument, is correct.

In fact, it is not. On closer scrutiny, the conflict is not really between two *moral* norms of equal weight and incompatible application in the Divestment controversy. True, the norms in conjunction with the relevant facts do lead in this instance to incompatible directives for group decision and action. Yet the two norms are not both *moral* norms (or not norms of equal moral weight). The moral norm that everyone ought to resist injustice, and the judgment that apartheid is unjust, conflict with the norm—cf. reason (c) above—that everyone who is part of the college community ought to favor investment policies for the college's endowment that yield the greatest possible safe return. But is the latter really a moral norm? No. Under it, the end to be sought is advancement of the college's program. This end is no doubt a *good* thing, and it is a perfectly reasonable and even praiseworthy end for persons to adopt and promote. Still, it is not the sort of good thing that, if not achieved (or not achieved to the fullest extent possible) would lead us to conclude that something wrong, immoral, or unfair had been allowed to occur.

In the present instance, however, our uncertainty should evaporate as soon as we recall that from the start the purpose of the group's decision in the Divestment controversy was to do the ethically correct thing. Under the empirical assumptions we have made for the sake of the argument, we see that doing the ethically correct thing evidently leads to acting in a way that does *not* further the college's best interests. And so we see that the college's interests must be to this extent sacrificed in favor of adopting the morally correct decision.

Such a result is not impossible, or even unlikely, nor should it surprise us. It would be extraordinary if action in the college's best interest (especially where its investments are concerned) turned out to be always and only action that is also fair, just, or morally right so far as everyone affected by its actions is concerned—in quite the same way that it would be amazing if action in *your* best interest always turned out to be fair, right, or morally correct.

Of course, it may be that as soon as the conflict is exposed between acting in the college's best interest (defined, always, in terms of maximizing its foreseeable return on investment) and doing the morally right thing in the Divestment controversy, some members of the group providing advice on or making the decision may decide to ignore the claims of morality and recommend instead a decision to act in the college's self-interest. This, too, should hardly be surprising. We know that we live in a world in which individuals and groups are often quite willing to act contrary to the requirements of morality, even when they believe they know what those requirements are.

A NOTE ON UTILITARIANISM

We are now at a juncture where we can see that a utilitarian's view of how to resolve the Divestment controversy is quite different from the viewpoint from which this discussion has been conducted so far. As a utilitarian might see it, in the Divestment controversy we have entered on one side of the ledger the good of opposing apartheid, albeit at a very remote distance, indirectly, and to a very slight degree, either through direct divestment or through leverage. On the other side of the ledger, there is the immediate and direct effect of lowering the college's annual income by $100,000 per year (on the facts assumed previously), if the college divests, or of increasing the risk to the currently secure investments in South Africa by trying to use leverage to fight apartheid. What the college ought to do is to act in the right way; and the right way to act is to act on the alternative from among those available that is calculated to produce the greatest good for the greatest number (see Smart & Williams, 1973). Thus, the utilitarian might well argue both in favor of not divesting and in favor of going ahead cautiously with any attempts to organize collective action to produce leverage. To be sure, such recommendations may rest on calculations that are quite conjectural. But the immediate and measurable effect of the loss of a sizable income (again, on the facts assumed earlier), judged against the remote and intangible effect of any act by the college aimed at putting apartheid on the defensive, is very likely to lead to the judgment that the former consideration outweighs the latter.

This, however, is a curious and unsettling result. Looked at in the current context of utilitarian moral thinking, the conclusion that we should not divest seems to emerge as an inference from the facts of the case (as assumed) plus the norm of general utility. Such a norm is surely a moral norm; at least, utilitarians think it is. If so, then the antidivestment conclusion (derived from the reasoning of the foregoing paragraph) is the *morally* correct decision to reach. But looked at from the perspective of the discussion in the previous section, and given exactly the same facts, the antidivestment conclusion is not a moral conclusion at all. Instead, it was seen as the decision reached by putting the college's self-interest ahead of any duty in the circumstances to act justly with respect to the nonwhites of South Africa.[7]

Now, this is admittedly confusing. How can one and the same decision be both morally correct and not even a moral decision at all, depending only on how the background for it is structured? In truth, this is typically what happens whenever utilitarianism defines what counts as correct moral reasoning. Our duties to others, their rights, considerations of fairness, mutual self-respect—all these become merely subsidiary aims or goals and no more than some among all the probable outcomes of alternative decisions and of the actions taken to implement those decisions. Thus, these distinctively ethical concepts and the norms that embody them are reduced in status to merely some among all of the factors to be taken into account in the effort to discover what we ought to do. To put it another way, the typical outcome of utilitarian moral thinking is to swallow up whatever is unique about ethical norms and goals and turn them into elements of some aggregate of goods.

In this way, utilitarianism is always shifting the goals of the decision to be made from what nonutilitarians would describe as the ethically correct action to a goal in which our moral duties, the rights of others, and so on, are simply weighed along with other (admittedly nonmoral) factors in the overall process of deliberation. To put this as bluntly as possible, we might say that the utilitarian simply does not understand (and in any case does not grant) that the proper role for ethical norms is to rule out, categorically and without any further discussion, certain otherwise possible (and perhaps even desirable) alternatives.

UNEQUAL STATUS OF GROUP MEMBERS

During the great campus upheavals of the late 1960s, one theme mentioned frequently by those in the community who were more or less hostile toward the campus radicals of that day was that the radicals, especially the students and junior faculty, were not full-fledged members of the campus community. They lacked (it was said) longevity of service, tenure, a demonstrated record of loyalty to the college, and the like. Instead, many of the most vocal had barely arrived on campus as freshmen, as first-year graduate students, or as newly appointed instructors; they and the college had yet to undertake any long-term commitment to each other. Their views and the right to express them were to this extent regarded as inferior to those of others. Even so, all members of the college's total community shared one important trait: For whatever reason, each knowingly had chosen to cast his or her lot with that community. All had freely consented to join, by accepting admission, faculty appointment, a job offer, or the like; and since any could theoretically leave whenever he or she wished, the failure to resign or withdraw had to be taken as a sign of some measure of loyalty to the ideals and purposes that defined the community.

These considerations raise again the general issue of the conditions of entry into the group, and the relevance of these conditions to the individual's moral responsibility for the procedures and the results of group decision making. As was observed in Chapter 1 and earlier in this chapter, if a person has volunteered to join a group, then that person's responsibility for the group's decisions is greater than if the membership has been co-opted or coercively or deceptively obtained. Similarly, if it is difficult or impossible to exit from the group when one wishes, a member is to that extent less responsible for the group's decisions (especially in the cases where he or she argued and voted against them). Consensual membership, in short, seems to be a necessary (although not a sufficient) condition of full responsibility for a group's decisions and for the actions taken to implement them.

In the Divestment controversy, these possible differences among members of the group are not likely to be of great importance. Factions defined by shared beliefs on one side or the other of the question whether to divest (and why) are likely to cut across the major campus groups (faculty, students, alumni, etc.). These groups within the college do differ, however, in the degree of their responsibility to act for the college. On curricular matters, final authority is generally conceded to lie with the faculty. The investment portfolio, however, is not controlled by the faculty, the student body, administration, or staff. Normally, the trustees and the trustees alone have the responsibility here, and all other campus constituencies at best remain in an advisory role. This leads immediately to differing degrees of responsibility for decision and action on this issue among these groups within the college.

Suppose that the board of trustees has sole responsibility for determining investment policies for the college's endowment, and that it normally delegates this responsibility to a special subcommittee of itself. This group in turn hires investment experts from the financial community for day-to-day decisions in managing the college's portfolio. In light of the Divestment controversy, however, the trustees (upon recommendation of the administration) request the formation of an advisory group composed of students, faculty, staff, and administration, each member of which is elected at large by the constituency represented. All are members of the college community, and all participate in the decision that resolves the Divestment controversy. However, some have purely advisory status, whereas others actually have the authority to decide. Some will vote for the alternative that turns out to be the final decision, whereas others will vote against it, and a few may even abstain from voting for any of several reasons.

Obviously, those who have least responsibility for the group's final decision are (a) those whose role is purely advisory and (b) those who also advised (and to that extent, voted) against the alternative that became the final decision. Those with the most responsibility were those (a') whose role was decisive, not merely advisory, and (b') who argued and voted for the alternative finally adopted. Because students and faculty typically do not have a vote in such matters, they are unlikely to be in the subgroup defined by factors (a') and (b'). Nor do we have exact measures for assessing the varying degrees to which individuals differently situated in a common group are differentially responsible for the group's decisions. Even so, although (a) and (b) may be true of most students and faculty where the Divestment controversy is concerned, they cannot entirely excuse themselves from the credit (or discredit, as the case may be) for the final decision, so long as they choose to remain identified, rather than to sever their connections, with the college.

Varieties of Decision Procedures

Throughout this chapter, we have proceeded as though there is only one possible, or desirable, general method of group decision making: An orderly deliberation, involving discussion of the issue on its merits, followed by a vote (either to decide what advice to give the decision maker or to make the decision itself) under the assumption of majority rule. There are, of course, other ways for groups to proceed (some of them have been described elsewhere in this volume), just as there are for individuals.[8] The group can let the issue be decided by whichever of its members wins some sort of contest, the winner's preference thereby becoming the group's decision; or the group could let the advocates of different views bargain with each other (by buying up votes, etc.). The group can delegate all its decision-making authority to its leader acting on his or her own, and the leader could decide by flipping a coin. We can even imagine a modern version of the ancient trial by combat. Except for the last, none of these other procedures has anything special to recommend it for our scrutiny here, because none is a method distinctive of group decision making.

Trial by combat, however, is different; when groups engage in it, we call it warfare. Interestingly enough, it is not the very antithesis of everything that an ethical process of decision making ought to involve, as the long struggle to establish the laws or rules of warfare show. The maxim, "All's fair in love and war," suggests the contrary, however; and no one can dispute that violence, destruction, and death are typical of war no matter what the scale and however scrupulous combatants may be in complying with certain norms. Nevertheless, documents, treaties, and international conferences have long recognized that certain types of conduct during warfare are legally and morally inexcusable and unjustifiable (e.g., the massacre of unarmed prisoners is a crime of war). The rules of war might thus be viewed as an effort of last resort to impose minimal ethical constraints on the behavior of groups that have already tried and abandoned any effort to resolve their disputes by discussion on the merits, negotiation, bargaining, or other nonviolent methods.[9] One might even argue that a group that must turn to warfare to resolve its differences is no longer a *group* at all. Warfare, on this view, fractures the minimal unity necessary to group cohesiveness and so is best viewed as an activity *between* two or more (warring) groups.

Nevertheless, it is sobering to realize that human history to date has not vindicated the proposition that discussion on the merits followed by fair voting is the best procedure for a group to determine its own will. Internecine struggle has often seemed the best thing to do because at least one side has found the stakes too high to be willing to lose by being outreasoned, outvoted, or outmaneuvered. And it is true that these peaceful methods can be used to inflict injustice, victimize minorities, violate group rights, and so forth; from the mere fact that a group comes to vote after lengthy discussion, it does not follow that the decision it makes is fair, just, or not in violation of anyone's rights. It is all the more important, therefore, when groups decide to fight it out, that they also do not abandon every civilized restraint on their conduct.

Majority Rule and Some Alternatives

In order to get a somewhat better grasp on the ethical considerations underlying majority rule, the chief decision-making mechanism favored throughout this chapter, it may prove helpful to look at the alternative of a *unanimity* rule. As a general method of decision making, unanimity is hopelessly unrealistic. Nevertheless, it is attractive from the moral point of view because everyone will grant that any group decision freely and knowingly consented to by every member is morally binding on each. Perhaps we can best understand the limitations of a unanimity rule by considering two kinds of cases where we permit one member of the group to veto a decision that everyone else favors. One such case involves the so-called hung jury. Another involves the practice of "blackballing."

THE HUNG JURY

Under the unanimity rule that prevails in most criminal trial jury deliberations, the jury cannot vote any verdict unless all its members explicitly agree on that verdict. In such situations, the recalcitrance of one person can force a group of twelve to fail in its task (viz., reaching a verdict of guilty or acquittal), thereby requiring either the trial to begin afresh or the plaintiff (or prosecutor) to drop the case. Intransigence of one juror may be based on an honest conviction and even a correct view of the evidence contrary to that held by all the other jurors.[10] Even so, this gives rise to the general question whether it is morally desirable to allow one member of a group to stymie a decision that all the rest favor, even where the dissent is sincere and reasonable.

So far as the jury system is concerned, the answer given by our legal system is that it is desirable for each juror to have the right to act in this way. The reason is not difficult to find. Since the sanctions that fall on a convicted defendant can be quite heavy, it is often said that it is better for ten guilty persons to go free than for one innocent person to be convicted and sentenced. The unanimity rule (like the "beyond a reasonable doubt" rule of evidence) is a simple and effective, even if extreme, way to give effect to such attitudes.

THE BLACKBALL

In situations of this sort, the refusal of one person again forces the rest of the group to go along. In this type of case, typically, the effect of the veto is to deny a candidate membership in some fraternity or club. One member's intransigence compels the rest of the committee to reject the applicant. However, the reason for the blackball rule (or, more precisely, for individual veto-power as the inverse of the rule of unanimity) is very different from the reason for the jury unanimity rule. In the blackball case, the reason is to preserve the moral, social, and ideological homogeneity of the group; to insure this, every member of the group is empowered to exclude anyone else from membership who the group member believes would dilute or destroy that homogeneity. (To put the point less charitably, blackballing permits unlimited exercise of mere prejudice and irrational dislike.) The value of group solidarity is thus placed well above whatever other values might be represented by the merits, talents, or status of the applicant.

It is not without interest to note that the practice of blackballing has come under severe criticism in recent decades, as an essentially undemocratic decision process. It is also increasingly recognized that individual self-esteem is a function of the important groups in which one is a member, and that many groups are really not "private" organizations; instead, they wield considerable political and economic power. The result is that blackballing is often a device for denying fair equality of opportunity, itself an ethical norm in public affairs of considerable importance. Perhaps one might say that the more trivial and inconsequential the powers and status of a group in a community, the less morally objectionable it is to permit it to use admission procedures that permit blackballing candidates or applicants.

MAJORITY RULE

What is the moral basis for resolving group deliberations over a given course of action by this familiar method, typically a majority of those present and voting, given a quorum of the group present?[11] Its effectiveness, compared to the alternative of unanimity, is obvious. At the same time, it is vulnerable to certain theoretical objections that make it unfit for rational decision making in certain situations; these have been reviewed in some detail in Chapter 4.[12] But in those cases where these objections do not apply, there may still arise moral objections to majority rule. One way to defend the moral merits of majority rule is to see it as the closest approximation to a unanimity rule and for precisely this reason superior to all other alternatives. This is the more obvious the nearer the majority approaches the whole number of those voting.

In this light, consider *minority* rule. It seems obviously unfair that a group's will should be determined by a minority of its members, since this amounts to dictatorship by a subgroup of the whole group. Moreover, there may be many minorities and there is no reason why the will of one minority should prevail over the others. This objection applies to rule by a minority of any size. It is simply unfair that if n plus 1 persons in a group want to do x, whereas exactly n persons (a minority) do not want to do x, then the group *for that reason* should decide not to do x. We might say that the ethical norm underlying simple majority rule is this: Each vote has the same *weight* as each other vote, because each member of the group who is voting has the same *worth* as every other member. Given that norm, the mechanics of implementing it are straightforward: The votes for and against a given proposal are to be treated equally; we do this if and only if they are paired up, each vote for matched with a vote against, until one reaches a vote for (or against) to which there is no cancelling vote the other way; and that vote should prevail.

Underlying the authority of majority rule is the (tacit or explicit) unanimous consent of the group to the principle that the group's will is to be determined in this way. This is why rule by majority works; the group as a whole accepts it. This is also why results of this method have authority even over the members who voted against what the majority favors. A group that cannot resolve its collective will by means of acknowledging the authority of majority rule either must find a way to tolerate very little disagreement (hence the use of blackballing is a symptom of considerable group homogeneity) or, like a trial jury that is "hung," must dissolve itself since it cannot act as a group.

There are, of course, special conditions that make plurality decision making, or a two-thirds majority decision, a better rule for some groups to follow than the simple majority rule defended above. Here, we may ignore these special cases.

Individual Versus Groups as Decision Makers

There remains one general question that ought to be asked even if it cannot be fully answered: Are group decisions more or less important from the ethical point of view than individual decisions?

The history of our culture and its most influential philosophies make individualistic attitudes and doctrines dominate over group-oriented or collectivist ones. The free, autonomous individual—his or her rights, aspirations, and projects—tends to be the center of focus for most ethical and political theories developed in Western thought. True, we know of societies in which the welfare and survival of the group (family, tribe, clan, city) is deemed of greater moral significance than the welfare and survival of any individual member of the group; but the opposite, individualistic outlook is one of the many features of modern life characteristic of Western culture and society. The result is that most of us firmly believe that no matter how important for our lives the decisions and actions of the groups in our midst are, including those groups of which we are members, it is still our own decisions and actions as individual persons (and not as the agents or representatives of any groups to which we belong) that matter most—to us. The plausible consequence of this line of reasoning is that it must be the ethical aspects of individual, rather than group, decisions that are of paramount importance.

However, running counter to such a view is the undeniable fact that it is groups and individuals acting through groups, not individuals acting by themselves, who wield the greatest power for good or ill. Nations, corporations, armies, courts, professional societies, and institutions of every sort have a staggering impact on the life of every individual, whether or not that individual is a member of the group in question. Evaluating and regulating the decisions of these groups is fundamental to human life because the impact the decisions of these groups can have is so enormous.

This suggests that we need to distinguish between the relative moral importance of individuals versus groups, and the relative importance of the decisions of individuals versus groups. Ethically, individuals may well be regarded as having greater worth than any of the groups to which they belong, whereas the decisions of groups may be far more important than those of all but a few individuals. There is no doubt that the power of certain groups—nation-states armed with nuclear weapons of mass destruction, in particular—is enormously greater than the power of any mere individual. Since the power can be more easily used for social harm than for social benefit, it is extremely important to most of us that these groups exercise their power in ways that are ethically responsible rather than irresponsible. We might even go so far as to say that, whereas individuals may use such power as they command more or less as they wish, groups and especially nations must be held accountable to a higher standard. The human race can survive the ethically unjustifiable decisions of many individuals acting individually (the race obviously has already survived millions of such decisions!) Whether it could survive certain ethically unjustifiable decisions of individuals acting as or on behalf of a group is doubtful. Only a fanatical and demonic group could have done what the Nazis did to the Jews, Poles, and other Europeans in the 1930s and 1940s. Criminal as genocide is, a greater threat—omnicide—now looms. It is within the power of several different groups, but no private individuals acting on their own, to perpetrate crimes on a planetary scale. If nothing else does, surely this should argue for the primary importance of the ethical aspects of group decisions making.

Making More Effective Decisions

Here are seven rules of thumb that summarize that main points of the foregoing discussion of the ethical aspects of group decision making, and which, if followed, should reduce complaints directed at the ethical quality of either the process or the result:

(1) Make the rules for membership in the group fair both to those who are already members and to those who may want to become members.

(2) Adopt fair rules for deliberation—that is, rules that give other members as much freedom to advocate their views as you want for the advocacy of your views.

(3) If you are in a position to propose a decision for a group, be prepared to support it with reasons; expect others to do the same for their recommendations, too. Do not expect your view to prevail and become the group's decision merely because you advocate it forcefully, or are the chairperson, or so on.

(4) During deliberations, make clear to yourself and to the others in the group what, if any, ethical aspects there are to each of the decision alternatives under discussion by the group.

(5) Distinguish between benefits and harms for the group that may be expected to result from various possible decisions, and benefits and harms for others outside the group; do not automatically disregard the latter or treat them as of little importance.

(6) Identify the ethical norm(s) that underlie the particular decision(s) you favor; pay close attention to whether you are prepared to apply the same norm in other situations.

(7) Adopt fair rules for decision making—that is, a voting procedure that counts your vote equal to (neither less nor more than) the vote of each other person in the group.

Notes

1. We should not overlook here the special case of the group member who loyally and unthinkingly executes whatever orders are given by the group leader(s), and thus acts as the instrument of the group. Although such a member may have played no role in group deliberation prior to the decision that he or she willingly executes, there cannot on that account be excusal from all moral responsibility for acts done on behalf of the group—unless the member acted under duress or in ignorance of what he or she was doing. See French (1972).

2. In this connection, it is useful to note the different kinds of guilt and responsibility that the Germans had from their involvement in the Nazi era (1933-1945). There was (1) the criminal guilt of particular Germans, for example, of brutal concentration camp guards; (2) the political guilt shared by the German people for acts of the Nazi government; (3) the moral guilt of each German for what he did or didn't do to avoid, assist, or resist the Nazis; (4) the sense of guilt among all Europeans for the Nazi era, even for things none of them could have prevented. See Jaspers (1947).

3. Other rules will of course also be needed; for discussion see Robert (1970), Johnson, Trustman, & Wadsworth (1962).

4. This is the idea that underlies the notion of "pure prodecural justice" central to the theory of social justice; see Rawls (1971).

5. Abnormal cases, where an individual or a group does not act in accord with the conclusion of its own practial reasoning, can be explained in several ways. One is to accuse the indecisive agent of hypocrisy—i.e., professing a major premise and the norm it expresses or relies on without really being committed to it. Another is to accuse the indecisive agent of weakness of will (*akrasia*)—i.e., an inability to act in accord with his or her real convictions and beliefs. Another possibility is that other considerations undermine the conclusion by challenging one or both of the premises, so that the conclusion does not really represent the agent's final judgment.

6. These and many other aspects of apartheid are extensively discussed especially for American readers in Study Commission (1981).

7. For the purposes of the present discussion, we may ignore the fact that a policy of not divesting is also the conclusion of the Leverage argument and that this is also a moral argument.

8. The discussion in the rest of this subsection is indebted to Barry (1965).

9. On the rules of war and the concept of a just war, see Walzer (1977).

10. See the modern classic drama and film, *Twelve Angry Men.*

11. For general defenses of majority rule on moral grounds, see Pennock (1968) and Rawls (1971).

12. A useful exercise would be to take the several criteria of rational social choice presented in Chapter 4 and identify the moral norms (if any) that each embodies. This would be the first step in testing the extent to which *rational* social choice is also *moral.*

References

Aristotle. *Nichomachean ethics* (W. D. Ross, trans.). Oxford University Press, 1925.

Barry, B. *Political argument.* London: Routledge & Kegan Paul, 1965.

Bedau, H. Ethical decision making. In P. Hill et al. (Eds.) *Making decisions: A multidisciplinary introduction.* Reading, MA: Addison-Wesley, 1979.

Bok, D. Reflections on divestment of stock. *Supplement to Harvard Gazette,* April 6, 1979.

Bok, D. *Beyond the ivory tower.* Cambridge, MA: Harvard University Press, 1982.

Bok, D. Statement on divestment. *Harvard Gazette,* May 6, 1983.

French, P. (Ed.) *Individual and collective responsibility.* Cambridge, MA: Schenkman, 1972.

Gauthier, D. *Practical reasoning.* Oxford University Press, 1963.

Jaspers, K. *The question of German guilt.* New York: Dial Press, 1947.

Johnson, R. B., Trustman, B. A., & Wadsworth, C. Y. *Town meeting time: A handbook of parliamentary law.* Boston: Little, Brown, 1962.

Litvak, L., DeGrasse, R., & McTigue K. *South Africa: Foreign investment and apartheid.* Washington, DC: Institute for Policy Studies, 1978.

Pennock, J. R. Majority rule. In the *International Encyclopedia of Social Sciences.* New York: Free Press, 1968.

Rawls, J. *A theory of justice.* Cambridge, MA: Harvard University Press, 1971.

Raz, J. (Ed.) *Practical reasoning.* Oxford University Press, 1978.

Robert, H. M. *Robert's rules of order newly revised.* Glenview, IL: Scott Foresman, 1970.

Schmidt, E. *Decoding corporate camouflage.* Washington, DC: Institute for Policy Studies, 1980.

Smart, J.J.C., & Williams, B. *Utilitarianism: For and against.* Cambridge University Press, 1973.

Study Commission on U.S. Policy Toward Southern Africa. *South Africa: Time running out.* Berkeley: University of California Press, 1981.

Von Wright, G. *Norm and action.* London: Routledge & Kegan Paul, 1963.

Walzer, M. *Just and unjust wars.* New York: Basic Books, 1977.

CHAPTER 6

SOCIAL RISK ASSESSMENT
AND GROUP PROCESS

Sheldon Krimsky

Public awareness of the hazards of new techniques and the by-products of industrial processes has made risk assessment a central part of policymaking. Agencies of government responsible for safeguarding the public's health and safety have established forms of technology assessment on environmental impact analysis as part of their decision-making procedures. To a great extent, these developments were prompted by the environmental, health, consumer protection, and occupational safety laws enacted during the 1970s.

The National Environmental Policy Act (NEPA), signed into law on January 1, 1970, was the earliest of this new generation of environmental legislation. NEPA makes federal agencies responsible for giving full consideration to environmental impacts of their programs and rulemaking. For the first time, major federal actions required the preparation and dissemination of an environmental impact statement. Its purpose was to draw attention to the adverse consequences and alternative proposals for the project under consideration. Other laws following NEPA in air and water pollution control, waste management, toxic substances control, and occupational health and safety demanded new standards of justification and public accountability from federal agencies. In response to these laws and the growing influence of the public interest lobby, many agencies have begun to use scientific and citizen advisory committees, or require that such committees be formed in local jurisdictions that are recipients of federal funds. And in 1972, Congress established the Office of Technology Assessment to advise its members on complex technological matters. With these recent developments, risk assessment and environmental impact analysis emerged as independent fields of study.

Many of the problems associated with the impacts of technologies warrant the attention of several disciplines. Consider, for example, the issues that arise when a chemical by-product of an industrial process is deposited in the ground and eventually enters the groundwater. The potential hazards associated with the chemical waste involve several determinations: the toxicologic or carcinogenic potential of the chemicals to humans, plants, and animals; the hydrogeology of the groundwater (groundwater motion and circulation); the effect of the chemicals on the local environment; the biodegradability and diffusion rate of the chemicals. In addition to contributions by those representing different fields of expertise, it has become increasingly important to involve nonexperts who may have a direct stake in the outcome of such decisions. For many areas of social decision making, citizen participation has become a formal part of a group process that eventually shapes public policy.

The purpose of this chapter is to examine group decision processes that assess technological risks. It discusses the extent to which rational and extrarational factors enter into the decision of technical advisory panels. To develop the thematic issues in social risk assessment, this chapter begins with a discussion of gene splicing, otherwise known as recombinant DNA technology. The case is referred to throughout the chapter to illustrate many of the conceptual distinctions of the analytical discussion.

The chapter then examines two competing models of social risk assessment that set the groundwork for a discussion of various decision modalities. Among the inventory of social decision processes, the public advisory committee is selected out for concentrated analysis. The chapter then turns to the role of rationality in social risk assessment, explores the distinction between subjective and objective risk, and examines the logic of comparative risk analysis. Finally, the chapter concludes by offering some prescriptive considerations on resolving controversies involving technological risks.

For those involved in risk assessment, there are unique problems and, at times, awesome responsibilities. Small groups of individuals make choices that affect million of people. They determine how we treat radioactive wastes; what drugs get marketed; which nuclear reactors get licensed; what types of pesticides are sprayed on our foods; which human experiments are approved; and which microorganisms are genetically engineered. In many instances, small group decisions are responsible for policies affecting two hundred million people. Before proceeding with the analytical discussion, let us turn to a brief case example involving the field of genetic engineering.

The Case of Recombinant DNA Technology

In 1973, a controversy erupted within the scientific community over the risks of a new research technique introduced to the field of molecular biology called gene splicing or recombinant DNA (rDNA) technology. With this new technique, biologists using chemical enzymes learned how to cut and splice pieces of genetic material from distantly related species thus enabling them to create new hybrid organisms. The initial concerns expressed by several eminent scientists included the possibility of the creation and accidental dissemination of a chimeric organism that would spread a dangerous toxin or introduce a new disease into the human population (Krimsky, 1982a).

After an international risk assessment congress met in February 1975 (Asilomar Conference), that drew nearly 150 scientists from many parts of the world, the National Institutes of Health (NIH) convened a panel of technical experts to turn the recommendations of the congress into workable guidelines. The risk assessment panel, which held its first meeting the day after the Asilomar Conference, was named the Recombinant DNA Molecule Program Advisory Committee, later changed to the Recombinant DNA Advisory Committee, or the RAC. The composition of this committee evolved over several years. It began with a membership of a dozen individuals comprised entirely of geneticists from the fields of virology and bacteriology. A short time afterwards, two lay members were added from the fields of public policy and bioethics. The RAC membership was increased to sixteen and remained that size until January 1979 when Secretary of Health Education and Welfare (now Health and Human Services) Joseph Califano expanded the membership to 25 with approximately one third of the committee consisting of nonbiologists. The RAC met four times a year for two- or three-day periods, assessing the risks of the new technology and making modifications to the guidelines that were first issued in June 1976. Although this committee was strictly advisory to NIH, the vast majority of its recommendations were adopted. The NIH director looked toward RAC as his principal source of guidance on regulating this new technology.

NIH is the largest funding source for biomedical research in the United States, and is thus a strong promotor of recombinant DNA technology as a powerful instrument in the study of human, plant, and animal genetics. In convening the RAC, NIH wished to provide assurances that gene splicing could be used safely when certain precautions were taken until additional knowledge was gained about the hypothetical risks. The committee, dominated by scientists, also insured those potential users of the technology that their interests and those who would benefit from its positive applications would weigh heavily in the risk assessment process. The public participation on the RAC was broadened as a result of intense lobbying of national environmental groups. The effect of this was to draw the external criticism of the risk assessment into the decision-making process, which was controlled by NIH. By internalizing the criticism, NIH was able to soften the impact of the environmental lobby and diffuse the controversy.

Some states and local municipalities were not satisfied with the federal guidelines for controlling the use of gene splicing. Cambridge, Massachusetts was the first city that passed its own ordinance regulating the use of this technology. To accomplish this, the city convened a committee of eight nonbiologists that reviewed the technical issues and reached a unanimous consensus on a local ordinance. This committee, in contrast to the panel of scientific experts comprising the RAC, was viewed as a citizen court and thus represented a new experiment in social risk assessment. Other communities established their own review panels, but unlike Cambridge, all had a mix of scientists and lay participation.

Further details of this case example will be cited throughout the chapter to illustrate different points about the use of groups in social risk assessment. But first the nature of this process is examined.

The Development of Risk Assessment as a Group Function

What is meant by social risk assessment? When policies or regulations are issued, or technologies are deployed that may have an effect on the health and safety of the public, the evaluation of these effects is referred to as risk assessment. The term social risk assessment is used to mean two things. First, it implies that the evaluation is of *social* risks, or the potential hazards to groups of individuals or large populations, in contrast to isolated risks to individuals. Second, it means that the assessment of risks is socialized; risks are evaluated by individuals who are designated to represent the interests of society.

Social risk assessment is distinguished from the kind of assessment that individuals make when they weigh the costs and benefits of certain actions. "Should I go skiing at the risk of an injury?" "Should I undergo this surgical procedure with its attendant risks and anticipated benefits?" In these individual decisions, the risks and benefits accrue to the same person. A far more complicated situation exists in social risk assessment. A decision-making body sets policy for a large population of individuals. In some cases, what is decided by a small panel of individuals in the United States will affect many peoples of the world. Value questions arise at the outset. What justifies the group speaking for the larger society? How much risk is worth how much benefit? What ought the distribution of risks and benefits in the society be?

Risk assessment serves multiple social functions. The *regulatory function* aids the environmental manager in setting standards, such as the permissible levels of chemical agents in the air, water, or in our food supply. Government bodies, like the Environmental Protection Agency and the Occupational Safety and Health Administration (OSHA) depend upon advisory groups in their efforts to set safe or acceptable levels of chemicals in the environment. The *political function* of social risk assessment comes into play when a group is convened to resolve a public controversy. Different groups in society may be heavily polarized over an issue of public health and safety. The skillful choice of a committee of experts and public interest representatives can go far to ease community tensions or to defuse a national controversy. In its *legitimating function*, social risk assessment is designed to justify a predetermined policy. Experts are chosen after some of the important choices are made. Decisions of this type are distinguished by their restricted scope, ad hoc character, and uncritical approaches to the problems they address.

The establishment of the RAC to assess the potential hazards of genetic engineering illustrates each of these functions to some degree. NIH needed a credible scientific body to grade the potential risks for a vast number of gene-splicing experiments, and to match those risks with commensurate safeguards. The RAC was also a political instrument for reducing public anxiety over the new technology. This was particularly evident when public members were brought into the assessment process. The committee charter and the selection of its members legitimated a particular manner of defining the issues. They were restricted to biohazards arising from laboratory research. Human genetic engineering, biological warfare, and the technological applications of the new technology were kept outside of the RAC's responsibility.

Two Approaches to Technological Risks

Risk assessment determinations are "wicked problems" (Rittel & Webber, 1973). Decisions are required when only limited information is available. Frequently, considerable divergence exists among experts on fundamental issues. The path between the scientific assessment of the problem and the policy alternatives is a murky one. And finally, it may not be possible to evaluate the final choice against the alternatives.

In addition to these formidable obstacles to a rational choice, there are also two competing views on the possibility of separating an issue into its scientific and policy components. The outcome of this debate has considerable bearing on what form of group process is used in social risk assessment.

THE DUALISTIC MODEL

One approach to a risk assessment problem begins by analyzing it into its subjective and objective components (Ashby, 1978). According to this view, the objective component consists of technical or scientific questions that are purely descriptive of the way nature behaves. Determinations made on the objective side of the issue are professed to be value-neutral and fall exclusively within the domain of experts. The principal determinations are causes, explanations, predictions, levels of risk, projected outcomes, and estimated probability of mishaps. In this model, the subjective side to the assessment of risks consist of policy choices that are acknowledged to be value-laden. After the objective part of the decision is made, a second stage is introduced where politics, social values, and the public have a legitimate role in the decision-making process.

In summary, the dualistic model of risk assessment divides the problem into a scientific or objective component and a policy or subjective component. It follows from this analysis that the composition of the decision-making groups should reflect the distinct types of questions raised in these independent domains of analysis.

As an example, consider the assessment of the artificial sweetener saccharin. The two-tiered decision process divides the inquiry as follows: (1) objective component: Does saccharin cause cancer? What are the epidemiological and toxicological data? How do we extrapolate animal studies to humans? What possible health benefits does the use of saccharin have in society? (2) subjective component: How much risk should we tolerate? Should government be involved in the regulation of saccharin use? Is the potential risk of human cancer outweighed by the real benefits of saccharin use?

Following our first model, different groups of decision makers treat the two categories of questions. The first group examines the scientific (objective) side to the issues of regulating saccharin use. It collects, analyzes, and evaluates the data. It determines the likelihood and severity of the hazards. Once these decisions are made, a second group takes up the policy issues such as the trade-offs between risks and benefits.

To illustrate this further, consider the following quotation from the history of the recombinant DNA controversy. It refers to the composition of the NIH recombinant DNA advisory committee (RAC). The statement, made by the first chairman of the RAC, a biologist, argues forcefully that the first stage of the problem is purely technical. As a result, input must come exclusively from scientific experts.

> Once the (genetic engineering) experiments have been decided upon, once a description at least of the risk and of the benefit can be given, even though we cannot prove in precise annotated terms, then the problem becomes a political issue as to what to do about it. But we weren't at that stage yet. . . . The person who never worked in a containment situation, and person who (has) never handled obnoxious microorganisms . . . can have very little sense of what's right and wrong. A lay judgment about surgical procedure is usually not very relevant [Krimsky, 1982a, p. 157].

THE INTEGRATIVE MODEL

A second approach to decision making involving risks under uncertain knowledge maintains that the dichotomy between technical and policy issues is a false one because there is no pure science of risks (Cumming, 1981). When technical experts analyze a problem, they carry to it ideological biases, special ways of defining the issues, and methodological assumptions for which universal acceptance is lacking (Douglas & Wildavsky, 1982, pp. 67-82). Another argument against the bifurcation of technical and policy decisions is that there is no clear demarcation between facts and theories, or between values and facts. All scientific facts are theory-laden, the argument goes. Facts do not present themselves as pure and timeless truths that provide the essential foundation of our knowledge. Scientific facts are already bits of interpreted information. Theories, on the other hand, vary in the degree of validation or confirmation they receive within the scientific community. While there are certainly some scientific judgments, both factual and theoretical, for which there is considerable consensus, many others lack unanimity.

Values also enter into scientific judgments (Myrdal, 1958, pp. 153-155). Scientists, after all, define the scope of a problem. Consider, as an example, the type of tests that should be carried out to determine whether a food additive is safe. Science doesn't provide us with that answer. That is a transscientific issue. Hidden in the question are the criteria for safety. Once the criteria are adopted, science may proceed.

These are some considerations against the two-tier system of risk assessment. Some group processes that address technological risks have been established with the more pluralistic view of decision making in mind. In this case, scientists are mixed with nonscientists at the stage when the problem is being defined, and questions about the nature of the risks are first being raised. When the criteria for the resolution of a technical problem are in dispute, the decision process takes on a more important role.

The Legal Analogy

The concept of due process originated in the field of jurisprudence. More recently, it has been applied to public decision making in general. The heads of public agencies have authority to hold administrative hearings as part of their responsibility to set environmental standards. The Freedom of Information Act and the federal requirements for "government in the sunshine" are designed to provide greater public access to governmental decisions. The Administrative Procedures Act makes available to the public the opinions, policy statements, rules, procedures, and records of federal agencies; and under the Federal Advisory Committee Act, deliberations and reports of federal advisory committees are also open to public review. Federal agencies are subject to citizen suits if they violate due process in their rule-making.

The legal model of decision making has only limited applications to the area of social risk assessment, however. When we select a jury to hear the evidence on the guilt or innocence of an individual under indictment, we seek an impartial panel of peers. The jury hears the case according to certain predetermined rules of evidence. To convict in criminal cases, the jury must render a unanimous decision. The burden of proof is on the prosecution to demonstrate "guilt without reasonable doubt." A lesser burden is placed on the plaintiff in a civil case where the preponderance of evidence is sufficient.

When public health and safety are at stake, there is no consensus about where the burden of proof lies. Does a product or technology have to be proven safe before it is permitted into general use, or do we have to show it is harmful before action is taken? There are instances where one or the other approach is used by decision makers. Most food additives, except a class generally regarded as safe (GRAS), require premarket clearance by the Food and Drug Administration before they can be marketed. The burden of proof is on the sponsor to demonstrate that the additive is safe. On the other hand, industrial chemicals may be introduced into the work place without proof that they are not harmful to workers. The common standard of administrative law places the burden of proof on the proponents of a rule that allegedly protects public health (Ricci & Molton, 1981).

Despite the differences between judicial and administrative bodies, the concept of due process does have a place in social risk assessment. It stems from the fact that the public wants assurances that its regulatory agencies render decisions that are not biased toward a particular group and that take account of all the relevant facts. Whether by law, agency mandate, or judicial precedent, a set of procedures is usually adopted, some prior to the deliberation of a body, some after it commences its work. These procedures include criteria for membership in the group; provisions for public input; protection against conflict of interest; adherence to open meeting laws; and responsiveness to different points of view. Due process applies to these and other procedural requirements.

Unlike group business decisions, where profit, engineering success, or market response can be used to evaluate the outcome, performance requirements for decisions of social risk taking involving public health and safety are usually not available. There are exceptions to this. The decision by the U.S. Public Health Service to administer swine flu vaccinations to tens of millions of people was found to be incorrect and was subsequently reversed. Early studies had underestimated the deleterious side effects of the vaccine. Many people were stricken with a disease called Guillain-Barre syndrome, when the vaccine program was in its early stages. Several expert panels were involved in assessing the risks and benefits of mass vaccinations. But public interest groups concerned about the risks of the vaccines had no access to the swine flu decision-making process. In this case, significant adverse effects of a poor decision came quickly and were widely publicized (Boffey, 1976; Berliner & Salmon, 1976; Schoenbaum et al., 1976). These early indicators are more the exception than the rule, however. As a result, more weight is usually given to the fairness of the decision process itself, including the full representation of divergent views on the advisory panel.

In the United States, the major responsibility for risk assessment is in the hands of a dozen federal agencies. It is with the director of these agencies that questions of due process and public participation rests. Public agencies employ several types of processes that utilize expertise, and to a greater or lesser extent, incorporate public input. I turn now to a discussion of several forms of group processes used, to varying degree, by governmental agencies.

Decision Modalities for Technology Assessment

The adoption by agency heads of advisory panels in setting policy accomplishes several things. First, it promotes a less centralized model of ironclad control by an agency. Bureaucrats can cite diverse inputs into the decision process. Second, it helps to diffuse the polarization among parties with competing interests, and different social and scientific perspectives. Third, it provides the government with expertise it may not find in-house or be able to get from public hearings. Fourth, it diffuses responsibility from the chief public official to his advisory panel. In this section, I shall review briefly the most commonly tried or discussed group decision modalities for assessing new technologies, new drugs, chemical exposures, and the like, in which social risks and benefits are at stake. The next section focuses on one of these forms, namely, public advisory bodies.

SINGLE DECISION MAKERS AND THEIR ADVISORS: THE INTRAMURAL MODEL

In one model of group decision making (developed fully in Chapter 10), an agency director frames policy after he or she has drawn upon the expertise and advise of his staff personnel. As an illustration, the head of the Environmental Protection Agency makes a determination to accept a new pesticide into general use after considerable staff work is completed and public hearings are held. What we have, in effect, is a hierarchical group. One person (the "responsible individual") clearly stands out as the authority with whom the final decision rests. Others in the decision-making process are in a dependency role with respect to their superior. The chief advantage of this process is that is may avoid long delays or deadlocks (that is, if the agency is not encumbered by protracted litigation) and places the responsibility for the decision directly in the hands of a single individual.

However, there are some important liabilities to the intramural model. Staff members cannot avoid thinking about pleasing their superiors. Tacit boundaries for acceptable dissent exist in any social institution. Hierarchical decision-making groups rarely provide diversity. They are limited by the values and politics of the agency or institution. "Groupthink" is pervasive in large government bureaucracies (see Chapter 3). Many agency directors have learned to use the intramural model in conjunction with other group processes that are more pluralistic in how they utilize expertise.

SPECIAL COMMISSIONS

Government bodies convene special commissions to assure society that a problem is being treated fairly and impartially, particularly when an in-house analysis would be viewed as self-serving or deficient. Short-term investigative commissions have been used extensively by Congress and the executive branch. They have been established in the aftermath of major accidents, environmental tragedies, or social upheavals. The role of these bodies includes identifying causes, assessing risks, and recommending policy changes. Federal commissions were established to study the nuclear power plant accident at Three Mile Island, the civil disorders of the 1960s, abuses of human subjects in scientific research, and many other areas of public policy affecting human health, bioethics, and environmental quality.

Commissions formed in the wake of crisis are convened in a highly charged political climate. Generally, these decision groups are comprised of technical experts as well as lay citizens. The latter, in addition to providing political window dressing, in theory are supposed to approach the issues from value perspectives and a set of interests that differ from those participants who are part of the technocratic infrastructure.

Another type of commission structure is mandated by law and serves a continuing regulatory function. Two examples are the Nuclear Regulatory Commission (NRC) that oversees the licensing of nuclear power plants, and the Interstate Commerce Commission (ICC) that determines policies on interstate transportation and trade. Unlike short-term commissions with advisory roles, decisions of the NRC and ICC are legally binding.

TECHNICAL PANELS

When the appeal to scientific or technical authority is considered the exclusive issue in risk assessment, it can override any effort to provide public participation in the decision process. The results are panels of experts. This country's most prestigious scientific body is the National Academy of Sciences (NAS). Leading figures in the natural and social sciences are admitted to the association upon recommendation by their peers. The NAS has convened scientific panels to assess the risks of chemical and biological agents, off-shore oil drilling, acid rain, and food additives, to mention a few (NAS, 1979; NAS, 1980). The public is entitled to assurances that its scientific experts are impartial and therefore receive no financial advantage from assessing the risks in one direction or the other. These assurances are not always satisfied. Although the government does require its special consultants to cite potential conflicts of interest in a signed declaration, that information is not usually made available to the public, and more surprisingly is often not available to other members of the committee. Consequently, experts who hold stock in certain industries, who have consulted for certain firms, or who have a financial interest in certain technologies, may become involved in decisions that examine the safety of systems or products in related areas.

PUBLIC ADVISORY BODIES

When technical advisory panels and commissions are seeded with public members, the decision process is significantly shaped by the scientists on the committee. Those with command of the technical knowledge possess a clear advantage in their ability to direct and influence opinion. Knowledge is an effective instrument for membership power (see Chapter 1).

When risk assessment decisions are carried out by panels made up exclusively of lay members, the group dynamics can be expected to differ from that of mixed panels consisting of experts and nonexperts. A freer and more open exchange of information is likely to occur if all members of a panel are at an equal disadvantage before the technical problem. In this case, mutual learning becomes the paramount concern. No single member of the group is in a position to declare a monopoly on truth.

There have been some, albeit extremely few, notable experiments in public decision making where a risk assessment panel dealing with a technical issue was comprised of all lay members. The aforementioned committee established in Cambridge to review gene-splicing research was a recent example (Krimsky, 1978). While internal control of such a committee by technical experts is clearly not a problem, the lay committee is faced with the enormous task of self-education—a task that may limit the effectiveness of the group without some form of technical assistance.

When deep divisions exist in the scientific community over the risks and benefits of some technology, a lay committee can provide a common sense view of the competing perspectives. The citizens serve as a jury listening to claims and counterclaims of the experts. A panel of lay citizens or "citizens court" is an alternative to the widely discussed science court made up exclusively of experts (Kantrowitz, 1975).

A mixture of scientists and lay persons may be an effective means of examining scientific activities that have ethical consequences. In the mid-1960s, institutions receiving funding from HEW were required to establish institutional review boards (IRBs) to oversee experiments that were performed on human subjects. These local committees consist of community representatives, physicians, scientists, lawyers, ethicists, and members of the clergy. The IRBs virtually have the final say in decisions pertaining to the protection of the rights of human subjects. Although nonexperts usually do not constitute a majority on such review boards, they do make a difference in the outcome of IRB deliberations (Gray, 1978).

REFERENDA ON RISK-BENEFIT DECISIONS

A direct vote is the purest form of democratic rule. Many communities and towns have used the voting booths to determine how they feel about a technology that carries risks and benefits. The troublesome part of risk assessment by plebescite is the difficulty in adequately informing the electorate on technically complex issues. However, the possibilities for educating the public on policy matters that possess a strong technical component have hardly been realized. We have seen local referenda on such issues as the construction of nuclear power plants, the location of hazardous waste sites, the use of fluoridation in the drinking water, and the building of dams.

Many opportunities exist in the mass electronic media for recording group preference in complex technical decisions. This could even be accomplished at a national scale for critical technological problems. However, the potential for abuse is so great that some critics feel such experiments could develop into a state propaganda machine, since the federal government controls the air waves and has access to considerable economic resources.

On the other hand, public officials are wary about promoting direct democracy for reaching technically complex decisions because they can easily lose control over the situation. Powerful economic interests or single-issue lobby groups can dominate media presentations and, as a result, influence the outcome of the vote regardless of how the risks and benefits appear from a scientific standpoint.

As previously indicated, variations exist in the structure, goals, and composition of group processes established to render decisions on technological risks. For the purpose of this chapter, it will be most useful to offer an in-depth examination of the most eclectic of these group structures, namely the public advisory committee. In this type of committee there is a mix of technical experts and lay persons. The problems of social interaction, exercise of influence and control, and consensus building are more pronounced than in groups where there is greater similarity among participants.

The Public Advisory Committee
as a Policy Instrument:
Factors Influencing Group Process

Let us suppose a panel is convened to render a decision that has important health and safety implications. The panel consists of a combination of technical experts and lay citizenry. (A person may be an expert in one field but a lay citizen in another.)

The following characteristics of a decision process define a group as a public advisory committee:

(1) Some form of public participation is established on the panel.
(2) Members are appointed by a chief administrative official and given terms of appointment.
(3) The decisions of the group are recommendations only, they are made to some administrative head of a public or nonprofit institution.
(4) For the most part, the committee's deliberations are open to the public.
(5) The group is given a mandate or specific charge.

When a politically sensitive issue develops and groups of individuals are in conflict with one another, an agency head may convene a citizen advisory committee as an alternative to acting as a sole arbiter to the conflicting sides. The selection of such a committee has two initial effects. First, it provides the public with an image and an expectation that an impartial risk assessment will be carried out. As we saw earlier in the discussion of the analogy to due process, perceived fairness of the panel and its group process may be very important. Second, by bringing together a range of viewpoints in the debate, issues are likely to become less polarized (Coates, 1975).

After an administrative head convenes a public advisory committee, boundary conditions provide constraints for the resolution of the problem. The conditions can be built into the charter or charges given to the committee. These charges will determine the types of questions the committee can pursue. Advisory panels formed to resolve technical conflicts will usually refrain from deliberations about social and ethical impacts. The administrative agency can exercise its control through the chairperson who sets the panel back on course if it departs from the given charge.

Another factor influencing the structure, composition, and performance of the group decision process is how the committee came into existence. Was it mandated by law? Did it arise because of some public controversy? Was it created exclusively to serve a public agency head? The conditions of its formation will determine whether a committee is short or long term, diverse or narrow in its composition, or under direct control of an agency head or free standing.

Individuals are chosen to fill positions on public advisory committees foremost to satisfy an overriding need of a chief administrator for a politically acceptable solution to a complex technological problem in a way that secures public confidence, brings praise from superiors, and maintains control of the situation. In cases where policy decisions depend upon scientific information, the agency head has the choice of initiating a one- or a two-tiered process. If the former is chosen, it must then be decided how best to use scientists and nonscientists on the advisory panel.

To illustrate a case where a one-tiered process used only nonscientists on an advisory committee, let us return to our example from the genetic engineering controversy. Although NIH issued guidelines for gene-splicing research, the city of Cambridge chose to convene its own citizen advisory panel. Despite the technical complexity of the problem, the city manager selected a committee of individuals who were nonexperts in the field of molecular biology. He justified his choice by arguing that nothing would be gained by having scientists who vehemently disagreed about the risks comprise an advisory committee. Futhermore, the city manager believed the public would be skeptical of such a committee.

A more typical example of the mix of scientists and nonscientists is illustrated at the national level, when RAC was expanded to 25 members in 1978 and took on a more heterogeneous form. Some new public members were chosen primarily because they had expressed concerns over the new technology. HEW Secretary Califano brought critics directly into the group process, in contrast to a legal model that depends upon the neutrality of participants rendering a decision. The new RAC experienced more conflict during its deliberations than it had previously, although scientists still held a majority, and the resulting policies were not significantly different from when public representation had been smaller. The expanded membership did help to diffuse the public controversy. The lay members had pushed some discussions into new areas, but a powerful chair kept the committee from straying from its mandate by effectively using the written charge as a signal that things were moving off course (see Chapter 2 on leadership effectiveness). However, by increasing the diversity of the committee, less opportunity existed for the "groupthink" phenomenon to prevail (see Chapter 3).

We turn now to some of the factors that distinguish the effectiveness of individual participants in advisory groups. Much of the discussion is appropriate to small group processes in general, but the conclusions have been drawn from the author's experience on risk-assessment panels.

The Exercise of Influence and Control

Individuals accept appointments to advisory committees for different reasons. Some enjoy the public visibility; some seek prestige; some wish to affect change; some enjoy the heat of controversy; some accept the appointment as a favor; some see it as a stepping stone to another position; some serve because they believe it is their civic duty. Since the motivations of participants differ, one expects them to play different roles in the process (see Chapter 1 on group composition). The social dynamics and group process factors in advisory panels can be illuminated by a general theory of small group interactions. The complex cognitive and theoretic activity of technical panels, in contradistinction to group function where there are strictly social objectives, does not reduce in importance the sociological and psychological factors that influence the outcome of the decision. Whether the decision-making group is a scientific body or a high school club, the factors of conformity, peer recognition, leadership, and rank come into play.

Among the most important elements of an advisory group process is the agenda. The selection of the agenda items determines the scope and range of investigations, the kind of information to be examined, the experts to be called, and the nature of the risk assessment needed. Individual committee members can exert a higher degree of influence if they can make effective use of the agenda rather than accept its determination by the committee chair and staff. Many committee members treat the agenda as fixed and outside of their direct control.

Advisory groups that mix technical experts and lay representatives are likely to exhibit hierarchical relationships that inhibit full participation by lay members. Scientific experts have a command over the technical knowledge. The nonexperts may find it difficult to distinguish dogma from conjecture and scientific consensus. When individuals are recognized as experts, they may be inclined to wield that confidence beyond the issues of science or their particular area of expertise.

If lay members are to have effective roles, they must be capable of raising fundamental issues about technical matters. They can require external review of certain conclusions by outside experts to determine the level of consensus. They can question the degree to which certain claims are generalizable. In short, they can force the technical experts to make explicit the assumptions and values underlying certain key decisions. Otherwise, the participation of lay representation on advisory boards is nothing more than window dressing in a process for which their contributions can make a difference.

Technical experts, having been socialized in their professional training, may not question certain conclusions or be open to new approaches to problem solving. Scientists on a mixed committee can benefit from the sophisticated naivete or the folk wisdom of the probing laity who may force deeper justifications of previously held beliefs (Krimsky, 1983).

Nonscientists can effect changes in how a meeting is run or express concerns about conflict of interest. In the recombinant DNA debates, public members of the RAC raised the following procedural issues: Are votes recorded in the minutes to make each individual accountable to the public? Are there rules for taking committee votes? Has the public had sufficient time to respond to proposed rule making or policy changes? Has there been ample opportunity to solicit responses to proposals from diverse members of the scientific community? The result of broader public involvement on the RAC led to a set of rules that formalized the committee's procedures insuring greater fairness in the decisions.

The involvement of lay participation in social risk assessment improves the chances that ethical problems and social impacts will be raised on the agenda since these are areas in which nonscientists have a legitimate standing. Scientists, on the other hand, may find such issues inappropriate for discussions as they tend to diminish their control over the outcome of deliberations.

In group decision, people become conscious of their own roles and powers to influence opinion. But regardless of the logic of an individual's position, there are many factors that can affect the efficacy of one's arguments. As a general rule, people demand consistency. Participants in a group process who show signs of duplicity may easily be dismissed as self-serving. Individuals targeted as ideologues may also lose the confidence of other participants. (See Chapter 3 on group deviates.) Some participants prefer not to fight every battle with the same vigor. The discriminating critic can avoid attracting the pejorative terms "noncompromising" and "nihilist."

This section has discussed influence and control through internal processes; but there are also external factors that affect the deliberation process. In highly politicized debates, individual committee members can exploit external pressures on the agency for influencing group opinion. Lobbying may be carried on internally and externally. Committee members who solicit support for their position from outside experts may gain a psychological advantage over their adversaries. Most people would like to know that their assessment of the risks is supported by some group of experts. Scientism has infected our culture; everyone needs an expert to be legitimate. Individuals who choose to fix their beliefs by other criteria would almost assuredly be branded a deviant and excluded from such processes.

Members holding minority positions can reach a wider audience by effective use of the media. A newspaper report on a critical vote that describes dissenting opinions can bring in letters of protest to public officials asking that they not support the "precipitous" action of the committee. The public agency head is likely to be responsive to public opinion even when his or her advisory committee is not. Foremost, one wants to avoid the embarrassment of having the issue co-opted by another agency or another branch of government. The media were used effectively by different members of RAC to build support for a proposal. Scientists and public members lobbied for their proposals by garnering support from their natural constituencies in the form of letters to the agency director.

Ethics and Responsibilities of Public Advisory Committees

Individuals serving on risk assessment panels that decide such things as how much exposure is permissible for toxic chemicals or what safeguards should be imposed on hazardous waste disposal sites, bear special responsibilities to society. Their votes may result in an exacerbation of certain diseases, a major catastrophe, or a redistribution of social resources. Chapter 5 in this volume discusses more fully the general ethical issues in group decision making. In the specific domain of decision making in public advisory groups, ethics and social responsibility become important in five areas: conflicts of interest, confidentiality, dual allegiances, the media, and redistributive issues.

CONFLICTS OF INTEREST

Federal law requires that advisors to the government file disclosure information on possible conflicts of interest. The information requested includes any activities or financial holdings and relationships that are related to the advisory activities of the individual. The responsibility for declaring that someone's role on the committee is compromised by their past or present affiliation lies with two individuals: the adviser himself and the chief administrative officer. Because of confidentiality provisions, individual members of an advisory panel may not be informed about the past and present affiliations of others, such as their industrial ties or personal investments. As a committee member, it is not possible to tell whether there is a hidden agenda or self-serving motives for a colleague who is advocating a position.

The question of what constitutes a conflict of interest becomes muddier when we go beyond the direct financial interests of decision makers. Consider the case where someone is called upon to advise the Food and Drug Administration on the potential risks of the salt content of baby foods. If this individual has consulted for one of the parent companies of the baby food manufacturer, does that constitute a conflict of interest? Does the length of time that one consulted matter? How distant should one's relationship to the industry be? And what should we say of a scientist serving on a risk assessment committee to investigate the hazards of a research technology he personally employs? This occurred with the Recombinant DNA Advisory Committee where some of those chosen to serve on the committee were themselves pursuing the gene-splicing techniques whose risks they were asked to evaluate. Beyond that, there were scientists on the committee reviewing industrial experiments who were at the same time on the payroll of commercial institutions.

In both cases, the general public was not aware of the potential conflicts of interest of committee members.[1]

CONFIDENTIALITY

People who serve on panels that provide advice on critical policy decisions are placed in the public trust no less than elected officials. It has been argued that the disclosure of their industrial affiliations—such as where they receive their grants, with whom they consult, and in which companies they hold stock—should take precedence over their right to privacy.

Some public advisory panels are made privy to information deemed confidential by their parent agency or their chief administrative head either for reasons of national security or because of its commercial proprietary nature. There are federal penalties for revealing such information. An ethical conflict can arise when a committee member believes that the public has a right to the information. (For a discussion of ethical norms, see Chapter 5.) That member has to balance his personal risks of prosecution with the overall benefits to society in having access to confidential reports. If he or she does decide to release information stamped confidential, the method of release must also be considered. The member could declare him or herself the source and resign, or release it anonymously. In either case the law may be violated. The public's reaction and the external political environment may be the key factors in determining whether the state prosecutes.

DUAL ALLEGIANCES

Some public advisory groups are formed under an adversarial principle that competing interests be represented in the decision-making process. Participants may be chosen because of their ties to industry, a community group, or an environmental organization. While participants know that they are there because of an institutional affiliation, ordinarily they are not on the committee as representatives of that organization. In the pluralistic model of group problem solving, points of view are represented, not organizations.

For individuals with strong institutional ties there is a dilemma: Whose views should be presented to the committee—the personal ones of the panel members or those of their organizations? Even if one intends to vote independently, the influence of one's organization can be significant. (Chapter 5 discusses the ethical responsibility of group members for their decisions.)

THE MEDIA

On controversial issues, individual members on special commissions will be besieged by the media. How should they respond? Should they direct the media to the committee? If they represent a minority view, should they use the media to insure that the public understands their perspective? Some committees try to impose a veil of silence on their members until a final recommendation is released, much in the way a jury functions. Since the media can exert external influence during a protracted deliberation process, members of the committee may view newspeople as part of their arsenal of strategies.

In situations where votes are taken in closed sessions, should the media be informed about the positions taken by individual members of the commission? The appropriate course of action in such situations depends upon the tacit contractual relationship that one makes with the group, and the importance placed on public disclosure.

REDISTRIBUTIVE ISSUES

The discussion has focused on group decisions of a special nature, namely those involving the assessment of technological risks. The outcome of such decisions frequently has a redistributive effect on our society. Some people will be paying more for things; others may get healthier or sicker. It may save lives or prevent illness. The policy changes that result usually involve a reallocation of social resources. One of the most difficult questions lawmakers face is how much society should pay to save an additional life (Baram, 1980; Howard, 1980; Jones-Lee, 1976). There is still substantial debate on how economic considerations should be factored into society's responses to technological risks. Decision makers should not only consider the aggregate effects of certain courses of action, but also their redistributive effects in the society (Krimsky, 1982b). Who reaps the benefits and who bears the risks? Will the decision place the most vulnerable in society in an even less favorable situation? There are no easy answers. But at the very least, one should expect a heightened sensitivity to problems of equity, and that includes a full accounting of the impacts and distributional effects of decisions.

Rationality and Acceptable Risk

Thus far, we have addressed the politics, ethical aspects, and structural characteristics of group decisions involving social risk taking. But where does rationality fit in? Is there a scientific approach to the determination of risk? Should we place a primary value on making a rational choice and assume it will take care of other issues such as democratic process, fairness, and equity? The utilization of rational models of social risk assessment reduces the need for participatory forms of group decision making. This section examines the extent to which science can be substituted for social process at the so-called objective stage of risk assessment. It illustrates the point that valuation cannot be avoided.

THE LOGIC OF CHOICE

Rational behavior under conditions of uncertain knowledge was the subject of intense study by economists in the 1950s. They sought a set of axioms that could serve as the logical foundations for the behavior of rational economic man in the face of risks (Arrow, 1951). The risks that motivated these early investigations were associated with public and private investment.

By the last 1960s and through the 1970s, government agencies were issuing extensive regulations in areas of health and safety. Considerable attention was given to setting reasonable and objective standards of controlling hazardous technologies and limiting human exposure to toxic substances. A new theoretical literature emerged, building on previous work by economists, but addressing the notion of acceptable risk of morbidity and mortality. In these investigations, the following questions were being raised: What risks need to be regulated? How should regulatory bodies deal with potential as contrasted with actual (proven) risks? What should be done when the public's perception of risk is at odds with actuarial determinations? How much social resources should be put into risk avoidance?

There have been serious limitations in efforts to develop a normative theory of social risk taking. Three troublesome areas are the calculation of risk, reconciling perceived or subjective risk with actuarial risk, and rational approaches to determining acceptable risk.

THE CALCULATION OF RISK

While mortality and morbidity data may provide information on the rates of occurrence of some diseases or technological mishaps, many areas of social risk assessment do not lend themselves to an actuarial determination of risk. Some events—for example, earthquakes—have too low a frequency of occurrence for statistics to offer reliable estimates of risk. For some classes of activity, adverse impacts have never occurred. In these cases, the risks are dependent upon untested and value-laden assumptions. Risks may be hypothetical, as in the recombinant DNA affair or in the scenario that astronauts returning from the moon might carry back a deadly organism. In another class of events, the measurement instruments may not be sensitive enough to pick up the effects. Human exposure to low-level radiation or low doses of carcinogens are such examples. Quantitative determinations of risk to human health are arrived at indirectly by data generated from animal studies where extremely high does of chemicals or radiation are administered over short periods of time.

There may be alternative ways to calculate the frequency of a hazardous outcome by the selection of different reference classes. The risks in flying may be framed as accidents per million miles or as accidents per flight. Or the risks of mortality from the Vietnam war may be measured against the normal death rate from disease for all ages, or against the death rate for U.S. males in the 18 to 24 age group. The relative or actual frequency of a hazardous event is affected by the choice of a baseline or reference class.

Problems of calculation and measurement, however, have hardly ever been obstacles to theory constuction. It is always left to the empiricists to find the measuring instruments so the theory can be applied. But the problem of constructing a rational choice theory that is not too far removed from the way reasonable people behave is critical. This brings us to our next problem:

RECONCILING PERCEIVED OR SUBJECTIVE RISK
WITH ACTUARIAL RISK

In the theoretical literature on social risk assessment, there is no method for reconciling the differences between the public perception of risks and the technical assessment of risks. More accurately, there is no *adequate method*, since some theorists would simply explain away certain subjective perceptions (otherwise known as revealed

preference) as inherently irrational, while treating technical calculations as rational and objective. People view flying as more
dangerous than driving despite the fact that, on the basis of actuarial
evidence, plane risks are lower than those of automobiles (Starr,
Rudman, & Whipple, 1976). Likewise, some experts bemoan the
fact that the public places a higher risk on nuclear power than is
justified by calculations, risk estimates, and actual frequency of
fatalities. One of the functions of theory is to explain the differences
between perceived and actuarial risk.

To illustrate some of the problems confronting the theorists,
consider the following example. Under a technical determination of
risk according to a measure of the frequency of fatalities, let us say
that events of type X are riskier than events of type Y, on the basis of
evidence E_1 (symbolized in A).

$$\text{(A)} \quad X \text{ riskier than } Y/E_1$$

Let us also assume that the social perception of risk for this class of
events, based upon another body of evidence E_0, and additional
background information, B, of an unspecific nature (which may vary
with individuals) gives the opposite result.

$$\text{(B)} \quad Y \text{ riskier than } X/E_0 + B$$

Now suppose we provide the public with the evidence on the basis of
which the technical risk was established, but the public perception
still yields the conclusion Y riskier than X.

$$\text{(C)} \quad Y \text{ riskier than } X/E_1 + B$$

In the background information, there may be a variety of factors
that are not included in the actuarial calculations, such as the
perceived value of the benefits, the magnitude of an accident or
disease that may result, or the extent to which the effects are delayed.
For example, low frequency, catastrophic events are often deemed
riskier by the public than high frequency, low magnitude hazards.
Similarly, hazards such as cigarette smoking where the adverse
effects are delayed for a number of years are perceived less risky than
hazards of lower magnitude where the effects are more proximate in
time with the causes.

Several explanations (not meant to be exhaustive) have been
advanced to account for differences in perceived and actuarial risks
as represented in A, B, and C above.

(1) People may accept the fact that X is riskier than Y when they learn of evidence E_1, but they continue to act as if Y is riskier than X. The background information contributes to irrational behavior.
(2) People act in a manner consistent with their beliefs; they do believe that Y is riskier than X because of the background information B.
(3) Those who conclude Y is riskier than X are acting irrationally because B is irrelevant to risk determination.
(4) Those who conclude Y is riskier than X are acting rationally when the background information is added to actuarial evidence E_1.
(5) Those who conclude Y is riskier than X are acting rationally when they do not accept the validity of E_1.

The concern for theoretical elegance has minimized the importance given to the background information, since it consists of nonactuarial subjective and nonquantifiable factors. If the theory views decision C as irrational, then one must draw the dismal conclusion that irrationality is pervasive in social attitudes about risk and democracy cannot work in social risk assessment.

Another problem in developing a normative theory of risk assessment relates directly to Arrow's paradox discussed in Chapter 4. Suppose we accept nonactuarial factors in assessing risks and wish to develop an aggregate risk assessment by either averaging over or totaling group preference. As previously shown, a transitive relation applied to three events with at least a three-person universe fails to exhibit transitivity for aggregate measures such as a simple majority. Let the relation be denoted by r = riskier than.

Person I   X r Y; Y r Z; X r Z

Person II   Y r Z; Z r X; Y r X

Person III Z r X; X r Y; Z r Y

Majority   X r Y; Y r Z; Z r X

According to the majority's determination of comparative risk, X is riskier than Y, Y is riskier than Z, but Z is riskier than X. However, "riskier than" is a transitive relation according to common usage. Thus, the use of subjective determinations of comparative risk in conjunction with voting procedures can transform a transitive relation into an intransitive one. The paradox is that voting preference should have no effect on the transitivity of a relation.

A theory that reduces risk assessment exclusively to preference can result in logical inconsistencies. Public policymakers often walk a narrow line between social preference behavior and technical assessments.

ACCEPTABLE RISK

In the social risk assessment literature it is frequently stated that a person does not act rationally if he or she refuses to accept a risk that is significantly less than the background risks one ordinarily faces in one's life. Richard Wilson, a strong proponent of quantifying risks, made a list of events, some quite ordinary, with equal probability of increasing the chance of death by one in a million (Wilson, 1979). The partial list includes the following.

Event	*Mortality Factor*
Smoking 1.4 cigarettes	cancer or heart disease
Living two days in New York or Boston	air pollution
Living two months in an average stone or brick building	cancer caused by natural radioactivity
Drinking thirty 12-oz cans of diet soda	cancer from saccharin
Eating a hundred charcoal-broiled steaks	cancer from benzopyrene
Living five miles from a nuclear power plant for fifty years	cancer caused by radiation from a nuclear reactor accident

Comparative risk analysis is used effectively by risk assessors to justify public acceptance of new technologies such as hazardous waste-processing facilities, nuclear power plants, and nuclear waste-storage facilities. The most extensive study, albeit controversial, of nuclear reactor safety led by MIT nuclear engineer Norman Rasmussen compared the risks of reactor accidents to those of meteorite impacts and other low frequency natural hazards (U.S. NRC, 1975).

Despite the compelling logic of comparative risk evaluation, people may act rationally as risk minimizers (Comar, 1979). They may not want to add additional risks to their lives, regardless of the imputed actuarial fatality figures. Furthermore, it is reasonable for people to react differently to risks not yet imposed upon them than to those already part of their technological culture.

Risk assessment based upon the comparative frequency of fatalities may be important to insurance companies, but for the field of public policy it fails to take account of the wide variation in the perception of benefits. A heavy smoker refuses to live near a nuclear power plant, although, on the basis of calculated risk, his or her dangers are far greater as a smoker. But the decision may be rational if we factor into his or her assessment the benefits derived from smoking compared to those derived from nuclear energy.

A theory of social risk assessment must also be capable of dealing with incummensurables. When do the social benefits of a technology outweigh the social risks? The benefit side can be given in terms of dollars, pleasures, more plentiful energy, or improved travel time, while the risk side is given in terms of the probability of fatalities, illness, or environmental damage. As pointed out in the previous section, policymakers are also faced with the problem of the just distribution of risks and benefits. As groups, asbestos miners and cotton mill workers exhibit higher incidences of cancer than other populations of workers. The benefits of their labor are enjoyed by all of us. What is the equitable equation for trading off worker exposure to harmful materials for societal benefits? A satisfactory solution is not found in the theoretical literature. Because of the limitations in rational models of acceptable risk, social processes and public perceptions will continue to play significant roles in setting social policies.

For the policymaker faced with an assessment of a technological risk, the following important consideration should guide the establishment of an advisory group. First, there should be a preliminary evaluation of the extent to which technical experts are, or are likely to be, in significant disagreement over key scientific aspects to the problem. If that is the case then a sound strategy calls for accepting the ambiguity of technical information and the politicization of the scientific issues. Under such circumstances it is incumbent on the policymaker to open the decision-making process to those who represent the public interest.

Second, once it is acknowledged that public consensus on the issue will not be achieved by a group process consisting of technical elites, the decision maker should consider the use of a one-tiered process where science and policy issues are recognized as interwoven. Public involvement should be built into the decision process at the earliest stage to counteract criticisms that technical assessments of policy alternatives have been biased.

Third, care should be taken to insure the fairness in the choice of advisory panel members. Participants should be chosen for their ability to offer different perspectives to the problem under review, as well as their capacity to study and understand the technical complexity of the problem in scientific terms. Safeguards should be built into the process to prevent undue influence by the technical members of the panel or outside interests on other members.

Finally, the policymaker should make a serious effort to avoid potential conflicts of interest in his or her selection of members of an advisory group. Since scientific unanimity may be difficult to find in many types of risk analysis, the emphasis on the process will insure that the broader society perceives as the ultimate goal of the decision the unconditional health and safety of the public.

Note

The author of this chapter was a member of the Recombinant DNA Advisory Committee from 1979 to 1981.

References

Arrow, K. J. *Social choice and individual values.* New Haven, CT: Yale University Press, 1951.

Ashby, E. *Reconciling man with the environment.* Stanford, CA: Stanford University Press, 1978.

Baram, M. S. Cost-benefit analysis: An inadequate basis for health, safety, and environmental regulatory decision making. *Ecology Law Quarterly,* 1980, 8, 473-531.

Boffey, P. M. Anatomy of a decision: How the nation declared war on swine flu. *Science,* 1976, 192, 636.

Berliner, H., & Salmon, J. W. Politics of prevention: Swine flu and the phantom threat. *Nation,* 1976, 223, 270.

Comar, C. Risk: A pragmatic *de minimus* approach. *Science,* 1979, 203, 319.

Coates, J. F. Why public participation is essential in technology assessment. *Public Administration Review,* 1975, 35, 67-69.

Cumming, R. B. Is risk assessment a science? *Risk Analysis,* 1981, 1, 1-3.

Douglas, M., & Wildavsky, A. *Risk and culture.* Berkeley: University of California Press, 1982.

Gray, B. H. Institutional review boards as an instrument of assessment: Research involving human subjects in the U.S. *Science, Technology and Human Values,* 1978, 25, 34-46.

Howard, R. A. On making life and death decisions. In R. C. Schoving & W. A. Albers, Jr. (Eds.), *Societal risk assessment: How safe is enough.* New York: Plenum Press, 1980.

Jones-Lee, M. *The value of life: An economic analysis.* Chicago: University of Chicago Press, 1976.

Kantrowitz, A. Controlling technology democratically. *American Scientist,* 1975, 63, 505-509.

Krimsky, S. The role of the citizen in the recombinant DNA debate. *Bulletin of the Atomic Scientists,* 1978, 34, 37-43.

Krimsky, S. *Genetic alchemy: The social history of the recombinant DNA controversy.* Cambridge, MA: MIT Press, 1982. (a)

Krimsky, S. Beyond technocracy: New routes for citizen involvement in social risk assessment, *Journal of Voluntary Action Research,* 1982, 11, 8-23. (b)

Krimsky, S. Scientists should listen to non-experts. *Science* 83, 1983, 4, 18.

Myrdal, G. Facts and valuations. *Value in Social Theory.* New York: Harper & Row, 1958.

National Academy of Sciences (NAS), National Research Council, Committee for a Study on Saccharin and Food Safety Policy. *Food safety policy: Scientific and societal considerations.* Washington, DC: NAS, 1979.

National Academy of Sciences (NAS), National Research Council, Committee on Prototype Explicit Analyses for Pesticides. *Regulating pesticides.* Washington, DC: NAS, 1980.

Ricci, P. F., & Molton, L. S. Risk and benefit in environmental law. *Science,* 1981, 214, 1096-1100.

Rittel, H.W.J., & Webber, M. W. Dilemmas in a general theory of planning. *Policy Sciences,* 1973, 4, 155-169.

Schoenbaum, S. C. et al. The swine influenza decision. *New England Journal of Medicine,* 1976, 295, 760.

Starr, C., Rudman, R., & Whipple, C. Philosophical basis for risk analysis. *Annual Review of Energy,* 1976, 1, 629-662.

U.S. Nuclear Regulatory Commission (NRC). *Reactor safety study: An assessment of accident risks in U.S. commercial nuclear power plants.* Washington, DC: NUREG-74/014, 1975.

Wilson, R. Analyzing the daily risks of life. *Technology Review,* 1979, 81, 41-46.

CHAPTER 7

CHOOSING PRESIDENTIAL NOMINEES
Decision Making on a Large Scale

Bradbury Seasholes

Two main procedures are used by American political parties in choosing their nominees for president: primaries and conventions.[1] Primaries are preliminary elections held by a party to select its nominees for the general election. Conventions, by contrast, bring together party representatives (delegates) under one roof to make such nominations. In the first part of this chapter, we will examine these two procedures, asking which of the two better fulfills the objectives of the parties. A theoretical discussion uses an apparently unrelated subject—where stores tend to be located—to cast light on how parties and voters interact in elections. This theoretical material is then juxtaposed with actual nomination and election history. In the later portions of the chapter, the decisions of candidates and especially delegates at conventions, acting as groups, are scrutinized, using the early chapters of this book as a framework.

This analysis of how presidential nominees are chosen has two purposes: first, to further understanding of an obviously important segment of American politics; and second, to contribute generally to an awareness of group decision making—that is, to raise in a particular (political) context larger questions about differences between "groups" defined simply as numbers of people acting simultaneously in response to a common stimulus (for example, a primary campaign), as compared to "groups" defined as interactive—having face-to-face communication, bargaining, forming coalitions, and so on (as in a convention).

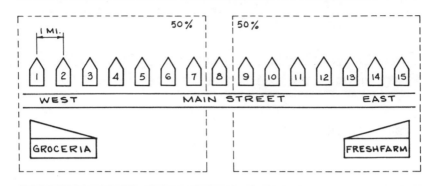

Figure 7.1   Two Stores at the Perimeter Divide Customers Equally

A Spatial Model

One type of noninteractive group—voters in an election—may have an unintended consequence. The following example will illustrate this consequence, and in so doing will illustrate the importance of the distinction between interactive and noninteractive groups. To start that example—and at the risk of creating some initial confusion—we examine what will seem to be quite a different subject: how grocery stores decide where to locate.

Figure 7.1 presents the decisional challenge. In a sharply simplified hypothetical town, fifteen families live in houses, each of which is spaced one mile from its neighbor. These families may differ in a number of respects, but they are exactly alike in their weekly food preferences and consumption.

In the real world, one grocery store could, of course, easily serve fifteen families. But for the purpose of making a point, we are going to introduce *two* stores, forcing each of them to make a decision about where to locate that has to take the other store into consideration.

Like their prospective customers, the two stores are unusual in their being exactly alike. Everything about them is the same—prices, decor, air conditioning, courtesy . . . everything. So, on Wednesdays, the traditional day for heavy grocery store advertising, they find it unnecessary to trumpet this week's price for cantaloupe; there is no way one of them can attract customers via price advantage. But there *is* something each of them can legitimately offer as an incentive for customers to choose one rather than its competitor: proximity. So, Wednesday's ads tend to say, "Shop Groceria—We're Closer!" or "Buy Freshfarms—We're Near!" With all else defined as exactly equal, nearness would indeed by the only criterion for choosing one store or the other. Accordingly, Groceria would end up with seven exclusive customers, with even number 7 realizing a trip of six miles is better than the eight miles to Freshfarms. Number 8, whose house is equidistant, would rationally split its shopping between the two stores, alternating weeks, The two stores, then, end up with 7½ customers' worth of business. That business outcome is clearly the consequence, however, of where they are located. If they were allowed to move their stores, experimenting with various locations on Main Street until each finds the one that seems best, the business outcomes would also vary. Figure 7.2 poses some of the other possibilities. For instance, the top deployment gives Freshfarms an 8- to -7 advantage, because customer 8 is now closer to it than to the other store. Locating a store at the far end of the town turns out to be the *least* desirable decision, because:

— higher numbers of customers are at least temporarily possible at other locations; and
— the store is vulnerable to its competitor moving, making it lose customers.

The logic of wanting to secure an advantage and at the same time protecting against losing customers forces each store to move toward the other, finally locating in exactly the same place, right at the center of town (the situation depicted at the bottom of Figure 7.2). When that happens, they again end up with 7½ "customers worth of business," now garnering half of all fifteen residents' trade (by alternation), rather than having any shopper exclusively use one store. Although that produces no more income that the end-of-town locations in the starting illustration, the center-of-town location has the advantage of security: Neither store lives with the danger of being hurt by a possible locational change by the other. Neither store can improve its business by moving away from the center, as long as the competition is at the center. (The first to try moving away, just a mile, would drop from 7½ to 7; see Figure 7.2, line B.)

Simplistic as this demonstration may appear, it is an application of the heart of some very important theories developed by Harold

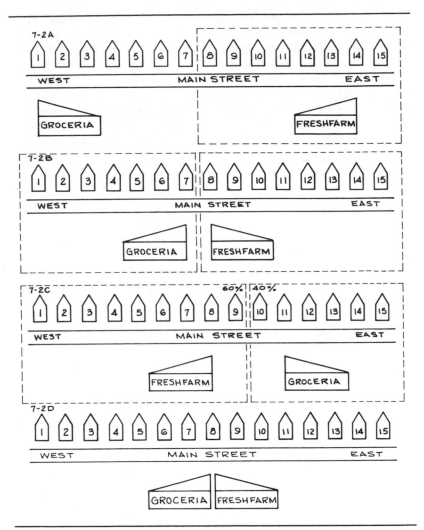

Figure 7.2   Location at Other Than the Center Makes Either Store Vulnerable to a
Loss of Customers to the Other

Hotelling (1929) and Arthur Smithies (1941) in an effort to
understand more systematically the reasoning underlying decisions
by retailers about where to place their enterprises. Intuitively one
might expect competitors to want to locate at a distance from one
another—to hinder customers interested in comparative shopping

and to establish exclusive geographic "spheres of influence" (be "the only store around"). Yet, empirically, we often encounter quite the opposite. Seeking out one movie theater, we are likely to find ourselves in a district of several theaters; or hunting out a car dealership, discover "car row." It is rare to find a solitary antique dealer in a city; a shopper is much more likely to discover a virtual rabbit hutch of competing dealers in the same general location.

Twenty-five years ago, the political scientist Anthony Downs (1957) saw in Smithies' and Hotelling's retail location theory a potential for understanding, by analogy, an important segment of our political life: the interplay between political parties and voters in elections. The nature of Downs's insight—and a revelation, at least, of the reason for this opening discussion of grocery stores—is perhaps most easily conveyed by just changing the labels of the elements in Figures 7.1 and 7.2. Main Street becomes "ideology," with east and west converted to left (liberal) and right (conservative). The residents/shoppers become voters; and the two stores, America's two major political parties (Figure 7.3). Just as the economic theory predicted that stores would tend to cluster, so Downs concluded that two parties are under enormous logical pressure to converge—now not geographically, but in ideas and programs. The implication is that any tendency of our election system to produce look-alike candidates (if that is in fact the case) should be viewed as expected, not accidentally or perverse. As with the original economic application, intuition might lead to quite a different expectation. After all, a two-party system is treasured (and that is the feeling many Americans have about it) because it is so suggestive of offering choice. Those citizens who periodically rally to preserve the two-party system (when one of the two seems to be getting weak) respond because they believe in choice, and hardly because of an attraction to the redundancy Downs attributes to two-party systems.

Do our elections bear out this theoretical expectation of ideological convergence? Confirmation would consist of, say, presidential elections in which both major candidates were in fact quite close in ideology, coupled with a very close margin of victory. The United States has had a surprising number of extremely close presidential contests; data since the Civil War are given in Table 7.1. How many of these, and which, also featured ideological closeness is harder to determine in the absence of conclusive means for measuring ideology. But in a study of several recent presidential

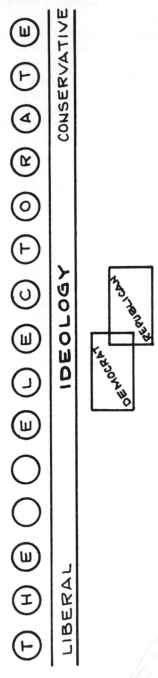

THE ELECTORATE

LIBERAL — IDEOLOGY — CONSERVATIVE

DEMOCRAT   REPUBLICAN

Figure 7.3   In Pursuit of Votes, Parties Converge

TABLE 7.1   Many Post-Civil War Elections for President
Have Been Close

Year	Winning Candidate	In Relation to Closest Competitor	
		Surplus (Deficit) of Popular Vote (to nearest 1,000)	Expressed as % of Total Vote for All Candidates
1868	Grant	305,000	5.4
1872	Grant	763,000	11.8
1876	Hayes	(251,000)[a]	3.0
1880	Garfield	7,000	0.1
1884	Cleveland	63,000	0.6
1888	Harrison	(96,000)[b]	0.8
1892	Cleveland	364,000	3.0
1896	McKinley	568,000	4.1
1900	McKinley	861,000	6.2
1904	Roosevelt	2,544,000	18.8
1908	Taft	1,270,000	8.5
[1912	Wilson	2,160,000	14.4][c]
1916	Wilson	591,000	3.2
1920	Harding	7,005,000	26.5
1924	Coolidge	7,339,000	25.3
1928	Hoover	6,376,000	17.4
1932	Roosevelt	7,060,000	17.7
1936	Roosevelt	11,070,000	24.3
1940	Roosevelt	4,939,000	9.9
1944	Roosevelt	3,596,000	8.3
1948	Truman	2,148,000	6.8
1952	Eisenhower	5,621,000	10.7
1956	Eisenhower	9,567,000	15.4
1960	Kennedy	119,000	0.2
1964	Johnson	15,951,000	22.6
1968	Nixon	511,000	0.7
1972	Nixon	17,998,000	23.2
1976	Carter	1,683,000	2.1
1980	Reagan	8,418,000	9.9

a. Loser, Tilden, received the larger popular vote.
b. Loser, Cleveland, received the larger popular vote.
c. A three-party election, not two; so data less germane to text.

campaigns, Benjamin Page (1978) did find evidence supporting
Downs's convergence thesis, both in party platforms and campaign
speeches. And at an illustrative level, the central charge made by
Harry Truman against Thomas Dewey in the 1948 campaign was

that Dewey was a "me-too" candidate. The 1960 nominees, Kennedy and Nixon, were quite different personalities, but from an ideological perspective were not far apart. The elections of 1968 and 1976, both close, featured the attempt of one of the parties to rectify an error of the previous election (1964 and 1972)—namely, the error of having strayed from the center.

Those two "error" elections suggest confirmation, too, by their being exceptions. In 1964, the Republicans nominated a candidate, Senator Barry Goldwater, who was noticeably to the ideological right of the candidate they knew the Democrats would be choosing (Lyndon Johnson, the incumbent president due to John Kennedy's death). Two slogans conveyed both Goldwater's absolute ideological position—"In your heart, you know he's right" (a delicious play on the last word)—and that position relative to Johnson's—"A choice, not an echo." Line C of Figure 7.2 can be thought of as representing the 1964 result. Much the same thing happened, it could be argued, in 1972—this time to the Democrats. George McGovern was distinctly to the left of other possible candidates in the party, including Muskie and Humphrey, the latter having fought Nixon four years earlier to a virtual draw. As their respective campaigns progressed, both Goldwater and McGovern tried moving more towards the center, but to no avail; the electorate had already "positioned" them (Page, 1978). McGovern, then, also offered more of a choice than usual, and, like Goldwater, paid the price: a 60% to 40% pasting in the balloting. (In America's presidential elections experience, a twenty-point loss is rather unfairly considered a landslide. McGovern had the misfortune of being the less favored candidate more-or-less uniformly in each state, in an election system that takes formal account of state-by-state results. So he will probably be better remembered as the man who lost every state but Massachusetts, a way of formulating his performance that conjures up a landslide of 98% to 2% proportions!)

So Downs's theory, combining the decisions reached separately by parties about whom to support, has at least some surface validity, sufficient to warrant further consideration of its assumptions and implications. These are the core assumptions:

(1) Parties are rational. Although they may have all sorts of programmatic preferences, their overriding objective is to have their candidates win.

(2) Voters are rational. People vote for the party or candidate which on balance is most likely to support, once elected, policies favorable to their interests.

(3) A voter's set of interests usually exhibit an underlying ideological consistency (consistently "liberal," "conservative," etc.).

(4) Voters' ideological positions are distributed uniformly; or if not that, then unimodally. The store illustration worked, in part, because the houses were uniformly spaced along Main Street. It would have also worked had the residents distributed their dwellings unevenly, yet unimodally (meaning one high point), as in Figure 7.4. In the same vein, the political equivalent does not necessitate a society whose voters include equal numbers at each ideological position—as many radical leftists as moderate liberals, for instance. The Downs model still works when ideological preferences, while unevenly distributed, still form one mode. That, in fact, has typically been the case with American voters.

(5) There are only two major parties. (In a system with three substantial parties, the three will move in toward the center, but not fully *to* it.)

A sixth assumption is fundamental to the remainder of this chapter:

(6) Voters vote "sincerely."

Imagine two Democratic voters in 1972, both in agreeement about how to rank their preference for President:

(1) Edmund Muskie, a moderate Democrat and a losing contender for the Democratic nomination;

(2) George McGovern, more left-leaning and the winner of the Democratic nomination, and,

(3) Richard Nixon, the Republican nominee.

The first voter, faced with a McGovern/Nixon choice on the ballot, votes for McGovern, despite her lingering bitterness toward him for having derailed Muskie in the preliminary stages. The second voter votes for Nixon, hoping McGovern will lose and be discredited— thus inducing the Democrats to return to Muskie or a Muskie type four years later. The behavior of the second is often called "strategic" voting. It doesn't reflect the voter's true rank preferences

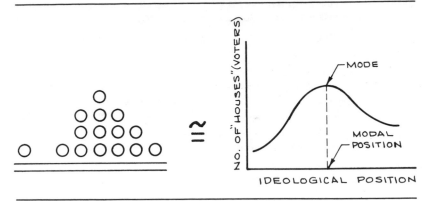

Figure 7.4   Houses or Voters Can Cluster in a Manner Forming a Single Mode

for the election at hand, yet is not irrational either (see Chapter 4).

For this analysis of pressure toward the center to be useful, it is not necessary that these assumptions be totally operative, but only that there be a substantial kernel of truth to them, enough to produce tendencies in the predicted direction. No one would seriously argue, for example, that (all) voters are (always and fully) rational; but it is possible, let us hope, that most are, mostly, and most of the time.

The first two assumptions—parties and voters are rational—answer the question as to why the parties move and the voters stay put. Where voters are located is an expression of their interests, drawn from their experiences collected over the years and their immediate calculation of what they want or need from government. They have no reason to try to accommodate one of the parties by changing their points of view. On the other hand, the parties have all the reason in the world to want to accommodate the voters, or as many of them as they can; above all, they want to win.

The logical conclusion to all this up to now is that the two major American parties are under tremendous pressure tp pick centrist candidates—candidates who have, perhaps, sufficient differences to allow the campaign to have something to talk about, but who are really quite alike.

Of course, one needn't accept Downs's spatial thesis wholesale. Page (1978) has stressed the need to expand and modify Downs to account for such determinants of nomination outcomes—besides ideology—as candidates' leadership skills, their images, and past performance; and the influence of such core party participants as financial contributors. Downs's heavy reliance on assumption 3 set off a cross fire of challenge and affirmation among students of elections. Judging by the commentaries of journalists and other knowledgeable observers (including candidates and other party professionals), assumption 3 does hold. One only has to consider how often our electoral and legislative politics are cast in liberal-conservative terms. Does any of us have difficulty in placing 1980 candidates Kennedy, Carter, and Reagan on a liberal-conservative continuum?

Nevertheless, some highly respected political science research has put this "obvious fact" about American politics into serious question. In the 1950s, the Survey Research Center of the University of Michigan carefully analyzed conversations with a random selection of voters, concluding that—even with the most generous interpretations of what was being said—only 16% were structuring their thoughts about a presidential election campaign along liberal-conservative lines (Campbell, 1960). In further work of the same genre, Philip Converse found an extraordinary lack of consistency in the opinions expressed by the same persons, interviewed several times during a short period of years (Converse, 1964). In the most exhaustive elections study to date, that of the 1968 election, a national group of scholars working through the University of North Carolina found that knowing a voter's ideological stance (by asking her or him) bore only a modest relationship to voting choice among Humphrey, Nixon, and Wallace (Kovenock, 1973). Researchers who have attempted to find liberal-conservative ideology *implied* (without asking voters directly) in the specific array of opinions voters express on topical issues (through the technique known as scale analysis) have likewise emerged less than overwhelmed by the evidence (Flanigan & Zingale, 1979).

But it is possible that such findings are more time-bound than first thought, more susceptible to such variables as the electorate's education level (dramatically higher now than in the 1950s), anticipated closeness of a campaign, and assorted "climate" conditions (war or peace, strong or weak economy, etc.), that in desperation we agglomerate as "the temper of the times." Simple correlations between ideological self-identification and choice of candidate increased dramatically, for example, from the time of Converse's studies up through the 1970s (Nie & Anderson, 1974).

Picking Presidential Candidates

Despite the challenges and qualifications, convergence theory remains powerfully persuasive, an inducement for parties to discover or invent procedures designs to locate and occupy "the center." The nomination procedures, however, that have in fact evolved historically have proven to be complex, changeable, and to some respects hindering to a rational selection.

At the time the Constitution was adopted, political parties did not exist in the form we know them. But from the start there were clear factions reflected in congressional behavior and—after Washington's two presidential terms—in presidential politics. The basic division, residual from the politics surrounding the adoption of the new Constitution itself, grew from different feelings about levels of government activism; about national versus states' responsibilities; about incompatibilities between commercial and agricultural enterprise, and even between types of agriculture; and about region (Ladd, 1970). Although the two Washington elections conformed to the idealistic premise of the Constitution that learned men—the electors of the electoral college—would pick, without crass partisan considerations, the best man ("men" and "man," regrettably the historically accurate way to refer to these persons), the elections of 1796 and 1800 quickly moved toward partisan contests, personified by the rivalry of John Adams and Thomas Jefferson. These two candidates were chosen largely by the urgings of their ideological allies in Congress, logically relying on a faction's or party's most important and electorally successful leaders to choose, in turn, a prospective national leader, It fell to them to select someone (1) who represented their point of view and (2) who would win. It is not clear, at this distance, whether they recognized that those two criteria might not always be wholly consonant.

This so-called caucus method of nominating a presidential candidate had the potential for a serious flaw. Congressmen were almost by definition from regions of the country where their own faction or party was strong; that is why they were in office. Their preference for a presidential nominee was likely to be congruent with the interests of their own districts and states. Consequently, they tended to support a person who could not easily broaden the party's appeal to areas of the country where other interests were more popular. To be sure, they were a relatively small number of persons, able and accustomed to meeting face-to-face, and thus capable of debating, cajoling, and negotiating. These are the sorts of activities that enable groups more easily to reach *strategic* decisions and not be limited by the sincere preferences of each of the group's members. Apparently, however, this opportunity to enhance their party's fortunes by transcending sincere preferences was largely missed. Historically, the course of presidential nomination techniques moved on to what became the convention system precisely to enlarge the involvement of more interests and in the choice regions. To this day, the number of party convention delegates assigned to a state is based both on how well the party fared in that state in earlier elections and on that state's total population. In this way the party can recognize its main sources of strength, yet also reach out for growth in areas of current weakness. To base delegates solely on population would give delegates from a region where the party is perpetually weak too much weight in nominating. To base them solely on prior areas of strength would deny the party opportunity to reach out into areas of past weakness yet future potential. Hence, the dual procedure.

The convention system brought together a group of decision makers designated as delegates by their party, using assorted devices for determining who warranted the honor; and why. The first such convention held for the purpose of selecting a single national presidential candidate took place in 1836, with the Democratic party choosing Martin Van Buren to succeed Andrew Jackson. The reason for taking the form of convention are those just discussed, already evolved and accepted in many individual states by that time. The innovation was its *national* character. The Whigs, lacking the device, challenged Van Buren with four regionally popular candidates. Their resulting defeat led them, too, to adopt the national nominating convention in 1840.

Nearly a century and a half later, this remains fundamentally the method our major parties use. It is not without critics, to put the matter mildly. Although originally conceived as a way of increasing more broadly based democratic participation, conventions came to be seen popularly as an opportunity for just the opposite. State delegations to national party conventions were increasingly populated—or so the belief became—by an array of party professionals ranging from powerful, manipulative bosses down to servile hacks whom they controlled. Votes may have continued to take place in plenary session on the convention floor, but the crucial maneuvering to structure the kind of choices those votes could address was accomplished by the power brokers in corridors and hotel rooms, accompanied by sufficient cigar consumption to give the term "smoke-filled room" its unshakable notoriety. Under the circumstances, it was and is difficult to remember that conventions were an eagerly welcomed reform in the pre-Civil War years.

Distress over the less attractive aspects of nomination by convention led to two sorts of reform in the late nineteenth and then the twentieth century. In some states, reformers simply did away with conventions, replacing them with party elections—"primaries"— to select candidates for governor and other lesser state offices, and often federal offices as well (congressmen and senators). The national party convention as the arena for choosing candidates for president and vice president has proven too hardy for that kind of displacement. Instead, reformers have focused on changing the way by which delegates to the conventions are chosen. Again, primaries have become the main tool. Perhaps presidential candidates couldn't (yet?) be chosen via primaries, but at least the choosers, delegates, could be. This century has seen a sequence of an increasing number of state delegations chosen by primary electorates; then, association of slates of primary candidates for delegates with particular presidential candidates (pledging); and then, pledging with a vengeance—the *binding* of delegates to their candidate through the first ballot of the presidential nomination voting at the national convention.

In its most clearly defined form, a primary is a preliminary election held just among members of one party, in order to narrow that party's number of contenders for a particular office down to one (in single-member districts). In the stream of events culminating in a presidential nomination, it is somehwat misleading that we call the elections that start in February in New Hampshire "primaries," because they are in fact final (that is, the only) elections for the choosing of convention delegates. They are primaries in the sense of "preliminaries" only to the extent that they give some clue as to the eventual convention winner. Sometimes that clue comes not so much from knowledge about which candidates for delegate have won (and whom they support) as from a concurrent "vote"—actually just a formal public opinion poll of a party's adherents—for various contenders, an exercise usually referred to as a "beauty contest." Other times, the clue is much stronger; states (or the parties within states) may require contenders for delegate to stipulate on the ballot who their preferred candidate for president is. In 1980, stricter Democratic party rules, specifying binding, led many states to adopt the following sequence for delegate selection:

— Within geographic districts of the state (for convenience, congressional districts), each major candidate's campaign organiza- tion held caucuses in separate locations, all on the same day. Attendance and participation were limited to registered Democrats willing to indicate their preference for the particular candidate. (A similar caucus for people wishing to be uncommitted was an option in some districts where interest in going that route was sufficient.) The product of any such caucus, by the voting of those attending, was a slate of possible delegates numerous enough to represent *all* the Democrats of the district at the national convention, should it turn out that all of them were in favor of just that one candidate. Put another way, three district caucuses, held separately on the same day by supporters of Carter, Kennedy, and Brown, produced three times as many potential delegates as would eventually attend the national convention.

— After these caucuses, but prior to the convention, the state held a primary, which had "beauty contest" flavor—but was used to make delegate selections. In a District entitled by party formula to ten delegates, a Kennedy-Carter-Brown division of the beauty contest vote of 50%-30%-20% would have led to designation of 5, 3, and 2 delegates drawn from the thirty potentials identified earlier in the caucuses. (The procedure described was used to fill 75% of a state's delegation. The remaining delegates were chosen after the primary by the state's Democratic Committee from its own roster of whom it considered important party professionals not already chosen, again making such choices correspond to the beauty contest percentages.)

With such rigorous attention to who was for whom, it should not have been surprising to find *binding* of delegates the rule at the end of the process. Delegates chosen not fundamentally on their own merits but because of whom they were pledged to support were required to vote for that candidate on the first ballot of the national convention. (A second ballot would only take place should no candidates receive 51% of the first ballot votes. Binding on the second ballot and beyond would be senseless, because change and securing of a majority would be foreclosed.) Yet there were loud complaints voiced in 1980 about binding. The argument ran: Although they associated themselves with presidential candidacies, delegates are thinking human beings who—since it was *they*, not a candidate, who were elected in the primaries—should be allowed to use their own intelligence and judgment. That judgment can change legitimately, because many delegates are elected months before the convention; and conditions affecting the desirability of holding to their pledge should be allowed to be taken into account. Among such conditions would be discovery that the candidate had a serious, disabling illness.

But what if the only "illness" were a growing panic that the candidate might lose in November? A few delegates in 1980, pledged to Carter earlier in the year, may have had some second thoughts as convention time approached. Certainly, the Kennedy forces hoped so, and openly advocated changing the convention rules to allow free choice by delegates on the first ballot, regardless of earlier pledges and binding. Their position in favor of what they called an "open convention" warrants serious consideration, independent of the transparent fact that its specific application in 1980 would have been the only way Kennedy could have had a chance of being nominated.

The "open convention" position has much to recommend it. Indeed, the main thrust of this chapter will turn out to be resonant with its defense. But as this juncture, a warning about clever titles is in order. The Kennedy forces skillfully labeled their position to give it a particularly honorable ring. Yet the "open convention" is philosophically a very close cousin to the venerable convention of smoke-filled rooms. The alleged virtue of the one is identical to the alleged vice of the other: separation of delegate action from the expressed preferences of "the people" (the party's voters).

Pragmatic and political considerations have led, in 1983 and 1984, to some alteration of the 1980 rules, eroding some of their logic in the process. Some reformers, shaking their heads in disbelief at the complexity and perversity of the nomination process in any of its most recent forms, have recommended a radical change, in the fuller spirit of the movement that originally invented primaries. Their proposal is to abandon national nominating conventions entirely, putting in their stead national presidential primaries, one of each party, held on the same day. Awesome pragmatic drawbacks—especially the overwhelming expenditure of money and of physical energy such a procedure would demand of each contender—have doomed the proposal from the start. Those sorts of considerations aside, the proposal also embodies a fundamental theoretical flaw, recognition of which is facilitated by the earlier Downs analysis. The flaw is that a national primary would tend to nominate someone who is less than the party's strongest candidate.

Figure 7.5 illustrates the problem. If a unimodal electorate encourages the selection of centrist candidates, a national primary in which only Democrats can vote would tend to produce a centrist winner—but someone at the ideological center of the party, not of the country (line A). Similarly, Republicans voting sincerely in their national primary (held the same day) would tend to generate a winner who is close to the center of that party (line B). Superimposing the two primaries emphasizes the point that national primaries would put the parties at vulnerable positions more distant from the country's center than they should be. The country's center, which would come into play in the November general election, is at the mode of a voter ideology distribution combining Distributions A and B, plus any Independents (who are usually in between, thus enhancing the mode). Each party needs a nominee who is close to the "ideal" position, line C.

The moral of this may be that party members participating in their respective national party primaries should think and act more *strategically*—set aside their most favored preference and vote instead for someone off-center (of the party) who they realize would have a better chance of winning the general election. But strategic voting is hard to perform—virtually impossible—when the decision makers have little or no opportunity for communication. Primaries (and general elections) by their nature present formidable obstacles to the kinds of interchanges strategic voting has to rely on. An electorate of hundreds of thousands or millions cannot be expected to negotiate, bargain, ascertain one another's second and third choices, gauge intensities of preferences, calculate contingencies, and so forth. The obstacles are the huge numbers of participants; geographic dispersion; money-, time-, and effort-costs of infor-

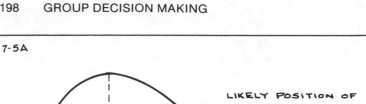

7-5A

LIKELY POSITION OF
DEMOCRATIC PRIMARY WINNER

IDEOLOGICAL POSITIONS OF DEMOCRATIC PRIMARY VOTERS

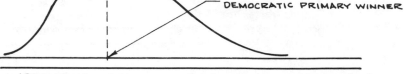

7-5B

LIKELY POSITION
OF REPUBLICAN
PRIMARY WINNER

IDEOLOGICAL POSITION OF REPUBLICAN PRIMARY VOTERS

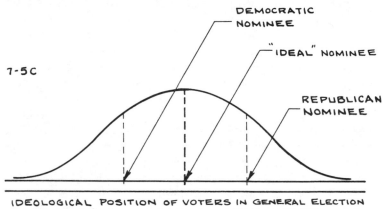

DEMOCRATIC
NOMINEE

"IDEAL" NOMINEE

7-5C

REPUBLICAN
NOMINEE

IDEOLOGICAL POSITION OF VOTERS IN GENERAL ELECTION
(NOVEMBER); A PLUS B PLUS INDEPENDENTS

Figure 7.5 Separate National Primaries Produce Less Than "Ideal" Nominees

mation sharing, so enormous as to be preposterous; and, because a national primary would take place on one day, no possibility of feedback, new learning, or mid-course revision.

National primaries can only be judged speculatively, since none has ever occurred. But state presidential primaries, which are real and numerous, share most of these same liabilities, save the last. Because state primaries occur at various times over several months, there does exist the opportunity for evolution of a final outcome that reflects feedback, learning, and revision. Nevertheless, a Republican primary in Illinois still taps the sincere voting preferences of its participants, admittedly given the likelihood that earlier primaries will have altered for some of them their candidate preferences.

Granted that Republican primary voters in, say, Illinois may be quite different from those in Florida, the parade of primaries still presses the national nomination process toward the error illustrated in Figure 7.5. The result may not be as pure and stark as it would be with a single national primary, but the push is in that direction.

These liabilities evaporate the moment a convention moves from a first ballot to a second. At that point, a profound shift in the mode of group decision making takes place, with delegates free to exercise their own judgments—including the decision, if they wish, to abandon their sincere preferences in order to nominate as strong a contender as possible. Getting over the boundary between first and second ballots has proven difficult, however, for the two parties in recent presidential nominating conventions. Over and over, the preliminary stages have narrowed the immediately pre-convention contenders down to two; or to one with a majority and others with just scattered support. If this is deemed a problem, its cure could take one of several forms. "Unbinding" delegates is one course, as we have earlier mentioned. Requiring that, of all delegates elected in a state primary, some portion must be uncommitted is another—their candidate preferences not known, not formally stated, or at least not legally or ethically binding. A third course could be to raise the majority requirement for nomination from 50% to some higher percentage— perhaps 65% on a first ballot, 60% on a second, 55% on a third, and 50% on any others—coupled, of course, with unbinding after the first ballot. (Before 1936, the Democratic party had a two-thirds majority requirement for any ballot. Because there was no provision for easing the requirement with each successive ballot, it gave powerful veto power to any cohesive minority faction able to control a third or more of delegate votes. The southern wing of the party constituted such a faction, causing the convention to suffer through 104 ballots in 1924 before a compromise candidate could be agreed upon.)

By clinging to a convention as the final decision-making body, the major political parties have implicitly acknowledged that the ethically appealing processes of choice by primary elections are to some degree in tension with the rationally compelling need to win. "Need to win," distasteful as the phrase may sound, serves a profoundly ethical purpose, too; the more parties heed that imperative, the more likely the presidential winner will represent the views of the largest portion of the electorate possible. It is not just to the parties' advantage to converge to the center; it is fully as much to the electorate's advantage.

Group Decision Making at the Convention

The foregoing theoretical and historical review makes a case that bringing nominators together under one roof has at least some potential merit. How well the potential is realized—the *quality* of decision making—depends on the specifics of the group or groups thus formed. An examination of those specifics can perhaps best proceed here by returning to the taxonomy of group decision making developed in the first two chapters of this book. Five major factors affecting group decision-making quality were identified there: a group's composition, its leadership, the nature of the task(s) facing it, decision rules and processes, and (in Chapter 2) forms of communication.

GROUP COMPOSITION

Chapter 1 identified these aspects of composition as important: size, member personality, member similarity, membership openness, member power within the group, and access to face-to-face contact among members.

In considering these factors, it is essential to recognize at the start that delegates to a national convention belong to at least three groups: (1) the convention body as a whole; (2) the particular state delegation; and (3) the nationwide agglomeration of delegates pledged to the same candidate. To simplify further discussion, these three groups will be referred to as the Whole, the States, and the Camps.

For most delegates, the Whole is the least influencing. Among the reasons are two related to composition. The Whole is so large (over 3,000), and encompasses so many dissimilar members (particularly dissimilar in candidate loyalty). Information is lacking on the sorts of delegate personality characteristics that undoubtedly enhance or impede a convention, such as patience, obedience, tolerance, and their opposites. All three group types are far more heterogeneous in demographic composition than used to be the case before the 1970s, because of relatively recent (and ever changing) rules governing representation among delegations of women and racial minorities. The diversity continues to be more pronounced at Democratic than at Republican conventions.

The three group types are also roughly equal in openness (it is very easy to run for delegate) and power (more and less powerful members can be found in all three). The availability of face-to-face contact is, of course, the prime advantage of a convention and the cornerstone of the thesis of this chapter. Realistically, however, the size of the Whole makes access for each member to every other member impractical—although voice-to-voice contact (that is, shout-to-shout) is possible and occasionally persuasive. States do caucus in a single small room and their members are the most likely to socialize among themselves. Surprisingly, Camps do not undertake full caucuses. A candidate will roam from State caucus to State caucus to plead his case, but will not typically ask to meet just with his Camp supporters from that State—although a campaign aide may do so if a situation warrants it. The absence of any general conclave of the Camp faithful to conduct business can be explained by two probable reasons: ungainly size, (perhaps a thousand or more) and a reluctance on the part of a candidate and his staff to let Camp members (pledged delegates) play an active part in crucial decisions. The preference is for obedience, with active decision making left to the candidate and a central few of his professional staff.

In addition to these three group types, functional groups based on such commonalities as race, gender, and youthfulness have tried to organize as caucuses at conventions, in attempts to influence both platform and nomination decisions. These efforts have not succeeded, however, even in the most supportive of environments, the 1972 Democratic Convention. Among reasons cited for the lack of success are inadequate time, scattering of delegates' housing, difficulty in defining a caucus' membership, internal disunity among members, and overlapping with the objectives of the other groups—especially candidate Camps (Sullivan, 1974).

GROUP LEADERSHIP

Selection of the chairman of the convention technically is made by vote of the Whole, but in fact the vote is almost always a ratification of an appointment made from without, by the National Committee (with considerable influence from the incumbent president, if there is one). The crucial leadership question, however, is the *tenor* of the appointment. The selection of a well-respected party professional like Gerald Ford will be seen as natural, "emergent" leadership, regardless of the actual procedure used in making the choice. A choice dictated by an incumbent president too intent on controlling things (or worried about restless natives) will be seen and reacted to as "appointed." A good choice is likely to be of a person with a lifetime of service to the party, including at least indirect service to many of the delegates themselves.

Although importantly biased direction by the chairman is possible from the dais (and behind the scenes)—for example, by determining how floor debate and votes on platform or delegate seating controversies are handled—a convention with several viable candidates is, almost by definition, one of decentralized leadership: leadership shared or divided up among those candidates and their staffs. When one of the candidates is the incumbent president, of course, centralization becomes powerful, even when that president is strongly challenged, as Carter was by Kennedy in 1980. (In 1968, President Johnson exercised enormous control over the convention that would nominate his preferred successor, Humphrey, even though Johnson himself had been forced out of the race several months earlier by antiwar pressures.) The size of the body he must lead, and the extreme shortness of time, virtually force him toward trying to be efficient (a task-oriented approach) at the expense of shortchanging actions meant to heighten delegates' morale. But the context is such that the latter would probably be resented rather than appreciated, as unduly impeding progress.

GROUP TASKS

The Whole and the Camps are task oriented—respectively, to produce a 50% + 1 nominee and to assure that the nominee is the Camp's choice. In the past, when the parties insisted on the "unit rule"—a State delegation had to cast all its votes for one candidate—

those delegations had, to put it modestly, a meaningful task. Without the unit rule, the orientation of a State group has reverted to process: maintain goodwill among persons who may interact in other contexts back home, and facilitate the mechanical process of producing a prompt and accurate tally during roll calls.

The tasks of State delegations are so mundane that analysis of that type of group will be minor for the remainder of this chapter. Yet there is an irony: Many delegates will remember the State group as the most meaningful emotionally of the three, the one recalled with some fondness. The reasons seem to be, for many, prior acquaintance with one another back home; pride in one's state, transcending division over candidates ("Mr. Chairman, North Carolina, the Tarheel State and home of the 1988 NCAA basketball champions, proudly casts 14 votes for . . . "); and loyalist identity reinforced in socializing settings—unacquainted delegates, in bars and dining rooms, quickly resort to talking about one another's cities and regional sights.

The task facing the Whole and the Camps are theoretically divisible. One portion of the delegates could, for example, work on the question of candidates' electability, another with campaign themes, another with ascertaining the likely impact of a particular nomination on relationships with other countries. But that is not the inclination. Delegates as members of the Whole and of a State tend to operate full time on a holistic basis, constantly weighing virtually all aspects of one or another candidate. The Camps are *serviced* by specialists—someone to handle the press, someone else to coordinate liaison with various State delegations, and so on—but these are likely not to be delegates themselves.

The Whole and especially the Camps have a strong preference for overkill, some nominee's winning not just by a hair over 50% but by a "convincing margin" to convert into a mandate; and to produce that effect as quickly as possible. A Camp, of course, wants the convincing winner to be its preference. The Whole says, in effect, "Regardless of who wins, let the win be clearcut."

The task facing the convention as a Whole is primarily competitive in character. The nomination of one candidate requires that all others fail. Similarly, within a Camp, a proposal to throw in the towel, and perhaps try to form a coalition favoring some other candidate, can create an internal competition with those wanting to stay the fight; and only one of the two factions can win.

Despite basic competitiveness, the convention is also deeply influenced by a "sink or swim" cooperative dynamic: the need eventually to nominate *someone*, not remain deadlocked indefinitely. Indeed, each delegate knows that with each succeeding ballot—necessitated by the failure of any candidate to obtain 50% + 1 of the vote—the chances for victory in November of any person nominated are likely to diminish. Prolonged balloting exhausts and further embitters members of Camps that eventually lose, and it signals to the electorate at large a party that is inept and/or helplessly unfocused. Once the first ballot is over, many delegates understand and respond to the imperative to throw their prime choices overboard (in favor of supporting second or third choices), lest the entire ship sink.

This strong impulse toward closure need not be cast solely as negative or defensive. All delegates can bask in the sun of having performed a task of national and international importance. By the end of the convention, most feel good about the nominee. Probably an even larger "most" can anticipate favorable spillovers into their own lives, from the successful act of nominating, since they will also be involved in campaigns, or will be eventual patronage beneficiaries, and so forth.

Of the three main convention groups, Whole, States, and Camps, only the Camps could be considered "ongoing." Candidates for nomination begin their campaigns two years or more before the convention, drawing in many of the persons who eventually become Camp members as delegates. The winning Camp members continue after the convention, in other roles than delegates; and with success in November, on into the indefinitely long future, as election machinery converts into governance machinery. The lifespan of the convention (the Whole) is technically just a few days. State delegations preexist the convention by several months, although very little interaction among members may transpire (except among intra-State Camp factions) until the Convention is imminent. Once the Convention closes, a delegation disbands; but many of its members have the prospect of continuing interaction in other roles (for example, as state legislators), a prospect which may color their actions in the delegation.

DECISION RULES AND PROCESSES

Two types of decision unit are involved in a convention. First, the nomination requires action by the Whole group of thousands.

Second, if events move to a second ballot, then the Camps must function as decision clusters, because one or more of them will have to shift from supporting their leader (for the nomination) to supporting one or more of the other candidates. In most cases, Camp leaders will allow members to base their shift on individual grounds, but the possibility exists of an attempt to shift the Camp as a unit, for strategic purposes: the promise of some reward other than the nomination.

Assume a first ballot situation with at least three substantial candidates, none of whom has a majority (50% + 1). Under those conditions, the fact that the decision rule for the Whole is 50% + 1, not simply a plurality (one more than anyone else), forces the candidate Camps to think beyond a first ballot, giving lesser-yet-substantial candidates hope for possible nomination, and probable *power* in the choice of someone else. A Camp's decision to continue its leader's candidacy or to help form a coalition for someone else is one usually made by the leader himself, not by the Camp's members. In effect, the group cedes its decision making to a single individual. The decision is "authoritarian," but expected to be so. (After all, it mainly concerns the life of the "author.") The nomination by the Whole is quite decidedly irreversible; the decisions of the Camps may or may not be. A decision to continue a candidacy beyond the first ballot can be reversed. Similarly, a decision to shift to another candidate, to create a coalition, can be carried out and then undone. But a Camp's decision *not* to continue their leader's candidacy is, for all practical purposes, irreversible.

The decision criteria for the Whole are heavily subjective, dependent to some extent on objective poll data but largely on optimistic guesswork colored by wishful thinking. Camp decisions to throw in the towel tend to be objective, precisely because they have to be made in the teeth of contrary desire.

The entire convention process is facilitated by the cultural context giving it cause to exist: a belief in the importance of the United States in the world, and of the presidency as its premier office; a belief in the moral necessity of democratic and representational procedures for filling that office; and a conviction that, as Jefferson saw it, "right" decisions emerge from open competition of ideas.

COMMUNICATION

In Chapter 2, several models of communications were identified: chain, Y, wheel, and circle. Formal communication for the convention as a Whole is of the wheel variety, from the podium directly and instantaneously to each and every delegate present—the most desirable model, if speed and openness are the objectives. The problem with convention information dissemination is not, then, the form, but rather the format, frequency, and forthcomingness of the messages. The format is largely oral (from the podium); hence slow, and particularly vulnerable to the distortions of selective perception (inability to review; mishearing and misremembering). Conventions have not mastered the art of efficient distribution of written messages; nor of messages of any sort to delegates other than when they are collected in the hall itself. And the sort of messages that *are* sent forth from the podium tend not to include informal and incomplete or fluid information, such as hints of inpending withdrawals— the sort of information most delegates are usually the most eager to obtain. As a result, rumors are rampant at conventions—rumors defined as information of uncertain accuracy and uncertain provenance. Communication of rumors takes the Y form typical of epidemic diffusion, with media newspersons entering the process at some point, vastly accelerating the diffusion. (Sometimes before the end of the century, conventions will surely include small television sets for each delegate, with, in addition to the national networks, specialized channels linked to the Whole, the State, and the Camp— the last, undoubtedly, with scrambler!)

Communication within a State and a Camp is likewise surprisingly primitive. The Kennedys in 1956 and 1960 made advances in intra-Camp communication substantial for the time, but based simply on a more thorough use of telephone and runners. On the floor, State delegates rely largely on passed (or shouted) messages, up and down rows of seats (the chain model). Outside the hall, there are occasional caucuses, plus possibly the most ubiquitous (and inefficient) form of group communication: the phone message at the hotel desk.

Evaluated all together, the communications procedures of conventions have to be recognized on balance as archaic, an awesome inpediment to the efficient performance of the task at hand: nomination.

Coalition Formation

That task is made considerably easier, obviating many of the complications just discussed, when by convention time there are not more than two contenders. Such is increasingly the case. Almost every time, of course, one of the two major parties is likely to have an incumbent president, which discourages other contenders. Why the out parties in recent times have also ended up with only one or two substantial contenders is unclear. The phenomenon has coincided with the expanding use of primaries to select delegates, but it is not clear why or whether the two might be causally linked.

However rare they have become, America's most exciting conventions are those with more than two major contenders, because they necessitate more than one ballot, unbinding delegates and opening up coalition building to produce the required majority. After a first ballot fails to produce a majority winner, each Camp has an opportunity to calculate its potential power in forming a winning coalition, decide which of the possible coalitions are more likely than others (because of ideological compatibility, perhaps, or geographic dissimilarity—the attraction of a "balanced" coalition); and must try to pin down what incentives it can expect to be given for joining a coalition.

MINIMUM WINNING COALITIONS

The power a Camp has—that it, the "right" to be wooed and to extract payoffs—is not as simply related to its size-of-membership as one might first expect (all this assuming, for the moment, that a Camp's members will all obey orders to shift as a unit from their leader to some other contender). Consider the hypothetical data in Table 7.2. How much effort should a front-running candidate such as A spend on trying to woo Camp C? Or Camp E? The numbers suggest that twice as much effort should be made on C than on E. But, in fact, *any* effort on E is wasted—and conversely, any hope on E's part to be wooed and to be offered inducements in mistaken. The reason lies within the concept, "minimum winning coalition" (MWC, for short). As Figure 7.6 shows, a Camp can be thought of as being (or not being) essential to a particular coalition—essential in that its presence puts the coalition over the 50% mark and—here is the crux—its removal drags the coalition down below 50%. A "winning coalition" is one of 50% or more. A "minimum winning coalition," then, is one over 50%, each and every member of which could pull it below 50% by withdrawing. The power of any given Camp can be thought of as the number of MWCs it can be a part of. In this example, D has the same power as C or B, and so warrants— despite its lower membership—the same attention as they, by any candidate trying to develop a winning coalition. E can be ignored,

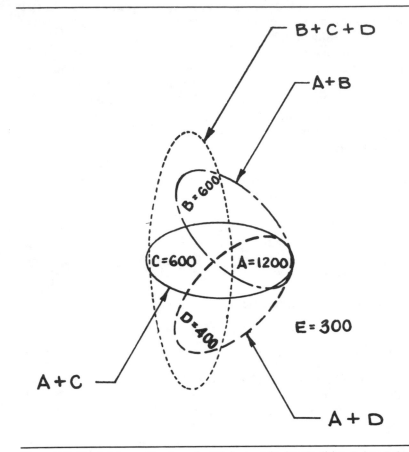

Figure 7.6 By Joining, a Member of a Minimum Winning Coalition Raises Delegate
        Strength from Below 50% to Above 50%

NOTE: Numbers are from Table 7.2.

and would find it futile to try building a coalition based on his own
candidacy. And A is not quite so important as the size of its
membership suggests.[2] (The desire to do more than win, to "win big"
in order to get a mandate, alters these calculations by changing the
definition of "winning" from the legal, technical 50% to some
psychologically defined higher percentage.)

Closer thinking though of the rationale underlying Figure 6 leads
to some alteration and refinement of the basic MWC calculations. D

TABLE 7.2   A Candidate's Coalition-Forming Potential Differs
from His or Her Delegate Strength

Candidate	Delegate strength (size of Camp) end of first ballot; = x	Numerical ratio; x: E	Power Index (from Figure 7.6)
A	1200	4	3 (I, II, III)
B	600	2	2 (II, IV)
C	600	2	2 (I, IV)
D	400	1-1/3	2 (III, IV)
E	300	1	0

NOTE: Total delegates, 3100; needed to win, 50% + 1 = 1551.

may actually be *more* attractive (have more power) than B or C because of its *smaller* size; the expense of time, effort, and money is less (or equal expenditure produces greater effect) when the target is 400 rather than 600, yet the payoff—winning—is the same. And the MWC analysis does not differentiate a coalition of three from a coalition of two, even though the former is presumably harder to pull off, needing as it does the willingness of two candidates to withdraw rather than one.

Given what is known about coalition formation, it is disappointing to find convention participants so inept at it in practice. A skillful Camp leadership would, one would think, devote a portion of its resources, starting months before the convention, to possible coalition strategies to be used if a first ballot is inconclusive. To maximize its ability to shift its members en masse to a single other candidate, it would work on developing Camp cohesion (perhaps especially inter-State cohesion) going well beyond the easy bonding of loyalty to the Camp's own candidate. It would develop a sense of the numbers needed to exercise at least a minimum of degree of coalition-forming power; in our illustration, at least 400. It would have a communications procedure "at the ready" for quick and effective negotiating with other camps in the breathtakingly short time for action between ballots. It would have clear, previously established criteria for what payoff it will demand in return for joining one or another coalition, ranging from insistence on being the coalition's candidate to lesser objectives such as an ambassadorship or cabinet post.

Actual convention experience indicates behavior far shy of this ideal. Wild improvisation is the more likely reality, with hectic unenforced appeals for a coherent shift at best, but more probably a simple devolution to individual delegate second choices.

The greatest potential in a convention for deviance and deviance control to arise is at the point when binding ends; that is, between the first and second ballots if party rules include binding. What sort of group pressure might a Camp exert on a deviant delegate threatening to bolt to another candidate at the same time the Camp's leader still intends to remain in the race? And how consciously do Camps anticipate the problem, develop tactics to deal with it? These are interesting questions to speculate about in the abstract. But there has yet to be a convention featuring both binding and a second ballot. What we know about delegates bound to Carter in 1980—people the Kennedy Camp desperately hoped included significant numbers of potential defectors—suggests that Camp delegates are, on the contrary, highly reliable loyalists, and that handling deviation need not be a significant Camp preoccupation.

THE BANDWAGON

Lack of careful contingency planning for coalition building beyond the first ballot abets one of the more notorious phenomena of some conventions—the bandwagon effect. A bandwagon is coalition building driven beyond rational calculation to produce, usually, a mandate greater than justified by underlying delegate predisposition. It leaves also-ran Camps on the short end with less payoff (ambassadorships, cabinet posts, etc.) than their years of effort and first-ballot strength warrant. The effect is, in short, largely (but not entirely) irrational, attributable at least in part to "deindividuation" (see Chapter 3) in a setting variously characterizable as a crowd or a mob.

In a bandwagon, delegates shift their votes from their first preference to the one person they urgently sense is on the verge of winning the nomination. For an individual delegate, the psychology of the moment may include any or all of the following: excitement, fear, euphoria, catharsis, panic, resignation. In some instances, jumping on the bandwagon *may* be an emotinally healthy transitional act moving a delegate from Camp loyalty to what he or she knows lies at the end of the convention: the ritual of unanimity.

For a Camp's leadership, the bandwagon engine is fueled not just by such irrationalities as panic but also by a rational imperative: not to end up superfluous to the emerging winner's coalition. (For instance, using our illustration in Table 7.2: if C, not to be third on board, after A and D have already coalesced.)

The vulnerability of conventions to bandwagons is, of course, exacerbated by the rumor-cultivating communications context described earlier.

THE RITUAL OF UNANIMITY

The penultimate group phenomenon (to consider it a group *decision* is stretching things a bit) is the nomination by unanimous acclamation of the person who has already won the hard way. This ritual gives individuals an enormous emotional satisfaction (and a hoarse voice to show for it), an experience repeated when the nominee makes his acceptance speech. For the winning Camp, and to a somewhat lesser degree the convention as a Whole, the acclamation is highly functional, creating the "united front" mentioned in Chapter 2. Given the intensely divided and competitive sentiments of the convention at its start, the Whole convention needs all the cohesion it can possibly muster before heading home.

HEADING HOME

Ironically, the final group phenomenon associated with the convention is one reinforcing its least significant group—the State delegation. Returning to their homes, delegates rediscover that "home" is the organizing rationale of State delegations. Many find themselves on the same plane or bus—localist attachments revived, Camp zealotry probably exhausted, and only one remaining decision to be reached: window or aisle.

Efficiency and Fairness

Is the underlying conviction defensible, that out of this process— the complex, uneven, sometimes boisterous, often boring, unquestionably imperfect process—emerges Jefferson's right decision? Or, more modestly, can it be said that the process meets the standards proposed in Chapter 1, of efficiency and fairness?

It could be argued that conventions are reasonably efficient. After all, they last for only a few days, and, since early in this century, for only a few ballots at the very most. They move quickly from sharp competition to, at the end, deafening shouts of heartfelt union. And they seem to exhibit careful development and analysis of decision alternatives. But the reason that the virtues of both speed and care can be claimed is, of course, the fact that the "development and analysis of alternatives" starts long, long before the convention itself takes place. The nomination process in its entirety, of which the convention is only the brief culmination, is highly *in*efficient, as any candidate, past or present, successful or not, will gladly affirm.

Whether convention decisions are *fair* is uniquely testable. The proof is in the pudding: the reasonable showing of the candidate in the November general election. By and large, the parties have selected well; for example, despite cries of "unfair," the choices of Eisenhower in 1952 and Humphrey in 1968 were stronger ones than the candidates preferred by the criers. The McGovern and Goldwater choices stand out just because they are exceptions. In short, the fairness answer seems to lie in the basic Downsian analysis that began this chapter, while the more particularistic examination of the convention in action with which we have concluded indicates room for innovation and improvement in the pursuit of efficiency.

Recommendations

To gain fuller efficiency, a number of recommendations emerge from our exposition and analysis of how nominations are made. One is to reduce the role of primaries in delegate selection. The parties might agree to limit the number of state presidential primaries to that sufficient to designate a maximum of 40% to 50% of the convention's delegates—the remainder to be chosen at state conventions. States holding primaries could be rotated from one presidential election year to the next. Delegates chosen by primaries could and should be bound for the first ballot; but delegates selected by state conventions should not be. To further encourage the interactive processes that are the strength of conventions, the definition of winning the nomination should be set at 65% on the first ballot, and then reduced to 50% by the fourth ballot, as discussed earlier.

To free a party to select *any* person as, presumably, its strongest candidate (as well as for reasons which transcend our concerns here), incumbent presidents should be permitted to run for three or more consecutive terms; that is, the two-term limitation imposed by the 22nd Amendment should be repealed. To facilitate calmer, more rational decision making, conventions should be lengthened. No more than one ballot should take place per day (at least until four ballots have been cast), with a minimum of say twelve hours between the end of one and the start of the next.

The mechanics of communication need vast improvement—among other ways, along the lines suggested in passing in this chapter. Given the enormous advances in electronic communication techniques in recent years, all that is needed is some ingenuity, the will, and alas, lots of money.

Finally, convention participants—officers, candidates, managers, delegates, even media commentators—need somehow to acquire heightened knowledge of and skill in coalition formation. In the continuing evolution of the professionalism of campaign management and election consulting, it is possible that in the future the presidential nomination process will reflect such knowledge and skill, bringing this particular form of large group decision making to a new, impressive level of efficiency and fairness.

Notes

1. A third, caucuses, is not analyzed here; caucuses are, in effect, conventions, the "delegates" for which are self-selected. Any person registered in the party may show up, participate, and vote for nominees.

2. The illustration is derived from a discussion of the Electoral College by Steven Brams (1978).

References

Brams, S. J. *The presidential election game.* New Haven, CT: Yale University Press, 1978.

Campbell, A., et al. *The American voter.* New York: John Wiley, 1960.

Converse, P. E. The nature of belief systems in mass publics. In D. Apter (Ed.), *Ideology and discontent.* New York: Free Press, 1964.

Downs, A. *An economic theory of democracy.* New York: Harper & Row, 1957.

Flanigan, W., & Zingale, N. *Political behavior of the American electorate.* Boston: Allyn and Bacon, 1979.

Hotelling, H. Stability in competition. *The Economic Journal,* 1929, 39, 41-57.

Kovenock, D., et al. *Explaining the vote* (Vol. 1). Chapel Hill, NC: Institute for Research in Social Science, 1973.

Ladd, C. E. *American political parties.* New York: Norton, 1970.

Nie, N., & Anderson, K. Mass belief systems revisited: Political change and attitude structure. *Journal of Politics,* 1974, f36, 540-587.

Page, B. *Choices and echoes in presidential elections.* Chicago: University of Chicago Press, 1978.

Smithies, A. Optimum location in spatial competition. *The Journal of Political Economy,* 1941, 49, 423-439.

Sullivan, D., et al. *The politics of representation.* New York: St. Martin's, 1974.

CHAPTER 8

GROUP DECISIONS AND FOREIGN POLICY

John S. Gibson

High officials in governments of all nations daily make decisions concerning relations between their states and others in the international system of nation states. We may be familiar with foreign policies of the United States, the Soviet Union, and other nations great or small, but we generally have little understanding of the *processes* that shaped those policies. Central to those processes are deliberations by individuals and groups of governing officials, who consider options and alternatives on international issues, and then make decisions. Once these decisions are approved by "higher-ups," they are converted into official state policy. An enlightened understanding of organizational structures and processes that lead to policy, especially the roles played by groups in shaping policy, is as important as understanding policy itself.

We focus in this chapter on group inputs and decision making in the shaping of United States foreign policy. We begin with an appraisal of structures and groups in the governing system of the United States that determine policy, and then analyze the dynamics of decision making. Emphasis is placed on decisions to meet three kinds of foreign policy situations: crisis situations, protracted or extended security issues, and the routine or programmed issues essential to all kinds of international relations. We then examine the basic steps in the decision-making process that lead to official policy and conclude with some prescriptions for enlightened group decision making in an open society.

Case studies on foreign policy decisions abound, with crisis situations and ensuing policy tending to dominate the electronic and printed media and the scholarly literature. Situations such as the

Iranian hostage crisis in 1979 to 1981 and decisions by the United States to escalate military activity in Central America in the summer of 1983 naturally comand attention because of the deep concerns about the issues affecting national security.

Decision making by President John F. Kennedy and his closest advisers during the Cuban missile crisis of October 1962 produced excellent case studies of crisis decision making, several of which will be cited in this chapter. But protracted and routine problems in foreign policy, while deemed less newsworthy than crises, nonetheless command the attention of thousands of individual and group decision makers. As a case study of such a situation, let us turn to the "European pipeline."

The oil crisis of 1973 and 1974, and especially the sudden quadrupling of the price of oil caused great concern in Western Europe, which relies extensively on Middle East oil for its energy needs. In order to augment its supplies of energy, the Europeans turned to the prospect of purchasing natural gas from the Soviet Union. By the mid-1980s, gas would be piped some 3,700 miles from Siberia to such Western European states as West Germany, France, Italy, the Netherlands, Belgium, and Austria. Contracts were signed for future gas deliveries between these states and the USSR with more than $200 billion involved in payments before the end of the twentieth century. Further, contracts were signed by several states including France, Italy, and Great Britain with the Soviet Union for Soviet purchase of Western technology and piping for construction of the pipeline. Some of this technology included United States exports to Europe as well as technology components licensed by the United States for further construction in Europe. In the mid-1970s, all of these transactions were considered routine or programmatic within the context of standard trade and licensing policies designed to broaden trade relations mutually beneficial to all parties. Clearly the vast majority of international relations and transactions are routine, not generally related to security issues, and designed to further the well-being of nations involved in such transactions.

With the Soviet intervention into Afghanistan in late 1979, United States officials made decisions to impose sanctions on the USSR for its aggressive policies. Among sanctions imposed by President Carter were embargoes on grain shipments to the Soviet Union and nonparticipation by the United States in the 1980 Moscow Olympics. Congress joined the president in tangibly condemning the Soviet Union with the passage in 1979 of the Export Administration

Act that restricts exports of material such as technology, deemed to adversely affect the security of the United States. This act also could preclude other nations such as France from exporting sensitive technology and United States licensed material to the USSR.

In December 1981, President Reagan invoked the 1979 act by banning American technology being sold to the USSR for pipeline construction. He held that the pipeline was dangerous to Western and United States security because it would earn hard currency for the Soviet Union and it would render the Western European states dependent on the USSR for a major source of energy which could be turned off at any time. Further, he argued that the actions of the Soviet Union in supporting the oppressive martial law in Poland as well as its aggressions in Afghanistan demanded that the United States seek all means to deny to Russia goods and services it might use to increase its own military and economic strength.

The Western European states disagreed, as did many groups in the United States. The Europeans argued that the pipeline construction and the sale and purchase of the natural gas would be beneficial to all, that only a small percentage of energy needs of Europe would be met by the Siberian natural gas, and that the American action only embittered rather than punished the Soviet Union. They argued that President Reagan's interpretation of "security" and threats to security was too intensely anti-Soviet.

For the Western Europeans, "security" was more identified with options for energy sources other than Middle East oil. A number of American firms engaged in technology exports agreed with the European perspective and were in opposition to what they felt were undue restrictive aspects of the Export Administration Act.

Much controversy was thus stirred by the American president's decision and definition of national security both within the United States and abroad. Tensions increased on June 18, 1982, when President Reagan issued a ban on technology licensed by the United States but manufactured in Europe for export to the Soviet Union. Certain European firms and subsidiaries of American firms in Europe now faced denial of trade with the United States and even possible fines and criminal penalties. On July 22, 1982, France told its firms to go ahead and produce technology with United States components and on the 24th, Italy said in no way would it sever any technology contracts with the Soviet Union. Early in August, the United Kingdom ordered its companies to honor contract on technology trade with the USSR and on August 12, 1982, the European

Economic Community issued a formal protest to the United States, declaring the United States policy was an unacceptable intrusion into European manufacture and trade policy.

Late in August, however, a United States federal court upheld the constitutionality of the act. President Reagan ordered immediate sanctions against a subsidiary (Dressser France) of a United States firm (Dresser Industries), and also against a French firm (Creusot-Loire) for the fact that Dresser France had built and sold three pipeline compressors to Creusot-Loire, which then shipped this technology to the Soviet Union. A routine and programmatic foreign policy issue now entered the domain of a security issue as perceived by the United States, and was beginning to reach crisis proportions in that the Western European states were defying the wishes of their strongest partner in NATO. By late fall, however, President Reagan was persuaded that his sanctions against the European firms and American subsidiaries in Europe were probably damaging the security of the United States more in weakening NATO than harming the Soviet Union by seeking to embargo pipeline technology. The sanctions were therefore lifted in November 1982.

In the United States, as we shall see, the president has prime authority in foreign policy decision making. However, he is advised by many groups within the executive branch and is constitutionally obliged to carry out legislation passed by Congress, which itself is a group within many subgroups. In the pipeline case, President Reagan's decisions resulted from three inputs: groups demands and advice within the nation, groups and events external to the nation, and the president's own definition of the issue and what is required for national security and well-being.

Groups within the United States agreeing and advising the president on the pipeline embargo included the Department of Defense and its secretary, Casper Weinberger, and those in Congress and throughout the nation who felt technology trade injured the United States by helping the Soviet Union. Groups opposed to the full extent of the embargo policy were the Department of State and its then-secretary, Alexander M. Haig, and groups viewing the embargo as counter-productive and damaging to United States relations with its close allies in Europe. Also opposed, naturally, were the many firms selling technology to Europe and the Soviet Union. No other nation in the external realm supported the United States in this policy. However, the policy was in close conformity with the president's own theory and hard position vis-à-vis the USSR—this, combined with the perception that economic ties between Russia and Europe damaged Western security and that the embargo was also one way of punishing the Soviet Union for its policies in Poland. Those advising the president to lift the sanctions prevailed, especially George Shultz, the new Secretary of State, who was warned by the Europeans that the president's policy was incorrect by virtually every measure of what determines national security and well-being. We will return later to some lessons of this case study.

Group Decisions and Foreign Policy: The Uniqueness of the United States

There is tremendous diversity among nations with respect to numbers and kinds of people making foreign policy decisions. Groups *make* foreign policy where there is an identifiable group, such as the Cabinet in the British parliamentary system, that tends to make, and jointly share responsibility for, foreign policy decisions. Such is generally the case in all parliamentary systems of government. Socialist nations such as the Soviet Union tend to arrive at decisions through a collective or collegial process, while juntas in authoritarian governments and top-level elite groups in other states often make collective decisions.

The United States, our exclusive focus of study in this chapter, is quite different. The Constitution of the United States in Article II delegates to the president authority, responsibility, and accountability for making the principal decisions in this nation's quest for security and well-being in the international system of states. When he takes the oath of office at noon on January 20th every fourth year, he assumes or renews specific powers in foreign policy shared with no other in government. The most important of these powers are his executive authority as the nation's chief executive officer, role as commander in chief of the nation's military, appointive and treaty-making power, his obligation to receive all foreign ambassadors and requirement that he commission all officers of the United States, and his authority to recommend legislation to Congress for conversion into policy and law.

Clearly the Congress, especially the Senate, has significant authority, such as in appropriations, investigations, impeachment, and other Constitutional obligations. In the process of making treaties, the American president must negotiate both with other nations and the United States Senate, which has the constitutional authority to give advice and consent before a treaty can be ratified by the United States. President Carter won in his negotiations with the Senate on the 1977 treaty with Panama concerning the Canal, and lost in his quest to have the senate approve the second Strategic Arms Limitation Treaty. Senate authority with respect to appointments is another power affecting foreign policy shared with the president. Other congressional authority such as giving approval to major sales of arms reflects presidential limitations in foreign policy decision making. The close November 1981 vote in the Congress concerning the sale of the Air Warning and Communications planes to Saudi Arabia reflects profound differences between some members of Congress and the executive on on foreign policy goals and processes. Among the many issues that have divided the Reagan administration and the Congress as the Reagan "midterm" was that of support the administration apparently wants to give for the destabilization of the Sandinista government in Nicaragua. To emphasize its opposition to such intrusion in Central American affairs, the House of Representatives voted in late December 1982, and again in July 1983, against providing military equipment, training advice, or other support for overthrowing the government of Nicaragua or for provoking a military exchange between Nicaragua and Honduras (*Time,* December 23, 1982; *Time,* July 28, 1983). In this manner, and through other prohibitive enactments, the Congress can certainly affect foreign policy.

The process of group decision making in Congress in the vast array of its committees and subcommittees and the important informal processes of bargaining and trade-offs is part of the total picture of group decision making in the United States government. However, as important as Congress is, the president usually gets what he wants, usually makes certain he has the votes before placing critical issues before Congress, seeks to employ his political leverage in steering group decisions his way, and remains as the key figure in Congress in the shaping of foreign policy. This is the case because, explicitly and implicitly, the Congress recognizes the constitutional authority of the president in the external realm.

Such is not the case, of course, in distinctively domestic issues where the Constitution delegates significant leadership and initiatory powers to Congress that the president cannot ignore. Further, in domestic policy, power must be shared by the courts and by state and local governments. Thus, in such areas as taxation, appropriations, fiscal and monetary policy, social and welfare issues, education, protection, and a realm of other governmental concerns, the interplay and responsibilities among many government structures and decision-making groups, renders domestic policy much less under the control of the White House.

Too often, however, domestic and foreign policy are viewed and studied as if they were in two different compartments. Excluding state and local governments, United States domestic and foreign policy are made by the same officials—both seek security and well-being for national interests, both draw upon the same pool of money, and both usually have many interconnections and dependencies that render false a separation between the two. Demands of the military on tax revenues directly affect money available for domestic policies and services. Production of steel, cars, and wheat is interwoven with domestic and foreign concerns, resources, and markets.

Foreign policy does have, of course, some of its own attributes. Officials within the nation have less control over the various factors affecting foreign policy than those in the domestic realm, since their authority is bounded by sovereign limits of their nation and the generally inviolable sovereignty of others. They cannot control adversaries and must cooperate in varying degrees with policies of allies as, for example, in the implanting of American missiles in Western Europe. Any foreign policy, however, has profound and compelling internal or domestic influences.

The categoric Constitutional role of the president, the separation of powers at the federal level, the federal structure of governance, and many other factors—including its comparative isolation in world affairs for about three-fourths of its national history—combine to make decision making on foreign policy in the United States quite unique among nations. We now turn to other singular facets of groups and decisions on American foreign policy.

Executive Branch Groups: Structures and Authority

"Reagan ponders lonely decision—with lots of help." This headline (*New York Times,* January 9, 1982) captures the essence of decisions in the United States on foreign policy issues. The president and only the president has the constitutional authority to convert advice and recommendations into official policy through the process of a decision. It is, indeed, a lonely condition, and while he has "lots of help," the responsibility and accountability are his and his alone for the decision and the ensuing policy.

The "lots of help" comes from the hundreds of departments, agencies, commissions, and other bureaucratic structures in the executive branch of government having some authority to consider and make recommendations on issues relating to foreign policy. The Constitution, while declaring that the "executive-power shall be vested in the President of the United States," is almost silent as to who shall assist the president in that enormous task. The Constitution mentions in Article II that the president "may require the opinion of the principal officer in each of the executive departments," which only emphasizes the exclusivity of the president in formulating national policy. "The opinion" of principal officers is input into policy by individuals and groups, both of which are indispensable for the president to carry out his awesome constitutional tasks.

Three points must be emphasized before turning to specific groups or governmental structures. How each president uses input from individuals and groups varies greatly. This becomes particularly clear when we appraise the principal policy group, the National Security Council. Because the Constitution is so specific about the singular authority of the president in foreign policy in the executive branch, each president is free to determine what is meant by requiring "the opinion of the principal officer in each of the executive departments." Secondly, we are not here concerned with inputs by individuals, whether in or out of government, in the president's determinations. Throughout the history of the United States, the president's decisions have been influenced by views and recommendations of a wide variety of individuals. The president always has the need for seeking individuals' opinions and recommendations and there are many who, whether sought out by the president or not, have felt free to offer advice. However, it is the official group, group processes, and group interactions that we are concerned with in this analysis. Finally, we say *official* because we are only concerned with groups in structures of the executive branch of government. We are not examining important groups such as vested interest groups, boards of corporations, or the Executive Committee of the AFL-CIO.

EXECUTIVE OFFICE OF THE WHITE HOUSE

The basic groups in the executive branch influencing the president are the officials in the executive office of the White House, the National Security Council, the executive departments, especially State and Defense, and the hundreds of other agencies such as the Central Intelligence Agency, the United States Information Agency, the Nuclear Energy Commission, and the International Trade Commission.

The executive office of the White House is essentially the group of advisers to the president that varies with each presidency. In the Reagan administration, the chief titles include Counsellor to the President, Chief of Staff, Deputy Chief of Staff, and a variety of presidential assistants. If we turn to studies of various presidencies, such as that of Theodore Sorenson (1963), we can gain a fairly good understanding of how these presidential intimates, as individuals and as groups, advise the president. But the executive office as such is hardly a formal group; it is rather an aggregate of people who are quite close to the president and his thinking and on whom he relies for daily inputs of information and advice in the constant process of decision making.

Executive office officials are particularly important in our study as they are the individuals who most clearly screen or filter input to the president. Many groups make recommendations; however, the presidential intimates in the White House process and judge input prior to its being received by the president. Presidential assistants may keep from the president input at variance with the president's thinking. President Johnson was not very receptive to view contrary to his own and his National Security Adviser, W. W. Rostow, usually was quite careful in screening information coming to the Oval Office that President Johnson might find incompatible with his thinking. On the other hand, President Kennedy eagerly sought group input from all sources, whether congenial to his thinking or not. One has the impression that President Reagan has information coming to him carefully screened by his immediate associates who have had delegated to them more screening and advisory authority than any White House group in recent history. Clearly,, how input from any source are conveyed to the president is at the discretion of each president.

NATIONAL SECURITY COUNCIL

The principal advisory group to the president in the vital area of national security is the National Security Council (NSC). Established by the National Security Act of 1947, the NSC is comprised of the president, vice president, and secretaries of state and defense. Its membership also generally includes the director of the Central Intelligence Agency, the chairman of the Joint Chiefs of Staff, the director of the Arms Control and Disarmament Agency, and other officials, when specific areas of policy relate to their responsibilities. The NSC has a series of committees to work on such functional areas as intelligence, covert activities, arms control, and crisis management. Committee members usually are cabinet or subcabinet officers. The NSC's chief administrative officer is the assistant to the president for National Security Affairs and he supervises a staff of about sixty experts in many areas of foreign policy and regions of the world.

The NSC was originally created to help the president plan, coordinate, and evaluate national security policy, given the global responsibilities assumed by the United States following World War II. Presidents Truman and Eisenhower relied more on strong secretaries of state and the cabinet for foreign policy advice and the NSC really came into its own with President Kennedy and his successors. The Assistant to the president for National Security Affairs (the "adviser"), the chief executive officer of the council, has more contact with the president than any other official in the foreign policy process and, with few exceptions in terms of personalities, is the most influential adviser to the President. Thus, the NSC as (1) a gathering of high officials and (2) the personal bureaucracy of the adviser is the most important single group structure in government in foreign policy decision making.

Each president determines the extent to which the NSC, as a group, is central to his authority. Some presidents such as Truman, Eisenhower, Nixon (in his last two years), and Ford drew upon strong secretaries of state and less on the NSC for the prime input into policy determination. Presidents Kennedy and Nixon (1969 to 1972) relied extensively on the assistant to the president for National Security Affairs, and thus, on the NSC to advise and coordinate foreign policy. The National Security Council and especially the adviser, William P. Clark, are probably more influential over

President Reagan than is Secretary of State Shultz and his department in terms of policy inputs to presidential decisions.

Although we turn later to the NSC as a government structure in which group decisions take place, we must mention the special role of the assistant to the president for National Security Affairs. Individuals chosen by the president have become household names in the past twenty years, largely because of the influence they have had on presidential decisions. The adviser does seek collegial patterns of policy and consideration from the NSC staff and committees of the council, but usually has been such a forceful person that group decision making often amounts to a ratification of the main policy sought by the adviser and the president. McGeorge Bundy for Presidents Kennedy and Johnson, Walt Rostow for President Johnson, Henry Kissinger for President Nixon, and Zbigniew Brzezinski for President Carter were strong, articulate, and broad-gauged advisers who had the confidence and support of the president. The controversy over Adviser Richard Allen in the Reagan administration was, in part, due to the fact that Dr. Allen had a role subordinate to the White House staff and did not have the clout or presidential support to plan or coordinate policy in any manner compared to his predecessors. In brief, the other advisers orchestrated groups and committees fairly effectively in collegial processes as input into decisions while Dr. Allen's role was confused, but certainly subordinate to other officials who dominated access to President Reagan.

THE CABINET

The presidential cabinet, comprised of chief executive officers of the major departments in the executive branch and a few others at the discretion of the president, has been a fixture in deliberations on national policy since the administration of George Washington. Each president determines for himself the extent to which the cabinet, as a group, becomes involved in policy deliberations. Some presidents have convened the Cabinet regularly and some others have virtually ignored it as a collegial decision-making group. The principal obstacle to the Cabinet's serving of this function, especially in foreign policy issues, is that each cabinet official is the chief officer of a vast bureaucracy, the problems of which, in terms of policy areas, are not those of the person sitting on each side of the

Cabinet Room at the White House. This is particularly the case since World War II when the United States' global responsibilities so significantly expanded, and when the intricate and manifold foreign policy issues demanded decision-making deliberation by those equipped with education and experience with high levels of expertise.

THE DEPARTMENTS OF STATE AND DEFENSE

The two principal departments with foreign policy responsibilities are clearly the Department of State and the Department of Defense. However, as we shall see, all other departments whose chiefs sit collectively in the presidential cabinet have today a variety of foreign policy responsibilities. Each department has its own "department of state" as foreign policy issues increasingly merge with domestic issues and policy in the total frame of national policy.

State and Defense have specific and traditional responsibilities and often collide in exercising their authority under the aegis of the president. State, historically, is responsible for the management of day-to-day relations between the United States and all other nations, as well as American concerns in the vast array of international organizations. Wired into State are all our missions and diplomatic structures abroad that carry out routine policy and relations, report back to State conditions and issues in all nations, and represent the president in negotiations and communication with officials in other governments. Defense, formed in 1947 as a merger of the former Department of War and Navy, administers a vast two hundred billion dollar-plus worldwide military apparatus, formulates basic military doctrine, mobilizes resources to meet military objectives, and through the secretary, advises the president on all aspects of military issues and crisis management.

State, Defense, and the National Security Council, as group structures in which foreign policy decisions are made, are often in the unfortunate position of competing with each other because each has different responsibilities. State is largely concerned with establishing and sustaining amicable relations with the maximum number of states in the international system, understanding other states' problems and policies, and seeking to harmonize United States aspirations toward security and well-being with similar aspirations by most other states. Defense is essentially concerned with defense and security affairs and tends to view international relations from the vantage point of quests for security and threats to American security, real or imagined. With few exceptions, the adviser for National Security Affairs is closer to the president than are the secretaries of State and Defense, sees the president much more often than the secretaries, and basically seeks to protect the president from positions at variance with the president's personal perspective on world affairs. The adviser can generally appraise issues that affect the president's foreign or domestic policies and, in general, is the president's man rather than one representative of the central mission of State or Defense.

Each of these three groups may define security and well-being in different ways, depending on the basic orientation and respon-sibilities of each group. In the European pipeline case, the secretary of state advised the president that the American embargo of tech-nology to the Soviet Union was harming United States security interests and relations with the European allies. The secretary of defense argued that the embargo was necessary to punish the Soviet Union for its behavior in Poland and to deny Western technology to the Soviets. The national security adviser in this case sided with the secretary of state and thus President Reagan lifted the embargo. Decisions always involve a costs-benefits judgment, with each group seeking to persuade the president that its perception of the issue has greater benefits than costs vis-à-vis the central policy goals of security and well-being.

Thus, "groups" and individuals in groups in foreign policy struc-tures are oriented toward the larger responsibility of the agency or bureaucracy. This was vividly demonstrated on the day after the presidential election in 1980, when officials at the Department of Defense toasted the election of Ronald Reagan with champagne, while those at State expressed concerns and were hardly as jubilant. This only reflects the happiness at Defense with the election of a hard-liner on Soviet relations, and one who clearly would support higher Defense expenditures, and those at State who saw in Ronald Reagan's foreign policy views, at that time, little concern for the broad sweep of foreign policies, arms control agreements, or problems relating to the new states in Africa and Asia.

Group structures at State and Defense are reflected in the organizational breakdown of both huge bureaucracies. The Office of International Organization Affairs at State and its assistant secretarycomprise a group advising the secretary and then the president on policy and decisions—often votes—in the vast array of international organizations of which the United States is a member. The Research and Engineering Division at Defense and its assistant secretary make up a group to develop and recommend policy on the production, procurement, and use of military hardware. The functional groups in all bureaucracies and their own subdivisions constantly engage in research, deliberations on policy, policy recommendations, and supports for these recommendations that move upward, ultimately to the White House.

Groups, therefore, do not make final decisions, but only group decisions that, in turn, are recommendations to higher authority. The basic exception to this observation are those decisions that are routine, not requiring day-to-day surveillance from higher officials. At the U.S. Information Agency, to give an example, the International Visitor Division can make decisions and announce policy on all kinds of issues affecting the official visitors coming to the United States, selected by our embassies abroad, and who are in this country for about thirty days to see and be seen. These, some 2,400 official visitors, are actual or prospective leaders from a variety of nations whose official visit to the United States is considered to be an important contribution to future good relations between the United States and other nations. It would be impossible for high authorities in the bureaucracies to supervise routine foreign policy issues, decision making, and policy implementation and thus, in reality, groups in major agencies not "at the top" have many delegated responsibilities and authority.

However, routine issue group decision making must be within the general framework of the definitions of national security and well-being emanating from the White House and this is the most important observation about group decision activity in the executive branch bureaucracies. Decision *recommendations* made by groups flow upward to the top in the important issues of foreign policy. Decision makers must take cues from superiors and function within the framework of what is understood to be the appropriate boundaries of definitions of security and well-being of national interests. Individual participation in group deliberations and policy recommendations is tempered by the fact that one's upward mobility and job security depend on staying within the bounds of the White House's view of the world, loyalty to superiors and to one's own department (e.g., State, Defense), and professionalism in the execution of one's duties.

Individuals enter the bureaucracy and become socialized by that agency with little opportunity to change the agency's orientation. A young person coming to work at State is expected to be loyal to State and its mission, and perhaps this is even more the case in the Pentagon where military behaviors and concerns demands strict compliance. As one rises the ladder in the bureaucracy, he or she assumes more responsibilities over group deliberations and recommendations and expects the new subordinates likewise to follow leadership and carry out tasks individually or collectively within the framework of overall foreign policy views and determinations as articulated by top leadership.

This all is not to suggest that group activity in foreign policy is a rubber stamp activity. Groups of officials meeting on specific issues, such as East-West trade, whether to install the neutron bomb in Europe, how much security aid should go to Egypt, or content of a Voice of America broadcast to Afghanistan, provide rational and informational input into the shaping of policy *decided* at higher echelons. Policy at the top would be impossible without group deliberations and upward flows of recommendations based on years of experience in foreign policy and international relations. Policy papers, briefings for officials going abroad, contents of treaty proposals, and specifications of military software and hardware are all the products of group meetings and deliberations in the bureaucracies.

OTHER CABINET DEPARTMENTS

All other cabinet departments have some responsibilities in the realm of foreign policy or their own "departments of state." Young people interested in careers with the government in foreign policy formerly considered only the departments of State or Defense or the Foreign Service. Today, foreign policy expertise is required and found in all cabinet departments with the ever expanding reletionships between foreign and domestic policy.

Examples abound. Treasury is concerned with customs, international trade issue, and monetary and financial policy relating to international trade and financing. Justice has authority in dealing with American corporations' operations abroad and antitrust issues, all kinds of international legal issues affecting the United States government, as well as its own Immigration and Naturalization Service and problems relating to the international flow of human beings. Interior is concerned with the nation's internal resources that are vital to the nation's reservoir of power in the international marketplace. Agriculture's International Affairs and Commodity Programs deals with all kinds of food transactions with the wheat sales to the Soviet Union as one key example.

Commerce has authority in maritime affairs, and international trade, and its office of East-West trade works with Agriculture and other agencies in that sensitive area. There is a deputy undersecretary for international affairs in the Department of Labor, and a bureaucracy dealing with labor issues in other nations, especially in assistance programs, the International Labor Organization in Geneva, and a host of issues affecting labor standards and union organizations throughout the world. The Department of Health and Human Services is concerned with international health and welfare problems, and the Department of Housing and Urban Development is also involved in urban issues at home and abroad. The Department of Transportation is the home of the United States Coast Guard. Energy is involved in many kinds of issues in resources, such as oil, which have profound international effects; and Education has long been working on issues of international education and exchanges.

All of this only demonstrates how groups, subgroups, and sub-subgroups in all kinds of federal agencies are involved in decisions and decision making in a vast area of international problems and issues. All of these departments are affiliated with international organizations, including the World Health Organization for Health and Human Services, the Food and Agricultural Organization for Agriculture, and the World Bank for Treasury. Most departments have officials working in United States missions or embassies abroad, especially in aid programs. All are under the overall supervision of the White House, function within the delegated policy guidelines of the president, and are accountable to the White House for all decisions and policy. Clearly, a study of groups and foreign policy in the American bureaucracy is a formidable task.

OTHER EXECUTIVE AGENCIES

Intelligence is a vital part of the foreign policy bureaucracy, but one that does not lend itself well to group policymaking, although groups of many kinds deliberate and recommend policy. We have in the "Intelligence Community" the Central Intelligence Agency, the Defense Intelligence Agency, the National Security Agency, and also the Bureau of Intelligence and Research (in the Department of State). Intelligence operations restate our basic observation that the more sensitive the foreign policy issue, the more authoritarian is the decision making—authoritarian in the sense that policy is made at the top, but on the basis of individual and group deliberations and recommendations as input up and down the bureaucratic ladder.

Among the dozens of other agencies is the United States information agency for global information about the United States, the Voice of America, educational exchanges, and many other informational and cultural aspects of policy. There are important commissions, such as the International Trade Commission and the Nuclear Regulatory Commission. The National Aeronautics and Space Administration has obvious international ramifications, as do the United States Trade Representative and the Council of Economic Advisers.

The Office of Management and Budget (OMB), headed by David Stockman under the Reagan administration, has extensive authority in foreign policy given its executive responsibilities over department budgets. OMB must approve of all budgets of bureaucracies before they go to Congress for deliberation and approval, is involved in the congressional hearings on all budgets, and also supervises the bureaucracy's spending of money during the fiscal year. In this manner, OMB, working directly under the president's supervision, is the central coordinating agency of the executive branch from the point of view of budget policy. However, decisions in OMB, based as they are on budget issues and constraints, usually are not concerned with policy per se, but rather with money. Here we have central decision making that often deals with finances and management, but not with the factual and issue-oriented problems of foreign policy. There is no necessary correlation here, and probably elsewhere, between the foreign policy affecting of decision makers and their authority to make decisions directly affecting the nation's quest for security and well-being in the international market-place.

This is the informational framework for foreign policy decision making in the executive branch. The president is the top authority and his views, ideology, and guidelines for policy prevail. Each president determines his own mode of operation and who his most intimate policy advisers are. Presidential appointees dominate the government agencies. While members of the foreign service and the civil service provide the bulk of federal personnel, they are constrained to follow the guidelines and policy orientation of the leader. Decisions may proceed up and down the organizational structure of the agency, and much authority is delegated by bureau chiefs to subgroups in the agency. However, decisions made by groups must be in harmony with the policy positions at the top. Decisions are informative and recommendatory, but rarely ones that really are converted into policy at levels below the top. The principal exception to this observation are decisions and policy that are routine and are generally made and managed by officials with delegated authority.

Group Decision Making and Varieties of Foreign Policy Issues

The *kind* of issue concerned with foreign policy generally dictates the structure and dynamics of group decision making. Crisis or direct security issues, protracted security issues, and routine or "programmatic" issues each have categories characteristics that tend to define the size of the group making decisions, the time frame for making decisions, flows of information for making decisions, and nonofficials or "outside" input into the decision-making arena.[1] Crisis or immediate security decisions arise when an immediate crisis is at hand or there is a perceived and/or direct threat to the nation's security. The North Korean invasion of June 1950, and the Tet offensive in Vietnam in January 1968, are cases in point. Protracted security decisions relate to the security of the nation over a period of time beyond an immediate crisis. The United States-USSR confrontation over decades or the Middle East series of hot and cold war are cases in point. Routine issue decisions, as we have noted, deal with trade relations, necessary treaties and commitments, daily operations of United States missions in other nations, decisions and votes in hundreds of official international organizations, appropriations for foreign aid, and many other commonplace but necessary and important issues.

Most research on foreign policy decision making concentrates on the immediate security-threat situations or "crisis decision making." Inadequate attention has been given to relationships between "crisis" and routine or protracted security issues that always precede a "crisis." About 95% of foreign policy decision making and relations between nations are in the domain of routine issues that generally are concerned with the nation's pursuit of "well-being" as a foreign policy goal, as compared to the quest for security that marks the protracted and immediate security issues.

Not only do we need more scholarship on routine protracted security issues and decision making, but we also must better understand that immediate security issues arise out of the continuum of issues from routine to protracted to the immediate. As we shall see later, in the routine or protracted phases of any issue, much can be done to reduce the likelihood of the issue moving on to crisis—much can be done to either plan for the crisis contingency or to reduce possibilities of the emergence of the immediate threat or crisis.

Graham Allison's *Essence of Decision: Explaining the Cuban Missile Crisis* (1971) is a penetrating analysis of perhaps the most important crisis issue of the post-World War II period. However, the focus is almost solely on the crisis with very little on this issue's routine phase from the Spanish American War to the advent of the Castro administration of January, 1959, or the protracted security period from that time to the United States discovery of the Soviet missiles in Cuba on Monday, October 15, 1962.

For the United States, Korea was a routine or almost nonexistent issue prior to the end of World War II, but became a protracted security issue with the division and occupation of North Korea by the Soviets and the South by the United States in 1945. The crisis erupted on June 25, 1950, but reverted to protracted with the 1953 armistice. Vietnam is another example of routine to protracted to several crises and back to a protracted security issue after 1975. The European pipeline situation began as clearly programmatic or routine but entered the protracted security domain when the United States related the pipeline to its security interests upon the Soviet incursion into Afghanistan and the worsening situation in Poland. It might have reached crisis proportions had the United States insisted on its embargo of technology and enforcement of its penalties for European technology to the USSR or its European allies. It is a wise decision maker who can see ahead of time that a protracted security situation might become a major crisis unless judicious measures are taken. In any event, the pipeline issue moved away from crisis and even protracted crisis and back to the routine level, although events may again reverse the process.

What is an immediate security issue for one nation may be only a protracted security issue for an adversary. The Cuban missile "crisis" for the United States was not considered an intense crisis or immediate security situation by the Soviet Union. Of course, the "immediate security threat" was *to* the United States *by* the Soviet Union. When the threatening state does not understand that its actions will evoke a crisis situation in the threatened state, the latter might take counteraction that would elevate the issue to crisis proportions for the threatening state. This would have been the case had President Kennedy ordered the United States armed forces to attack Cuba rather than call for a defensive quarantine of Soviet missile-carrying ships steaming toward Cuba. A military strike may have escalated to a counter-strike upon the United States. Allison's study of this "crisis" demonstrates how President Kennedy moved away from the reciprocal or dual crisis situation and back to a protracted situation where the United States-Cuban relationship remains today. It was the president's handling of the group deliberation process by the executive committee of the National Security Council that brought about the immediate security threat situation to a more acceptable protracted situation.

What is an immediate security issue for one ally may not be for its friend. Egypt's President Nasser nationalized the Suez Canal on July 26, 1956, and this act was perceived as an immediate security crisis by the United Kingdom, but only as a protracted security event by the United States. England's Prime Minister Eden utterly failed to persuade President Eisenhower of the intensity of this matter, which led, eventually, to Eden's resignation as Prime Minister in January, 1957, after his policies to unseat Nasser by use of armed intervention by England, France, and Israel met with total failure. As we have noted, the United States perceived the shipment of Western technology to the USSR as a direct security issue while the Western Europe allies basically disagreed. Clearly, it is advisable for allies to be in central agreement on their definition of security and threats thereto.

Whether a situation is viewed as crisis, protracted, or routine determines the management of the decision making process and thus the dynamics of group participation. Those dynamics include the number and roles of the actors of the decision makers, the time frame and agenda for the decision process, the information flow and base, and input into the decision process from outside the official structure or decision making arena.

Actors, or officials making decisions, all have life experience that have much to do with their behavior when they assume high office. Those experiences and perspectives have a profound impact on how actors and especially presidents act and react in group situations, with generally the more authoritarian personality less willing to draw from group discussion and advice information and direction for making decisions. Strong egos of presidents, such as Lyndon Johnson and Ronald Reagan, forged over many decades, are not always amenable to group processes for shaping decisions.

In general, the more serious the crisis, the more limited the time frame for making decisions, while the more routine the issue, the more spacious the time frame. Timing, or the relation between a decision and a major event such as an election, a vote in the security council, or an alert signaling detonation of a nuclear device, may also be important.

Information is the data base essential for decisions. Information may be sought, offered, or ignored, and its function in group processes is usually subject to close examination and verifiability. Information may be sought from "outside" the specific decision-making group, for example from public opinion polls during routine or protracted situations, or from specialists or experts. As was seen in Chapter 3, during crisis situations, when expert opinion is often most valuable, decision-making groups may insulate themselves as part of the "groupthink" process, resulting in a less than optimal decision. Outside input may also be offered from "opinion publics" such as political interest groups, the media, elites, other nations, and a host of other sources demanding certain decisions or support for the "right" decisions and support withdrawal for the "wrong" decisions. These four major factors in foreign policy group decision making—actors, time, information, and outside input—will now be examined in more detail.

ACTORS

Immediate security issues involve a very small number of actors and always those in the intimate entourage of the president. Scholarship on actors in crisis gives us many case studies of who these people are and how they behave in crisis situations.

Allison's study of the Cuban missile crisis examines three models of decision making: rational, organizational, and bureaucratic. The rational man considers categories of options in response to the threat, as well as the consequences and impact upon others of each option, ranging from doing nothing to a military strike on Cuba. The organizational model examines the decision maker from a specific agency whose input into the decision process represent and reflect his or her bureau's central tasks and orientations. "You stand where you sit," or, "protect your turf." In the pipeline case, the secretary of state perceived the issue from the perspective of diplomacy and harmony among members of the Atlantic Alliance while the secretary of defense was more concerned with denial of Western technology to the USSR, which was viewed as aiding the Soviet military capability. The bureaucratic-political model views decision makers as upwardly mobile political creatures, who may be more concerned with power and status than broader issues, and will therefore tend to act on these concerns.

The president or top official must understand these models of decision making, and thus, roles and perceptions of decision makers in group decision making, because he must evaluate and reconcile options, agency perspective, and political consideration. Further, each of Allison's models has important implications for groups other than those in the decision-making arena. The rational actor model must take into consideration the impact of a specific option-decision on other groups such as Congress, allies, and political interest groups. The organizational model decision, once made, may have an adverse impact on an official's bureaucracy if the official, say from department of defense, voted in a collegial context to support a "soft" reply to the source of a threat. The bureaucratic model decision, once made, may adversely affect an official's future if his contribution to a decision recommendation was at variance with a top official in the White House. The decision maker in the group usually is quite concerned with the anticipated impact of his or her recommendation on important agencies and officials.

Protracted security issues generally involve only actors and groups with specific assignments or concerns in security and regional issues. However, other kinds of groups and actors make their contribution to decision deliberation. Iran's taking of the embassy personnel in Teheran on November 4, 1979, was an immediate security issue for the United States, but it moved into a protracted situation in short order. Actors and groups dealing with how to get the hostages released were, in general, those in security affairs, as well as Middle East specialists. Group deliberation and planning came to a head in April 1980, with the abortive American military incursion in Iran to release the hostages. But others became involved in the Iranian situation, including Americans having business interests in Iran, actors from the United States and other countries at the United Nations, and allies in group deliberations with the United States and its allies. Nevertheless, protracted security issues do involve fewer individuals and groups than do routine issues because the problem is more specific, although economic, political, cultural, and legal factors among others always enter into protracted security situations.

As a rule, routine issues involve many actors and government structures, protracted security issues far few, and immediate security issues, only those at the top. Routine issues cover the broad gamut of international relations and thus necessitate many and varied areas of decision-making expertise. Groups are comprised of people with different backgrounds and bureaucratic responsibilities and obligations. Political and bureaucratic interests compete in decision-making processes and often the actor in the group fights for his or her political and/or bureaucratic interest rather than the national interest.

Should or should not the United States sell wheat to the Soviet Union? This is a routine trade issue for some in the American bureaucracy such as the Department of Agriculture, but a protracted security issue involving United States-Soviet relationships for the United States trade representative in the White House and the office of East-West trade in the Department of Commerce. Agriculture "represents" interests of Midwest farmers who want to sell the wheat, while U.S. trade representative down the hall from the national security advisor in the White House may argue that such trade only strengthens the economy of our adversary. Congressmen may be equally divided. Thus, politics and bureaucratic in-fighting take place in group activities with only the president able to make the final decision. Thus, groups will differ in definitions of the dual goals of foreign policy—threats to national security and needs for national well-being—and these differences are exposed in the large number of officals and groups concerned with routine policy issues.

TIME

The immediate security issue has a tight time frame because action must be taken. In the Cuban missile crisis, if the missiles are there, they must be removed, and immediately. The reciprocal messages between the United States and the Soviet Union during the crisis all had time price tags on them. The pressure of time may have a considerable impact upon the group process because of psychological pressures and understandings of the huge impact of the crisis on national security. Often the very existence of the group, however, bolsters morale, reduces tension by the fact that it is shared, and inclines one not to show his or her real feeling of apprehension. Time may be more generous in the protracted security issue. However, there will always be decision makers seeking support for their view that "time is running short" and that this matter cannot drag on forever. Such was the case in the protracted Iranian hostage crisis with those calling for a military penetration of Teheran to release the hostages as against President Carter's view that time was on the side of the United States. Some declared that the timing of the United States' abortive armed intervention in Iran in April 1980 was dictated by the forthcoming presidential campaign and election. The actual timing of the agreement to release the hostages, only hours before the end of the Carter administration, is another example of the intricate relationship between clocks and decisions. For routine issues, the time frame is generally dictated by the fiscal year, the legislative session and its adjournment, or some other regularly occurring event.

INFORMATION

In the immediate security situation, decisions must be made and the time frame is such that the adequacy of the information base may be less important than reaching and implementing the decision. There may not be enough information, too much information, or flawed information. There usually is never enough information about the intent and capability of the adversary. There may be so much information put forth by group participants that it is exceedingly difficult to sift through it all to identify the critical mass of accurate information. There may be flawed information such as the contention expressed during the April 1961, Bay of Pigs crisis that once the Cuban exiles are landed in Cuba, thousands of Cubans will rise up and overthrow Castro. Director of the United States Information Agency, Edward R. Murrow, had an extensive memorandum based on wide inquiry and fact that the Cubans would not so rise in rebellion, but this memorandum, while in the White House, never got to the president's desk. As was discussed in Chapter 3, groups characterized by premature consensus-seeking ("groupthink") are prone to *select* the information that is most consistent with their preferred solutions.

In the protracted security situation, there is more time to gain more accurate information, but this again depends on who wants what information. President Reagan tends not to go far to gain information or group input on issues for which he feels his knowledge and immediate advisers' views are essentially correct. In a projected Department of Defense budget cut in January 1983, only two or three people were involved in deciding that there should be a freeze on pay for military personnel. As a group, the joint chiefs of staff were not consulted, and when they heard the news, they felt that the cuts should be in weapons and research and not in morale-damaging military pay. Air Force General Charles A. Gabriel declared that "I would have appreciated, as the other chiefs would have, having a part in that [decision-making] process" (*New York Times*, January 14, 1983). Top leadership in Congress also was not consulted, which evoked some strong statements of dissent from Capitol Hill. The question is, then, how much information do you want, and from whom?

In any event, the president and his associates must be extremely careful in gauging the flow of information to and from the decision arena to avoid affecting adversely the decision process or future bargaining situations. In response to a question at a January 1983 news conference about possible arms reductions in Europe, President Reagan turned off the reporter with a no comment. He pointed out that

> here you are getting dangerously into the area that cannot be opened for discussion, which is the tactics of negotiating and the strategy of negotiating. If you discuss that openly, then there is no strategy and you have your hands tied with regard to attaining anything.[2]

As far as routine issues are concerned, information is abundant, open, and usually unclassified, and multifaceted in terms of views and positions.

OUTSIDE INPUT

In the immediate security situation, the doors of the decision-making arena, such as the Cabinet Room of the White House, are usually tightly closed. If there is input outside the realm of officialdom at home and abroad, it is sought rather than freely received. Studies of crisis decision making, such as those of the Cuban missile crisis, have described the processes of accentuating secrecy and sealing off the outside from the processes of decision. ABC Correspondent John Scali, an outsider and, indeed, a gentleman of the press, was solicited to play a key role in the communications process in the Cuban missile crisis. However, such an individual would never be used unless it were quite clear that his or her confidence and discretion were unimpeachable.

In the protracted security situation, outside inputs are often sought by official decision makers and they are received in abundance as well. In late January 1968, President Johnson brought in for consultation a variety of seasoned foreign policy experts from outside of government (although most were former high officials) to advise him on the future course of the war. Their general recommendation was to begin negotiations with North Vietnam and the president accepted that advice. Council on Foreign Relations President Winston Lord was invited by Secretary of State Shultz to bring in a group of specialists on China in January 1983 to advise the secretary on some key issues and trends he should know in detail prior to his forthcoming trip to the People's Republic of China. Groups of people with specialized and seasoned experience are often used to offer important inputs and advice to the policy process.

In both protracted security and routine issue situations, the outside inputs are a most significant component of official group decision making. Any democracy is characterized by intensive inputs into the processes of governance by those outside officialdom, as this is a manifest attribute of governing by consent of the governed. Consent, in part, is the right "to petition the government," guaranteed in the First Ammendment to the Constitution. The United States is probably unique, however, in the powerful role played by public opinion and the opinion polls in political interest groups, the media, all kinds of economic and social institutions, and elites in seeking to demand and give support or deny support to officials to further the interests of the outside group in shaping and inplementation of decisions and policy. The federal structure of government and the separation of powers at the national level provide many points of access for outside inputs and for playing off one branch against another in the tortuous process of shaping national policy. The outside or nonofficial groups have their own definitions of national security and well-being, what constitutes threats to security and what is essential for well-being, and thus what policies they feel are appropriate to advance security and well-being as defined by the outside group.

Outside groups representing business and labor, national and ethnic entities of all kinds, other nations' interests, farmers and producers of armaments, and a host of others make demands and provide support or support-denials in seeking to impose their version of national security and well-being on the official decision makers. Some praise this intense out-side activity as the essence of democracy, as a vivid manifestation of the "governed" registering the democratic right to influence and, in part, determine the dual goals of national security and well-being. Some officials are strongly guided by the outside inputs and others nicely finesse them, but no official can ignore the political significance of these demands. Others condemn this external pressure on the grounds that it politicizes foreign policymaking and often substitutes the special interest group's version of security and well-being for the more accurate determination of security and well-being by those within the framework of government. Walter Lippman (1955), in echoing the views of ˋAlexis de Tocqueville of the 1830s, declared that democracy and the making of effective foreign policy are quite incompatible.[3] Spainer and Uslaner suggest that immediate security and even protracted security issues involving few actors and outside interventions provide the best model for foreign policy decision making. (Spanier & Uslaner, 1978). It therefore might be convenient for purposes of efficiency to place a "security" label on as many foreign policy issues as possible. However, in an open democracy with a free and probing press, such a procedure would be quite unacceptable. Chapter 3 also raises more practical objections to excluding the opinions of "outsiders." The security-democracy dilemma in foreign policy decision making continues to call for fresh insights and high levels of wisdom in statesmanship.

Groups and the Decision Process

We next consider the role of groups in the decision process in immediate security and to a lesser extent, protracted security issues and situations. Routine issues in United States foreign policy involve a much wider variety of groups, including the committee and subcommittee structure of the Congress. The time frame, number of actors, high involvement of outside inputs, and abundant sources of information are quite different from issues involving the nation's security, thus rendering an examination of such issues beyond the scope of this chapter. The two basic segments of groups and the decision process for security issues involve preplanning or contingency planning, and the actual process when it becomes necessary to decide and implement policy.

PREPLANNING

The National Security Council and groups at State and Defense give much consideration to probabilities of threats to security and what decision and policies might be necessary to meet those threats. This is contingency planning or anticipatory security analysis and often takes the form of simulating the threat to security and appropriate responses. Preplanning is a damage-reduction exercise in that if groups anticipate security threats and prepare policy options, the groups and White House are better prepared to respond should the eventuality occur. This is particularly the case when preplanning can make the time frame more efficient during the actual decision making process. We have observed that time is quite precious in proportion to the intensity of the crisis or threat, and a plan that does fit or approximate the facts of the crisis reduces the necessity and thus the time to search for information and to develop options for consideration as policy.

In the late summer and early fall of 1962, the Department of Justice, Department of State, and Department of Defense all gave consideration to issues that might arise would it be discovered that the Soviet Union was placing offensive missiles in Cuba (Chayes, 1974, pp. 17-24). Because of these studies and preplanning, the executive committee of the National Security Council had before it extensive paperwork that made the ultimate decision of a defensive quarantine around Cuba easier to reach and implement.

At Defense, there is constant simulation concerning what options might be considered in the event of various kinds of conventional and/or nuclear attacks against the United States of its allies. The American military has orders to respond in various ways *if* a contingency takes place. For instance, United States aircraft apparently had such orders when it shot down Libyan planes attacking United States aircraft in the Mediterranean Sea in August 1981. President Reagan was not informed of the American responsive action until well after it took place; therefore, one can infer that the contingency was preplanned, as was the almost automatic American response.

This raises the question, of course, of the extent to which "preplanning" is, in effect, the actual decision in immediate security issues. If this is the case in some instances, it certainly would be advisable continually to review preplanning activity to make certain that conditions and situations that might arise between the contingency action plan and the actual event do not make it undesirable to implement the plan. Some have expressed the view that the United States overreacted in the Libyan case, and that United States action took place in an area of the Mediterranean that Libya considers within its territorial jurisdiction. Thus, concern was expressed that the contingency plan, in becoming the actual decision and policy, was too hasty and not subject to review and consideration by a group such as the National Security Council.

Lack of contingency planning may lead to group decision activity and policy that raises some questions about overreaction and the appropriateness of the decision. In May 1975, an American merchant ship, the *Mayaguez,* was attacked by Cambodian gun boats. President Ford, Security Adviser Kissinger, and other security officials met in the White House Situation Room to consider the input of information and possible responses to this crisis. The United States military activity that ensured did bring about the release of the *Mayaguez* and its crew, but also led to the death of almost forty American military personnel, as well as an unknown number of Cambodians. Criticisms of this action included American overreaction, perhaps American compensating its record in Vietnam, and poor processing of information looping in and out of the White House Situation Room as a short-lived crisis moved toward its termination. A security threat, as this was perceived to be, is not always obvious, and preplanning often does not exist. However, extensive planning of all kinds of security threats, and the availability of time and intelligence to consider possible responses, decision, and policy, are important group activities in any foreign policy issue of situation.[4]

THE DECISION PROCESS

The standard scenario for the decision process has a small number of high officials chaired by the president meeting in a specific restricted area, such as the Cabinet Room or the Situation Room of the White House. The group process involves consideration of information about the relevant issue, exchanges of views, development of options, review of messages coming into the decision-making arena from other nations, including the adversary, and the gradual emergence of a policy position that is recommended for the decision and implementation by the president. Any of these steps and others may be recycled in the logistics of reaching a bottom-line decision, including consideration of the consequences of each option and the impact of those consequences on many audiences, including the decision makers themselves. Some salient aspects of this scenario are as follows:

The decision-making arena is close to sources of information, especially primary and confidential information. Facilities for full and rapid communications are necessary. The security of the arena and the exclusion of all but top officials and modest support staff is directly proportional to the group's ability to manage the process immune from outside influences, demands, or supports.

The high officials probably have top security clearance and the confidence of the president as full actors in the decision process. Usually, each official is the principal officer of his or her government structure or bureaucracy, and thus tends to represent the interests and objectives of that structure. As Graham Allision (1971) has observed, much of the group process revolves around group members developing options that will protect their turf or their bureaucratic base of power and authority, then moving toward a specific position that may or may not be compatible with the bureau or the turf of one or more members of the group.

The president, of course, has the authority to repudiate a group member who, because of ego or fear of reprisal from within his or her bureau, holds to a position in opposition to the emerging policy position. After all, each person in the arena is appointed by the president and may be relieved from office by the president. However, it is usually far better to draw upon all the resources of discussion and persuasion to develop a group consensus rather than to permit an adversary proceeding divide the group. The individual option of the group participant who may feel he or she cannot accept the emerging policy position may be to resign, but history records that this is quite rare and that as all officials know that the president is the final authority, they generally conform to the emerging consensus rather than stand their ground to the point of resignation, voluntary or requested.[5] Of course, as was discussed at length in Chapter 3, a *premature* consensus, in the euphoria of group cohesiveness, can be even more disastrous than a rancorous adversary proceeding.

Ideally, the group will eventually reach consensus after careful, deliberate weighing of all relevant alternatives.

Such a prescription, however, ignores the realities of group deliberations headed by the President of the United States. In the absence of clearly spelled-out rules permitting the free flow of opinions, group members may be inhibited from expressing views that seem to go against the prevailing sentiment. Some may be intimidated by the senior status of others in the room, as was Professor Arthur Schlesinger upon the occasion in April 1961, or the group deliberation and recommendation to the president to proceed with the invasion of the Bay of Pigs in Cuba. It was Schlesinger's personal opinion that the invasion was doomed to defeat, but the military brass in the Cabinet Room, with braid and ribbons galore, impelled Schlesinger to hold his tongue. Irving L. Janis (1982) aptly observes in his superb analysis of group decision process in foreign policy that group participants may gradually go along with the "we-feeling" of solidarity as a tidy way of resolving personal or agency objections to the drift of deliberations and the emergence of a consensual policy position. (see also de Rivera, 1968; Schlesinger, 1965).

In returning to our scenario, we find that there is rarely a common consideration by the group. Rather, each member of the group has his or her information base, which may be placed on the table as the most accurate or most recent. Exchange of information and discussion of differences over the validity of information are often critical in the development of a consensus on the validity of the information on the issue itself. Further, information that is in addition to that available at the beginning of the group process is also subjected to close scrutiny, especially by group members who find new information damaging to their own position.

In no orderly manner, unless there is a strict chairman in the room, exchanges take place among group members in the gradual shaping of options for decisions. Allison's rational actor model deals extensively with the shaping of options, their significance if they become *the* policy, and consequences of each option with respect to the adversary, allies, publics within the nation, other branches of government, especially the Congress, and the decision-making officials themselves. Throughout all of this process, information loops in and out of the decision-making arena, which may bring about changes in positions, advance or retard relevance of various options, and clarify emerging policy positions.

All of this leads, according to the neat scenario, to bargaining between and among the group participants as a basic position or policy begins to emerge. Group members with differing opinions must weigh the benefits and costs of joining the consensus. The chair of the group, whether the president or his surrogate, performs the necessary task of engineering support for the developing consensus— a process which, as Theodore Sorenson (1963) stated, is an art and not a science. Whether this process is one of clear rationality or not is an interesting question, depending on one's definition of rationality. Herbert Simon suggests that often group participants do not always approach the task and the emerging policy position with high levels of rationality, in line with Allison's "rational actor" model. Simon states that the actor may take an acceptable stand without offending anyone because this is the least complicated and damaging approach to making decisions. He calls this approach "satisficing" to the actor and his bureaucratic base and also in line with the views of others. Another term for this concept is "the easy way out" (Simon, 1959; see also Dougherty & Pfaltzgraff, 1981, pp. 476-480).

And thus emerges a consensus among group members for a policy position that is submitted to the president for final decision and implementation. Those not accepting the consensus, as we have noted, have their own options, ranging from silently assenting and publicly defending the position at a later time to the other extreme of resignation and protest.

The basic problem with this scenario is that while all of its elements do take place in the group decision process, there is no neat order to this process. The various steps may be plateaus or in reverse order. The president and/or his secretary of state or national security adviser may have an immediate policy solution to a security issue and thus the group and its processes may be a charade. A policy may be publically articulated, such as "the United States will respond with nuclear weapons if there is a Soviet conventional attack on the Persian Gulf." Is that policy engraved in stone? Or, might it be tempered in group decisions should the Soviet conventional attack take place? No one close to immediate or protracted security decision making at the White House level has written that there is a science or a completely orderly procedure to the process of high officials reaching positions and policy recommendations. However, most would agree that the essential pieces of the action are involved in the scenario we set forth in this chapter.

Some Prescriptions

Group decisions and inputs into foreign policy may be enhanced if we draw from what are considered successful examples of how such inputs and decisions have advanced national security and well-being. The converse is also the case. The Bay of Pigs fiasco offers many examples of wholly inadequate group processes and recommendations to the president (see Chapter 3). The Cuban missile crisis decisions of almost a year and a half later identify some very effective group processes and group management by the president. Key participants in the missile crisis noted some twenty years later that certain actions and activities led to what most consider was a decision not only advancing United States security but international security as well. Among judicious actions and choices were the following: accurate mutual assessment of interests by and between the two superpowers; determination to gain accurate information; careful and confidential group processes; effective communication between the two superpowers; determination by both powers not to leave the other with no way out but war or humiliation; and certainly that each power knows the intention of the other.

These former members of the executive committee of the National Security Council pointed out that the president set the tone and climate for their group participation and thus it is he who both receives and orchestrates group inputs and processes. They praised President Kennedy as one "whose cautious determination, steady composure, deep-seated compassion and, above all, continuously attentive control of our options and actions brilliantly served his country and all mankind" (*Time*, September 27, 1982).

Drawing upon what are considered effective group processes in foreign policy decision making, some prescriptions for making effective decisions include the following: Intelligence and experience are essential for group participants, as are open and frank exchanges in the group interactions so that a growing consensus might reflect wisdom and mutuality in sharing that wisdom. Respect for inputs of officals below the level of cabinet secretaries and other high officials is valuable. Overprotection of one's bureau's position and responsibility is to be avoided, as is a position that may reflect an outside vested interest, such as demands by ethnic or other interest groups, that their perception of security should be that of the group and the president. Generous information to the media tends to inform publics, generate loops of support or criticism that must be considered in an open society, and convey a broad feeling in the public of being respected and appreciated.

In *crisis* situations, the handling of the Cuban missile crisis offers valuable lessons. Full consideration should be given to two key audiences perhaps not in the decision making room—the Congress and the nation's allies. When President Eisenhower and his advisers were considering aiding the French who were fighting their last battle against the forces of North Vietnam in May 1954, strong recommendations were made to the president for United States armed intervention. The president replied that he would order intervention providing the congressional leadership and key allies were in support of such action. Neither was, and the intervention never took place. In the summer of 1983, some felt that without support from the Congress and major allies, United States military intervention in Central America would be a huge mistake. Closed doors, maximum and accurate information, simulations, cool heads, full exchange of views, time and timing, and effective leadership are all essential for crisis decision making.

In *protracted security* situations, experience suggests strong teamwork between the executive branch and the Congress is important, along with continual planning simulations and open communications. Overemphasis on the external threat as a tactic to gain consensus is to be avoided. Uses by the president of broad-gauged commissions or groups of experts, as was the case of the group advising President Johnson in the Vietnam situation in February 1968, is a most useful mechanism to gain seasoned and nonpolitical or bureaucratic judgment. Above all, group inputs in protracted security situations should explore all possible channels to keep the issue protracted, not immediate security or crisis, which appeared to be the case with the European pipeline situation.

In *routine* and *programmatic* situations that usually are rooted in legislation, complete familiarity with that legislation and standard procedures is essential. Lessons must be learned from legislation to improve group planning and decision making. For instance, the Export Administration Act of 1979 that was central in the European pipeline issue must be continually examined and possibly altered in view of experience of policy under that act. Maximum openness in group processes, diplomacy in reconciling the vested interests of groups seeking to have a foreign policy that matches the group policy, constant evaluation of group processes, effective coordination of groups within the executive branch and between the executive and Congress are all obvious but important components to group decision making in advancing effective foreign policies.

Enlightenment, experience, common sense, respect for views of others, and a constant search for consensus on definition of foreign policy goals of security and well-being, as well as what constitutes threats to security and what advances national well-being, are essential as groups meet to consider policy choices. Above all, however, is understanding the limits of national policy. Increasingly, the international system of states becomes more complex and inter-dependent and no nation, even the United States, can consider and make wise foreign policy decisions without full consideration of relations between decisions and policy in the global community. Group participants who seek to understand the nature and patterns of the international system will contribute far more to wise policy than those who truly believe this nation can ignore the broader concerns and aspirations of the global community.

Notes

1. Spanier and Uslaner distinguish between two kinds of decisions—crisis and program. For present purposes, "program" is referred to as "routine," or regular and necessary issues such as annual budgets, which officials must process and decide on as part of standard government operations. See Spanier & Uslaner (1978).

2. *New York Times,* January 15, 1983. This brings up, of course, the group of representatives from two different countries (e.g., the United States and the USSR) in group decision making to reach an arms limitation agreement. While this kind of group context is not within the scope of this chapter, it does suggest a group process within each nation to come to a position that then will be discussed and negotiated by the group comprised of each state's representatives.

3. de Tocqueville (1945, p. 243) wrote that "in the conduct of foreign relations, democracies appear to me to be decidedly inferior to other governments." Lippman (1955, p. 20) declared that "mass opinion . . . has shown itself to be a dangerous master of decisions when the stakes are life and death."

4. Other terms and processes in preplanning include gaming and simulation. See, in particular, "Learning Through Gaming," in Lincoln Bloomfield's excellent study excellent (1982, pp. 193ff.).

5. In the emerging policy position that the United States should militarily intervene in Iran in April 1980, Secretary of State Cyrus Vance became increasingly certain that such a policy would not be successful in the long run even if the short-term intervention were successful. He told the president that if the intervention were under-taken, he would resign. The abortive attempt to rescue the hostages did fail and the secretary immediately resigned. So did many members of the British Cabinet after the failure of the British intervention in Egypt in late October, 1956.

References

Allison, G. T. *Essence of decision: Explaining the Cuban missile crisis.* Boston: Little Brown, 1971.

Bloomfield, L. *The foreign policy process: A modern primer.* Englewood Cliffs, NJ: Prentice-Hall, 1978.

Chayes, A. *The Cuban missile crisis.* New York: Oxford University Press, 1974.

Dougherty, J. E., & Pfaltzgraff, R. L. Decision-making theories. In *Contending theories of international relations.* New York: Harper & Row, 1981.

Janis, I. *Victims of groupthink.* Boston: Little, Brown, 1982.

Lippman, W. *The public philosophy.* Boston: Little, Brown, 1955.

Paige, G. D. *The Korean decision.* New York: Free Press, 1968.

Simon, H. *Administrative behavior.* New York: Macmillan, 1959.

Snyder, R. C. et al. *Foreign policy decision making.* New York: Free Press, 1962.

Sorenson, T. *Decision-making in the White House.* New York: Columbia University Press, 1963.

Spanier, J., & Uslaner, E. *How American foreign policy is made.* New York: Holt, Rinehart & Winston, 1976.

Sullivan, M. P. Decision-making. In *International relations: Theories and evidence.* Englewood Cliffs, NJ: Prentice-Hall, 1976.

Toqueville, A. de *Democracy in America.* New York: Vintage, 1945.

White, B. P. Decision-making analysis. In T. Taylor (Ed.), *Approaches and theory in international relations.* London: Longman, 1978.

CHAPTER 9

DECISIONS INVOLVING
THE CORPORATE ENVIRONMENT

Percy H. Hill

"To date, millions of dollars have been spent in legal expenses and out-of-court settlements in compensation for those killed or maimed in the Corvair. The corporation steadfastly defends the car's safety, despite the internal engineering records which indicate it was not safe, and the ghastly toll in deaths and injury it recorded.

"There wasn't a man in top GM management who had anything to do with the Corvair who would purposely build a car that he knew would hurt or kill people. But, as part of a management team pushing for increased sales and profits, each gave his individual approval in a group to decisions which produced the car in the face of the serious doubts that were raised about its safety, and then later sought to squelch information which might prove the car's deficiencies" [DeLorean & Wright, 1979, p. 67]. (The Corvair launched in the fall of 1959 had a six-year record as a dangerous car, yet it contained more innovative features than any other car of its time. Production of the Corvair was halted in 1969, four years after it was made a safe car.)

"Within our own organizations, the day of the autocratic chief executive officer has passed. The management problems we face today are simply too complex to be decided by any one individual, however wise, however brilliant, however experienced. In our business, the ultimate responsibility and the ultimate accountability to the Board of Directors, who represent our owners, rests with me. However, my decisions aren't reached in a vacuum. In reaching them I have the benefit of the views of our Executive Policy Committee, which consists of myself, the President, two Vice

Chairmen, three Executive Vice Presidents, and the Vice President and General Counsel ...

"We are assisted, of course, by specialists from the various departments and by our Corporate Planning Division.

"But the specialists don't make our decisions. Top management must decide, as every chief executive officer knows all too well. The questions we face, even with the help of quantitative analysis, characteristically involve a high degree of uncertainty and therefore risk. When the experts have departed, we are left to ponder the imponderables, to weigh uncertain consequences against unforeseeable costs, to balance the interests of opposed constituencies, and finally, to decide" [Burger, 1978, p. xi].

These two points of view will give the reader some insight into the corporate environment. On the one hand it is pointed out that perhaps there would have been a different decision in building the Corvair if top management had made the decisions as individuals, rather than as members of a group. Here is a clear case where a group decision was wrong, and where the company continued to produce the car even after they knew it was a bad product. How does a group admit that it is wrong and change its decision? No one member wants to take the blame for the group. Due to the number of individuals that make up a group and their corporate pride, it is often said that group decisions at the corporate level are irreversible.

The second point of view states that top-level decisions are made by individuals but are based on information supplied by groups. In other words, the information that forms the basis of a decision is provided through a group activity, with the ultimate decision made by an individual who assesses the opinions and data provided. According to this view, the responsibility for the outcome is the decision maker's, and that is why the board of directors elects the manager or chief executive. In this case, the group providing the information could recommend one course of action. The chief executive, after reviewing the information, could very well decide just the opposite, and he or she has the power to implement it. (See Chapter 10 for a full discussion of the responsible individual in the context of administrative decision making.)

It is beyond the scope of this book (or any other for that matter) to determine which style—the group as actual decision maker or the group in an advisory capacity—results in the best decision. This chapter, therefore, will discuss both styles and try to point out measures by which each may be used effectively. But first, it is important to understand the corporate environment. The decision makers at the corporate level are managers. Their single motivation is that of company growth for the corporation, which in most cases is the stockholders. There are few rewards given for manufacturing an attractive product, a safe product, an efficient product. The rewards are great, however, for showing a profit. In fact, many business schools teach that the only responsibility of a corporate manager is to make a profit. Managers are really up against a difficult job. To keep their positions, they must see to it that new products are introduced regularly to the marketplace, that these products sell, and that profit margins continue to rise from quarter to quarter. If one makes the right decisions and thereby shows an increase in profit over a number of quarters, one can be sure that the corporate directors will target an even higher margin for the next quarter and for the one that follows. Unfortunately, this has been industry's style of operation for the past twenty years when dealing with consumer products and services. One or two wrong decisions, and the corporate manager is out of a job. At this level, the risks are too great for many wrong decisions. Chrysler is a good example of a company that almost went under in 1980 because its managers continued to build bigger cars where unit profits were better, rather than enter the small car market to satisfy the needs of the public and national economy.

The Corporate Manager

THEORIES OF MANAGEMENT

Management is the magic of combining individuals who are fulfilling their potential as human beings into groups that enjoy success in achievement. A manager develops himself—others may guide, inspire, motivate, or teach—but he does all the developing. A good manager plans and controls his plans. The poor manager never plans and then tries to control people [Hayes, 1974].

A manager gets people to do what he or she wants them to do in such a manner that they enjoy it. A good manager causes things to happen through people making them happen. He or she creates a dynamic environment that is exciting and enjoyable, as opposed to a static one that is drab, boring, and often doomed to failure. It is to the manager's advantage that the people who report to him or her want to be members of a winning team, to be proud of their division, to be a cut above the others.

There are now three identifiable techniques of management or styles of operation known as McGregor's (1960) Theory X and Theory Y, and the more recent Theory Z by Ouchi (1981). *Theory X* assumes: (a) the average human being has an inherent dislike of work and will avoid it if he or she can; (b) because of this characteristic dislike of work, most people must be coerced, controlled, directed, and threatened with punishment to get them to put forth adequate effort toward the achievement of corporate objectives; (c) the average human being prefers to be directed, wishes to avoid responsibility, has relatively little ambition, and wants security above all. Such a management technique often results in directives, unions, arguments, restriction of output, sabotage, missed days, and dissent (gathering in small groups).

Theory Y assumes (a) expenditure of physical and mental effort in work is as natural as play and rest; (b) external control and the threat of punishment are not the only means of bringing about effort toward organizational objectives. People will exercise self-direction and self-control in the service of objectives to which there is a commitment; (c) commitment to objectives is a function of the rewards associated with their achievement; (d) the average human being learns, under proper conditions, not only to accept but to seek responsibility; (e) the capacity to exercise a relatively high degree of imagination, ingenuity, and creativity in the solution of organizational problems is widely, not narrowly, distributed in the population. When a manager exercises this technique of directing people, the results may include harmony, less effort and productivity, a "happy family" feeling, everyone will want to get into the act, and many will take advantage of the situation.

From the foregoing discussion, one might hypothesize that the path to good and effective management lies somewhere between these theories. Good managers want to create harmony among personnel, but at the same time induce a moderate level of stress to promote effort and productivity. They should give responsibility and authority, but at the same time require progress reports. A good manager should expect people to *want* to produce, but at the same time should set productive quotas or targets and reward the workers when they have achieved it. There is nothing wrong with expecting a continual rise in this quota during periods of economic growth.

When one considers that Japanese productivity is the highest anywhere is the world and that American industries are desperately trying to catch up, the Japanese must be doing something right. The *Theory Z* technique of management practiced in Japan may very well shed some light on their success. In most if not all companies in Japan there is (a) *lifetime employment* as opposed to short-term in the United States. This means that the individual can be trained for a job and stay around long enough to see the fruits of this training pay off; (b) there is *slow evaluation and promotion* in Theory Z companies. A manager of a Japanese company has time to develop his or her full potential in a division and to make plans for growth, instead of the hysterical attitude among managers in U.S. companies who feel that three years without a significant promotion means they have failed. In many American companies, new MBAs are placed in specialty positions and rarely have the opportunity of knowing what happens in other divisions. They must depend upon inter-departmental directives and records in order to fulfill corporate goals. Theory Z suggests that there be (c) *nonspecialized career paths* in which young executives are assigned to one division, then moved to another and another until he or she has a rather broad understanding and more important experience in each division of a company before being assigned a permanent position of respon-sibility. There is (d) an *implicit control mechanism* within Theory Z companies in which all managers and workers know that the goals of the company are both short and long range. In the United States, we tend to be explicit as far as communicating companies' plans. Another major difference between Theory Z and U.S. techniques of management is (e) *collective decision making* by groups as opposed to individuals. Many Japanese companies will place a number of top level officials in the same office, so that decisions can be voted on as a group. This leads to (f) *collective responsibility* for the outcome of the decision. Finally, Theory Z suggests (g) *holistic concern* for company growth and development.

It is easy to see, when comparing the seemingly opposite tech-niques of management, why the Japanese lead the world in productivity. It would be difficult for U.S. companies to totally adopt Theory Z, for we are of a different culture. They could profit, however, by altering present styles of management in favor of many of the methods suggested by the Theory Z approach.

THE PROCESS OF MANAGEMENT

As stated earlier, a good manager makes things happen through people; people do what the manager wants them to do and are happy about doing it. The following process outlines a plan for the management of people that could cause the right things to happen:

(1) Planning—It is important that managers have a clear understanding of what subordinates are to do and communicate this in the form of job descriptions to the individuals involved as well as others.

(2) Organization of Human Resources—Knowing what people are to do, the manager's next step is to determine which people are needed to do it. This involves identifying the kinds and numbers of personnel required to carry out the plan.

(3) Organization of Physical Resources—Once the manager knows what the people are to do and the type of people needed, he can turn to identifying and acquiring the material to accomplish the task. Particular tools, raw materials, work space, transportation, and so on, will be necessary for carrying out the plan.

(4) Standards of Performance—This important step in the process answers the question; How well do you want people to perform the assigned task with given resources? Simply put, standards of performance establish a yardstick by which productivity can be measured.

(5) Progress Reviews—Some review is necessary to determine the rate of progress and to establish whether standards (item 4) have been set too high or too low.

(6) Personal Development—Once standards of performance have been established, it is important to teach or coach each individual so that performance approaches potential. A personal development program involves training, conditioning (mental and physical), satisfaction measures, incentives, and other enrichment programs to stimulate individual productivity and pride in one's work.

(7) Rewards—The process ends with the establishment of rewards for productive work. In descending order of importance to the individual, these rewards are:
     (a) Position (Title)
     (b) Recognition
     (c) Money (Raise)
     (d) Praise
     (e) Encouragement
     (f) Respect

(8) Turn-Off—On the other hand, if a manager wants to cause an employee to leave an organization voluntarily rather than by outright dismissal, the following actions are recommended in descending order:
  (a) Neglect
  (b) Discouragement
  (c) Criticism
  (d) "One-Upmanship"

ATTRIBUTES OF AN EFFECTIVE MANAGER

A list of the desirable attributes of a corporate leader would include honesty, industry, technical capability, company loyalty, leadership, imagination, and responsibility. Other desirable attributes will depend on the particular theory of management subscribed to or other specific features of the work environment (see Chapter 2 for a discussion of the fit between leadership style and situational characteristics). Beyond this there are five characteristics of an individual that more generally separate excellence from mediocrity.

(1) A Record of Attainment—He or she must have already achieved something by virtue of prior leadership. This may have occurred in a previous job, in college, in the community, in church, or even in a remote activity.
(2) A Mission—The candidate for a leadership role as a manager ought to have some purpose in life, some things to be accomplished, a goal, something to be achieved beyond just making money.
(3) Consultative Supervision—A good manager believes his colleagues have ideas, are creative, and so he is willing to listen to them. No one manages effectively alone, but most depend upon the ideas of others to carry out a successful plan. The good manager is modest and encourages and rewards others for their ideas.
(4) Intellectual Maturity—The effective manager will be true to his word, will hold his ground, and will be willing to stand up and be counted. Such an individual has a deep and basic conviction in relation to those issues having an important impact upon life.
(5) Emotional Stability—The best managers are able to "roll with the punches," willing to take risks, unafraid of failure, able to make decisions, without excessive stress, and have a relatively low anxiety level. In other words, the individual must be able to take some "lumps" and never be overwhelmed by the problem.

Management Through Group Participation in Decisions

Now that we have discussed the process of management and the attributes of a good manager, it is appropriate to elaborate on the phase of management decisions that constitutes group interaction. This discussion will deal with group structure, organization, and the effectiveness of a group as a decision-making body.

SETTING UP A GROUP

The diagram is Figure 9.1 shows the mechanics of establishing an effective group in a profitmaking enterprise. Such a group should consist of from five to fifteen people. Somewhere around ten provides for ease of communication among members, which is important for productive results (see Chapter 1 for further discussion of group size). A group will listen, but members will play a passive role and very little, if anything, will get accomplished. Give a group a purpose (a goal), however, and it is transformed into an organization. The group now has an identity, something to work for. This is not enough, however, for an organization (group with a purpose) will produce very little. If now the organization is given a structure, a productive organization will result. This requires a leader, assigned responsibility, scheduled progress reports, and time limits to induce a certain amount of stress among members. Such an organization will produce the kinds of information required by management to conduct a successful business and make the right and timely decisions.

Group meetings should be scheduled during the morning period when everyone is alert, attentive, and energetic. This is prime time and shows that management feels this activity is important. The meeting should be held at a round table rather than the customary rectangular one, where junior persons usually sit at the foot with seniors at the head, automatically dividing the group. A round table tends to place members on a more equal level and facilitates a more open discussion.

Decisions to be made at a group meeting should be made by those to be involved in the action, in the implementation of the decision, and in the consequences. "The charge of the Light Brigade was ordered by an officer who wasn't there" (Townsend, 1970).

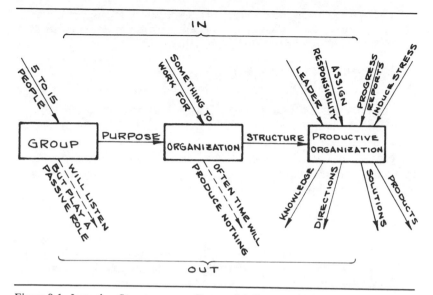

Figure 9.1 Imposing Structure on a Purposeful Group Will Transform That Group into a Productive Organization

GUIDELINES FOR CONSENSUS IN GROUP DECISION MAKING

One of the most difficult tasks of a group leader is to reach a consensus among the members. A consensual decision is one on which all members can at least partially agree. Group consensus has important functions, as discussed in Chapter 3. The danger lies in a rush to consensus, producing the "groupthink" effect discussed at length also in Chapter 3. To avoid premature group consensus, it is suggested that the following advice be circulated to members prior to a meeting (Hall & Watson, 1970):

(1) Avoid arguing for your own individual position or point of view merely because it is your own.
(2) Approach each issue or question on the basis of reasonable evidence rather than on who presents a particular argument. (Often a group member will vote against a proposal presented by a disliked colleague or will vote for a question when presented by a friend.)
(3) Avoid changing your mind only in order to prevent conflict and reach agreement. Moreover, avoid conflict-reducing techniques, such as majority vote, averaging, or trading-off.

(4) Support only proposals with which you are in strong agreement.
(5) View differences of opinion as helpful in exploring issues rather than as a hindrance in reaching a group decision.

**WHEN GROUP DECISIONS ARE EFFECTIVE
AND WHEN THEY ARE NOT**

When one has a choice between letting a group make a decision or confining the group to an advisory capacity only, it is a good idea to examine the effectiveness of each alternative. There are certain advantages in having a group discuss a problem on which they are informed and which they will then decide to solve in their own way. Some of these follow:

Advantages

(1) There is safety in numbers. Group members tend to bring out different aspects of a problem and can detect invalid reasoning.
(2) Groups tend to take more risks and innovative (off-beat) approaches to solving problems.
(3) Groups, by their very nature, will usually arrive at a decision rather than postponing action.
(4) There is more discussion with more expertise brought to bear on a problem than in individual decision making.

Many of the advantages of a group decision are sometimes outweighed in particular cases by the following disadvantages:

Disadvantages

(1) Group decisions are usually irreversible. Once a decision has been reached, it is difficult to reconvene a group and go through the process again.
(2) Groups are sometimes led to the decision by a strong leader type who dominates the discussion.
(3) Members of a group will often vote with their friends, identified authorities, or business superiors, even though they may feel just the opposite on an issue. (See Chapter 3 for a discussion of ways to combat disadvantages 2 and 3.)
(4) The decision maker, to be at all effective, must accept responsibility for a decision. It is difficult if not impossible to fix responsibility on a group.

An effective manager who has knowledge of and some experience with the group decision process as well as the independent decision should choose the most effective style in reaching a conclusion on an issue. Tasks that often require studies along with the careful weighing of alternatives seem to adapt themselves to the group process, where decisions of a lesser magnitude based on evident facts fit the individual or executive's choice. It is quite proper in the case of the Corvair discussed earlier to reach a decision through the group process, since its outcome could (and did) effect many of the divisions at GM. A decision concerning the purchase of an injection moulding machine in order to commercialize a product should be made by the chief executive officer based on facts provided by concerned divisions within the company.

Group Decision-Making Techniques

This section will deal with a number of decision-making techniques suitable for groups in situations where the group plays the dominant role. That is, one presents a problem and expects a decision as the output within a fixed period of time. This is simply illustrated in Figure 9.2 below.

A PROCESS OF GROUP DECISIONS

Effective group action can be brought about through management, giving some thought to an orderly process of managing a group. Figure 9.3 is an attempt to outline a process in which the final decision outcome may approach the ideal if followed with suitable modification to fit each company's profile. The arrows between steps point in two directions to indicate an iterative process. If a manager finds it difficult to complete a phase, it may be a good idea to go back and restructure the previous one.

(1) Define the Problem—It is important for management to define the decision problem in such a way that all can understand. It might be a good idea to analyze the definition so that it addresses the cause and not the symptom. There are cases in which a group has made a decision that is intended to provide a solution, but it is addressed to the wrong problem.

(2) Select Group Members—Once the problem has been defined, the process of selecting members to the group follows. Here, one should identify members who are knowledgable in the problem area. It is always a good idea to select two or three members outside of the area to provide more balance, thus insuring that some questions will be asked that the "experts" might overlook. The responsible manager should also be a member of the group.

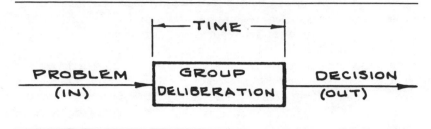

Figure 9.2 Effective Group Action

(3) Charge the Group—This next step is one of instructing the group as to what is expected of them. Given the problem definition, what does one expect the group to accomplish—Reach a conclusion? Provide information? Generate ideas?

(4) Structure the Group—As discussed earlier, a group becomes a productive organization when it is given structure. A group must have a leader, it must be assigned responsibility, given an identity, and required to make periodic reports.

(5) Establish a Deadline—Any group will work more effectively when given a target date to complete it proceedings. Many industries and agencies manage group activities through the use of PERT/CPM (Program Evaluation Review Technique/Critical Path Method) whereby a flowchart begins with the start date and ends with an end date or event. All events in between are there to help accomplish the final end action. A discussion of this technique will be found in the next section.

(6) Decision—Considering a well-run and efficient management unit that has chosen a group with care, one should expect an effective decision to be made on or before the deadline date.

PERT/CPM TECHNIQUE OF PROJECT MANAGEMENT

The ability to make the right decision at the right time involving numbers of people with diverse interests requires an understanding and some insight into the full scope of a problem (job or project). This is the responsibility of corporate managers, division heads, and their advisors. Good decisions require detailed knowledge and methods of accounting for a series of sequentially related events necessary to complete the project, assign responsibility and resources, and establish an overview of the entire program. Here managers really earn their way when a problem area can be detected that may be preventing project progress and, through the application of

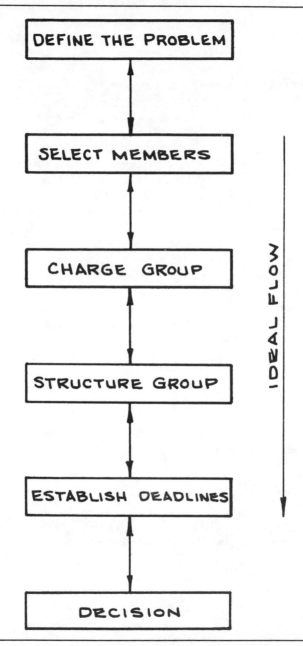

Figure 9.3 Group Process—A Group Decision Emerges from an Orderly Process of Group Management

additional resources or change in personnel or equipment, they can cause it to move along according to schedule. Many projects have failed through lack of attention to such detail or because complexities of the program became overbearing. In response to the complex nature of present-day programs, from the production of the Reach toothbrush by Johnson & Johnson to the Lisa home computer system by Apple, to the prototype of a new jet transport by Boeing, techniques have been developed to assist management in an orderly process of program coordination.

Of the many techniques for program management of large-scale systems (large numbers of people involved), Program Evaluation Review Technique (PERT)/Critical Path Method (CPM) stands out as the most effective. PERT/CPM was developed by the management firm of Booz, Allen, and Hamilton in 1958 for the U.S. Navy to be employed in the Polaris program. PERT/CPM is now recognized by the Navy as the single most important feature in completing the Polaris program ahead of schedule. This is significant when one considers that the average weapons system program exceeds the predicted schedule by 36%.

The use of PERT/CPM involves the generation of a network of events and activities to aid in the scheduling of projects. An example of such a network is shown in Figure 9.4. Each key member of the network has been identified and defined below so that the reader will be acquainted with the terms used in the case study to follow.

Definition of Terms

Event—Represents an instant in time when something happens (either a beginning or an end) at which the programmer can measure the plan against reality. The event does not consume time or resources. It is represented on the network by an oval with a letter designating the event legend.

Activity—An arrow between two events on the network illustrating dependency one to the other and representing the work effort in time and resources from the preceding to the succeeding event.

Serial Activities—When events are strung out in a single line and the start of one is directly dependent upon the completion of its predecessor, the work effort of activities results in a serial pattern. One should avoid this in the design of a network.

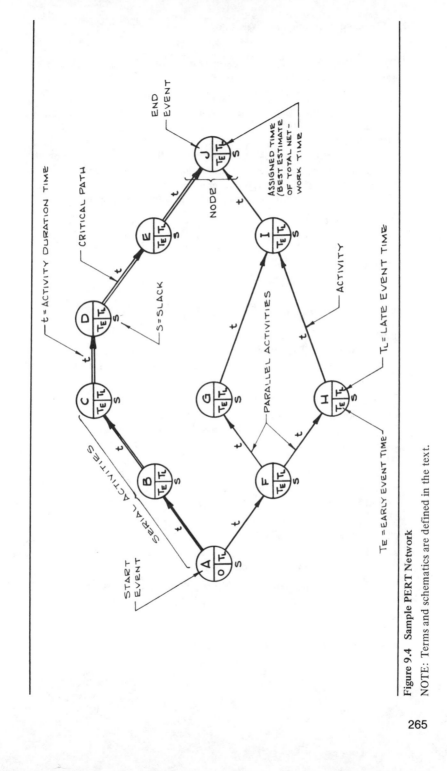

Figure 9.4   Sample PERT Network

NOTE: Terms and schematics are defined in the text.

265

Parallel Activities—Results when two or more work efforts can be carried out simultaneously. Such an arrangement in a network is desirable so as to maximize personnel and resources.

Node—An event with multiple activities leading either into it or away from it.

Dependency—The PERT principle describes the constraint placed upon each specific event and activity by the requirement that all earlier events and activities be completed prior to the commencement of the next one. Later events are dependent upon their earlier activities; every activity is dependent upon its earlier event.

Activity Duration Time—The quantity (minutes, hours, days, months, or years) that measure activity duration. and whose accumulated result is an event. Determined by estimating the optimistic (t_o), pessimistic (t_p), and most likely time (t_m) for an activity, and calculating the result through a quadratic average:

$$t = \frac{t_o + 4\ t_m + t_p}{6}$$

Earliest Event Completion Time (T_E)—The earliest time to have an event completed from the start. It is found by adding the activity duration times (t) from the start and in case of nodal activity, taking the largest number.

Latest Event Completion Time (T_L)—The latest time for the completion of an event without delaying the schedule. Determined by first finding all of the T_E's, then assigning a time (best estimates of time required to do the complete project) to the end event. Now working back through the network, each early time (T_E) is subtracted from the previous T_L to determine new T_L until the start event is reached. The smallest time is recorded when there is a node (more than on path to an event).

Slack(s)—The difference between the latest event completion time (T_L) and the earliest (T_E): $S = T_L - T_E$. Slack must always be either zero or a positive number. If a negative number, simply assign a greater value to T_L at the end event.

Critical Path—The path of activities beginning at the start event and terminating at the end event, which is the path of least slack. It is shown as a double activity line in the network. The critical path must be managed carefully, for if any activity is allowed to run over in time, the entire network (project) is apt to fall behind schedule.

Design of a PERT Network

You are project director for a small company of design consultants dealing in innovative solutions to technical problems. Problem solutions provided by your engineering personnel usually take the form of a technical report and a feasibility prototype. Your company has recently been engaged by a large commercial airline to handle passenger luggage from the check-in area to the airplane and from the airplane to the passenger at his or her destination. The system should be automatic if possible, harmless to luggage, and require a minimum of installation modifications. Management has agreed to accept the problem and has suggested that work begin on March 10, with a formal presentation to airline officials on July 16. Six design engineers have been assigned to the project and you as project director must prepare a PERT network so that the group will function efficiently, and so that each member understands the full scope of the program. You are also expected to manage the project so that it will be completed on time.

The first step in the preparation of a PERT network is to compile a list of events and arrange them in some logical order. This list is best prepared through an informal discussion with engineering and management personnel who are assigned to the project. These people should suggest events to the project director, who in turn lists them on a blackboard or flip chart.

Once a list of events has been finalized, a first trial PERT network is designed. This first trial, known as a skeleton network, is shown in Figure 9.5. Obviously this network is too nodal and contains a four-event series at the end that is undesirable. In designing a network one would like to schedule as much work as possible to be conducted simultaneously, which will result in parallel activities.

The network shown in Figure 9.5 is then revised (often a number of trials are required) until a final one results that represents optimal planning. Such a network is shown in Figure 9.6. Dates and times have been estimated (all times shown are in days) and final calculations made. The final network may now be used in managing the project and in assisting in the making of decisions required to keep the project on time.

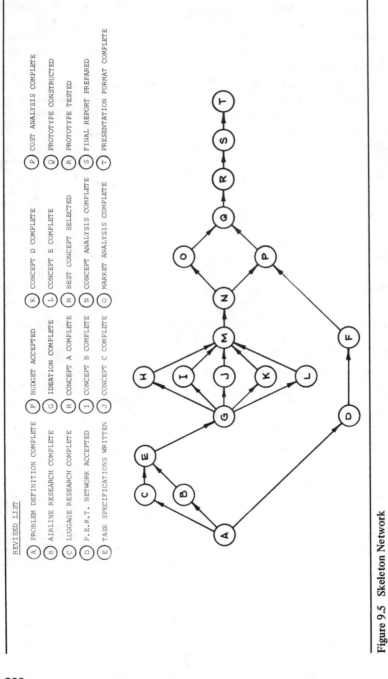

REVISED LIST

(A) PROBLEM DEFINITION COMPLETE (F) BUDGET ACCEPTED (K) CONCEPT D COMPLETE (P) COST ANALYSIS COMPLETE
(B) AIRLINE RESEARCH COMPLETE (G) IDEATION COMPLETE (L) CONCEPT E COMPLETE (Q) PROTOTYPE CONSTRUCTED
(C) LUGGAGE RESEARCH COMPLETE (H) CONCEPT A COMPLETE (M) BEST CONCEPT SELECTED (R) PROTOTYPE TESTED
(D) P.E.R.T. NETWORK ACCEPTED (I) CONCEPT B COMPLETE (N) CONCEPT ANALYSIS COMPLETE (S) FINAL REPORT PREPARED
(E) TASK SPECIFICATIONS WRITTEN (J) CONCEPT C COMPLETE (O) MARKET ANALYSIS COMPLETE (T) PRESENTATION FORMAT COMPLETE

Figure 9.5 Skeleton Network

NOTE: The skeleton network represents a first-trial PERT network, subject to modification.

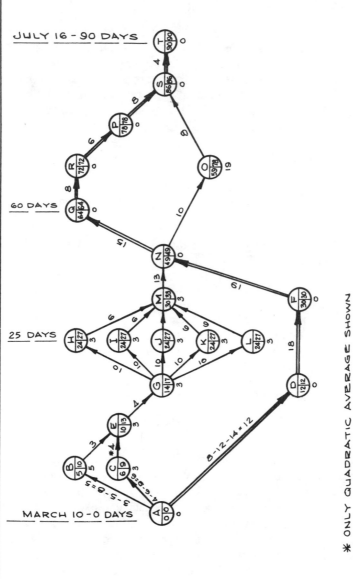

Figure 9.6 Final Network

NOTE: Numbers refer to work days. The final network may now be used to coordinate groups and manage the project through to completion.

269

Project Management With PERT/CPM

It goes without saying that the PERT/CPM technique is an excellent scheme for managing a project in which time of completion is critical. Consider developing a new product to be commercialized on a predetermined date, delivery of a process to the Air Force within a fixed time, construction of a large building at a time of spiraling inflation. In summary, PERT/CPM is intended to accomplish the following objectives:

(a) Provide Organization From the Onset
    Force definition of goals
    Promote detailed planning at the beginning
    Provide a ready-made framework for documentation and presentation
(b) Be a Planning Tool
    Segment planning problems to an easily-handled size
    Force detailed planning
    Require definition of all necessary work
    Display relationship of each work effort to the entire plan
    Promote consideration of alternate methods
    Make resource deficiencies apparent
    Aid in delegating and fixing responsibility
(c) Be a Communication Tool
    Standardize vocabulary, precise terms
    Use pictures whenever possible
    Explain status and changes quickly

CREATIVE PROBLEM SOLVING TECHNIQUES THROUGH GROUP PARTICIPATION

The life blood of almost all organizations and particularly those that are profit making depends upon a continuous flow of new ideas and novel approaches to problems, as well as new products. Management often expects this form of creative thinking to originate from individuals, especially engineering and marketing personnel. Even though it has been argued (Taylor, Berry, & Block, 1958) that the individual when working alone is capable of better ideas than when involved in a group, he or she just does not function in this way for a variety of reasons. Among them are fear of ridicule, dependency on authority, overspecialization, and practical-mindedness. But when involved in a group, something happens to stimulate the individual's imagination above a specific problem situation

(Bouchard, 1971). One idea may lead to another, which in turn forms a basis for further ideas. A large number of ideas may be listed through group participation that would otherwise be difficult or impossible to assemble by one individual without extensive literature searches and research. The following sections will discuss the three better known group creative problem-solving techniques.

Brainstorming

Brainstorming (Osborn, 1963) is a technique of originating new ideas through an organized group's creative collaboration. The term is derived from using the brain to storm creative solutions to given problems—to do so vigorously, with each person focusing his attention on the same objective. This technique was invented in 1939 by Alex F. Osborn, co-founder of Batten, Barton, Durstine, and Osborn Advertising Agency; Vice-Chairman of the University of Buffalo; trustee of several banks; director of four manufacturing corporations; and founder of the Creative Educational Institute.

A number of brainstorming sessions have been held throughout the country, spanning a multitude of problem areas, and nearly all have been successful in terms of the ideas generated. Leading companies as well as civic groups have found this technique useful. General Motors, General Electric, Westinghouse, federal agencies, state and city governments, the armed forces, and educational institutions are among those using these sessions. If a brainstorming session proves unsuccessful or results in chaos, its failure can usually be traced directly to the chairman. The chair must under no condition flaunt his or her knowledge of a subject or attempt to dominate the group, for this may result in silence, particularly among the more timid members. It is also important for the leader to suppress any criticism that tends to creep into the proceedings, such as comments to the effect that "It won't work," "They already make those," "It won't sell," or "Whoever heard of doing it that way?" The chairman must insist at the onset that ideas produced during the session are not to be judged immediately but only after a period of rest following the session. An informal gathering with all members tossing out ideas about a stated problem area and the chair acting in the capacity of moderator and sometimes adding stimulus to get things started usually results in a worthwhile and productive session.

Brainstorming is not a bull session but a concentrated group effort to produce creative ideas. Each member of the group must focus his or her attention on the stated task and not get carried away with opinions and speculations. A group of five to ten seems to work best during a period not to exceed one hour. If the organizer finds he or she has more than the optimum number interested in participating, they may split into two or more groups and compete to see which one comes up with the greater number of ideas. The session requires a chair moderator, a recorder (human or mechanical), and a member who has been previously assigned to bring in a few ideas to stimulate initial thought. In some cases the chair can fill this role. The technique is effective because one idea builds on another, combines with another, and triggers another, until ideas seems to spill forth with little effort. There must be few if any inhibitions among group members. They must be loose (flexible) in their thinking, and imaginations must be allowed to soar, with people speaking out what is on their minds. Ideas revealed in the session are reviewed later, obviously bad ones are discarded, and a list is prepared in hierarchical form from good to poor for intensive study. The following rules are considered basic for fruitful sessions:

Criticism of Ideas is Not Permitted—This rule should be stated early in the session, and if violated the violator should be reprimanded or asked to leave. Premature criticism often leads to ridicule, which stifles creative thinking.

"Free-Wheeling" or "Loose Thinking" is Welcome—Alex Osborn (1971) states, "The wilder the idea, the better; it is easier to tame down than to think up."

Ideas Are Wanted in Quantity—The mathematical probability of one or more ideas proving truly significant is a function of the number of ideas generated.

Transpose Thoughts and Combine Ideas—Group members should try to improve ideas of others, allow one idea to build on another, and attempt to divide certain ideas into several alternate possibilities.

Programmed Invention

One of the primary disadvantages of brainstorming is the possibility that someone will get credit for another's ideas. For example, person A comes up with an original thought that B builds on. Let's say that B's improved idea is recognized as something special and is praised by group members. Member A's original thought is lost in the discussion and no credit is given. A will probably remain silent for the duration of the session with the attitude, "I'll be damned if I will help out this group." Unfortunately, this is the nature of brainstorming and its main drawback.

Programmed Invention (PI) attempts to correct this obvious defect. The PI session is conducted much like brainstorming, in which ideas are wanted in quantity with "blue sky" thinking encouraged. The PI session differs, however, in one important step. When a member of the group suggests an original thought (say member A), all idea generation stops upon a signal from the chairman and every member focuses on A's idea to make it better, extend it, and build on it. During this discussion, A records all pertinent constructive extensions of the idea on index cards (9 x 7) and signs and dates them. In this way the group truly works to the benefit of the individual, who gets full credit for the original thought.

Synectics

The technique of group idea generation or solving problems in a creative way know as "synectics" was developed by William J. J. Gordon (1961). Synectics is a Greek work meaning the fitting together of seemingly diverse elements. The technique involves the use of metaphorical and analogous information exchanges within a carefully selected group of individuals of varying personalities and areas of specialization, with the chairman or leader playing a dominant role during the discussion.

The problem or task is first explained to the group (chair, five to ten members, and a recorder) in detail and repeated until all understand it thoroughly. The chair then begins the session by selecting the method of attack, such as role-playing, an investigation of certain minute details of the problem, or presentation of an analogous situation that may or may not have an obvious bearing on the problem. When an interesting idea of possible significance is suggested by someone in the group, the chair attempts to steer the discussion into an elaboration of and sometimes an analysis of the idea.

The synectic technique might be used, for example, in designing space tools; more specifically, designing a device for an astronaut to use when drilling a hole in an orbiting platform. The chair would review the problems relating to such a device, such as need for portable power sources, lubrication at extremely low temperatures, zero reaction force devices, and storage of the tool. The analogy approach may be used, for example, making the strange familiar by suspending a piece of styrofoam from a length of thread attached to the ceiling and attempting to drill a hole through it with an electric drill without steadying the styrofoam with his free hand. Of course, the styrofoam will sway as drill force is applied and the hole cannot be made. A live and sometimes dramatic demonstration such as this is usually strongly motivating to any observer. The group is now instructed to suggest methods of producing a hole in the styrofoam and sooner or later someone will suggest burning it with a cigarette. The chair will then lead the group to focus in on this idea with an attempt to force fit the solution to achieve the same objective in space.

In general, the technique of synectics is based on the fact that the mind is more productive when dealing with a new or foreign environment. The analogous situation quickly takes one away from the exact problem at hand (with traditional approaches to a solution) and requires one to consider a related problem. This has a tendency to make the strange familiar, or in another situation, when appropriate, the familiar strange. If a group were considering a novel snow removal system, they might discuss how the soil is filled or fallen leaves disposed of. Considering the design of an office building, the group might profitably discuss how a beehive is constructed. Trees might be studied when dealing with structural shapes. Novel methods of mowing a lawn might take the form of a detailed analysis of the process of cutting and tearing.

Managing Through the Group Providing Information

The two previous sections discussed techniques and the style of managing through group participation in the decision-making process. Here the group plays an active role and actually makes the decision (i.e., the GM style of operation). The second style of management is to place the responsibility of the ultimate decision with the manager (e.g., the chief executive at AT & T). The group in this case provides information to the manager in the form of data and analysis of criteria so that the decision will be made on a rational basis. (See Chapter 10 on administrative decision making by the "responsible individual.") This section will discuss techniques employed by groups as a decision aid to management.

SELECTION CRITERIA	CRITERIA, ORDERED	WEIGHTING SCORE	WEIGHTING FACTOR
TECH. CAPABILITY	MATURITY	7 ⟶ $7/28$ =	0.25
RECORD OF ATTAINMENT	STABILITY	6 ⟶ $6/28$ =	0.21
IMAGINATION	RECORD	5 ⟶ $5/28$ =	0.18
HAS A MISSION	IMAGINATION	4 ⟶ $4/28$ =	0.14
CONSULTATIVE SUPERVISION	TECH. CAPABILITY	3 ⟶ $3/28$ =	0.11
INTELLECTUAL MATURITY	MISSION	2 ⟶ $2/28$ =	0.07
EMOTIONAL STABILITY	CONSULT. SUPER.	1 ⟶ $1/28$ =	0.04
	TOTAL =	28 ⟶ $28/28$ =	1.00

Figure 9.7 Calculation of Weighting Factors for a Decision Matrix

NOTE: Each selection criterion is weighted in terms of its ranked utility or importance, and this rank is converted to a weighting factor. The weighting factors are then entered into the decision matrix (Figure 9.8).

DECISION MATRIX

An excellent technique to serve as a guide in making the best decision among alternatives is a scoring matrix that forces a more penetrating study of each alternative against specific selection criteria (Hill, 1970; Hill et al., 1979). The use of the matrix can best be illustrated through an example. Consider that a search committee has been formed to recommend the selection of a top level manager from among four candidates, with the ultimate decision resting with the committee's chair. The committee has listed several criteria to use in evaluating each candidate. Once the criteria have been decided upon, they are ordered by rank and a weighting score is assigned to each in descending numerical order. It is important to have the total of weighting factors equal to 1.0, which will be explained later. After dividing each score by the total, one arrives at a weighting factor (similar to utility, discussed in Chapter 1), which adjusts each criterion to its ranking position of importance as shown in Figure 9.7.

Next a matrix chart is drawn with "Alternatives" (candidates) listed in the left column and "Selection Criteria" across the top. The chart used in this example is shown in Table 9.8.

Each candidate is now rated on a 10-point scale (10 = high and 1 = low) against each criterion. In this example, candidate White is

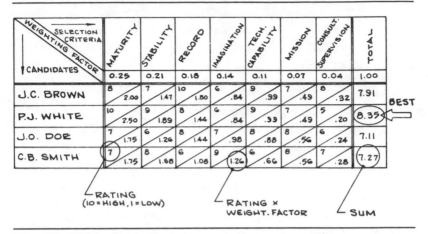

Figure 9.8 Decision Matrix Chart

NOTE: Each candidate is rated on each criterion. Each rating is multiplied by the weighting factor of the criterion. These products are then summed to yield a total score for each candidate.

considered very mature (10), with Brown weighted 9, and Doe and Smith about the same at 7. When all ratings have been made, they are adjusted by multiplying each by weighting factors. A sum of all adjusted scores is now made and the highest total score reveals the best candidate, as established by this technique. Considering that all judgments are perfect (and they never are), a perfect score of 10.00 indicates complete confidence in the decision. This score would be arrived at when each rating factor equals 10 and is then multiplied by weighting factors whose total is 1.0. Totals of 9.00 and 8.00 show reasonable confidence. Totals of around 6.00 and below might discourage placing much confidence in any of the decision alternatives.

This technique provides an excellent documentation when recommending courses of action to top level management, forces an in-depth investigation of alternatives, and shows visually the analysis procedure for purposes of presentation.

THE DECISION TO COMMERCIALIZE

Competition for new product sales today is overwhelming, as American companies compete not only with one another but, increasingly, in a world market. As with most managerial decisions discussed in this chapter, the decision to commercialize a new product (bring it to the market) rests with the top-level managers, but the information is provided through a complex network of associates, advisory groups, and ad hoc groups such as potential consumers. To commercialize often means the spending of millions of dollars on inventory, quality control, distribution channels, and advertising. To make the wrong decision can cost a company these millions of dollars and may jeopardize the careers of the decision makers. Prior to the advent of computers and sophisticated marketing techniques, the decision to commercialize was made on what many chief executives expressed as a "gut feeling." In other words, they sensed if a product would sell or not. There were many product failures, but at the same time there was less competition. Today we hear of many product successes—mini-calculators, microwave ovens, range-finding cameras, recreation vehicles, and digital watches, to name a few—but hear very little of product failures. The successful executive is able to minimize failures through the technique of market analysis. Once a new product has been conceived and constructed in sufficient numbers, one or more of the following data collecting methods are employed:

(1) Use Test—A number of products are given to individuals to use for a predetermined period of time. These people are then interviewed and questioned about their opinions of the good and bad features of the products. The outcome of these interviews represents a "pseudo-group decision" (see Chapter 1), in which noninteracting participants provide information that is pooled and acted upon by an executive.

(2) Focus Groups—A group of potential product purchasers is assembled and a brainstorming session is conducted regarding the new product and its competitors. Advertising strategy is often presented to the group, so as to get a feeling for customer reaction.

(3) Market Test—The product is marketed on a limited basis and sales are closely monitored. A community is located somewhat similar to where the product will eventually be sold and local stores are contracted to offer the product for sale. Selling a product in a test market (say, a town the size of Stamford, Connecticut) is like selling nationwide, but on a smaller scale and, more importantly, without a commitment to continual sales at the national level (which is risky and often requires an investment of several millions of dollars). The

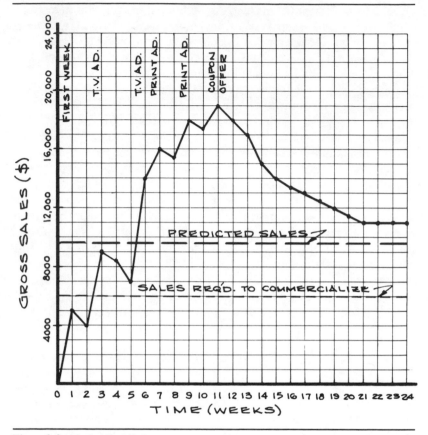

Figure 9.9   Market Test Data

NOTE: The effects on sales of various promotional efforts can be inferred from the graph.

selective market test reveals information on ability to deliver the product (inventory), distribution channels, quality control, selling price, advertising, and, most important, the ability of the product to sell.

Figure 9.9 shows the kinds of information gained through a market test. Here a product is monitored weekly against gross sales. One can see the effects of advertising, special coupon, and other promotional efforts to enhance sales.

Finally, the market analyst summarizes the information provided by use tests, focus groups, questionnaires, market tests, and so on, and presents a commercialization plan to the manager along with the cost and predicted profits. The manager must then make the ultimate decision of whether the product will be brought to the market.

To say that it is "lonely at the top" has become a truism in describing the jobs of top corporate executives. As this chapter has illustrated, however, although ultimate decisions and the responsibility for those decisions rest with executives, they would have great difficulty making effective decisions without the inputs of various groups. Perhaps just as important as making the decisions, the successful executive must learn to select, structure, and direct these groups to provide the information that will result in the best decisions for the company.

References

Bouchard, T. J. Whatever happened to brainstorming? *Journal of Creative Behavior,* 1971, 5, 182-189.

deButts, J. D. Foreword. in C. Burger *The chief executive.* Boston: CBI, 1978.

DeLorean, J. Z., & Wright, J. P. *On a clear day you can see General Motors.* New York: Avon, 1979.

Gordon, W.J.J. *Synectics.* New York: Collier Books, 1961.

Hall, J., & Watson, W. H. The effects of a normative intervention on group decision-making performance. *Human Relations,* 1970, 23, 299-317.

Hayes, J. L. Personal communication, 1974.

Hill, P. H. *The science of engineering design.* New York: Holt, Rinehart & Winston, 1970.

Hill, P. H. et al. *Making decisions: A multidisciplinary introduction.* Reading, MA: Addison-Wesley, 1979.

McGregor, D. *The human side of enterprise.* New York: McGraw-Hill, 1960.

Osborn, A. F. *Applied imagination.* New York: Scribner, 1963.

Ouchi, W. *Theory Z.* Reading, MA: Addison-Wesley, 1981.

Taylor, D. W., Berry, P. C., & Block, C. H. Does group participation when using brainstorming facilitate or inhibit creative thinking? *Administrative Science Quarterly,* 1958, 3, 23-47.

Townsend, R. *Up the organization.* New York: Knopf, 1970.

CHAPTER 10

ORGANIZATIONAL DECISION MAKING

John A. Dunn, Jr.

Most of the work of the modern world is carried on through organizations, from administering the national social security system or operating the Chase Manhattan Bank, to selling milk through cooperatives or publishing this book. No single individual has the range of expertise or the time needed to carry on all the functions; groups of people must work together, formally or informally, if major missions are to be accomplished.

The overall work of each organization, however, has to be divided into tasks that individuals can handle. Those tasks must be related to each other in systematic ways so as to minimize confusion and duplication. Most organizations have developed formal hierarchical structures to handle the administrative tasks of relating the work of the various branches, assigning responsibilities, setting schedules, and making other decisions that affect the organization as a whole.

This chapter deals with the way groups of people in organizations make decisions. Typically, there is someone in the organizational structure—a boss or a leader—with an assigned responsibility for making decisions in each major area. The responsible individual often recognizes that the people he or she works with may be able to contribute to a good decision, and will be affected by whatever decision is made. He or she may seek to involve the group in the decision process in some fashion. This is our area of interest: the relationships between the responsible individual and the group in decision making in organizations.

The chapter starts with a case study, to provide a concrete example for the analyses of organizational theories and of the role of the responsible individual. After examining some of the characteristics of organizational groups and of the sorts of decisions they are called on to make, the chapter closes with a review of practical steps the responsible leader and group members can take to improve their organizational decision making.

Case Study: The New Library

Many of the concepts explored in this chapter will be easier to understand in reference to a specific example. Jefferson University, described below, is a mythical institution. Any similarity in the events or people portrayed here to events or individuals in existing institutions is intended only to give plausibility to the case, and not to reflect on any individuals. Jefferson is a sizable and complex institution with an enrollment of over 10,000 students in a number of undergraduate, graduate, and professional programs. The formal organization of the senior administration is shown in Figure 10.1.

Ralph White, the executive vice-president, had called the meeting. "I've asked each of you to look at the proposal for the new library for our health sciences campus from your own points of view," he said. "I have to make my recommendation to the president and the board tomorrow. What position should we take?" Having posed the question, he sat back and listened.

When the vice-president for development came in, the rest of the group was sitting around the big table on the fourth floor of Jefferson Hall. "Evelyn," said Al Benson, the vice-president for plant and services, "we've already set your target for you." Evelyn grinned; somehow, lately, all the big decisions seemed to rest on the ability of her shop to find new money. This time, however, she wasn't sure she could deliver.

The problem was the size of the project. Conversations about the need for a major library-learning resources center on the health sciences campus had been going on for years. A fund-raising campaign had been started four years before, but, aside from about $3,000,000 in major gifts, had not produced anything like the funds to cover the project. Changes in the medical school's leadership and in faculty ideas about the sort of facility needed had muddied the water.

During those four years, a good deal of money had been spent on the project. An architectural programmer had been hired to work

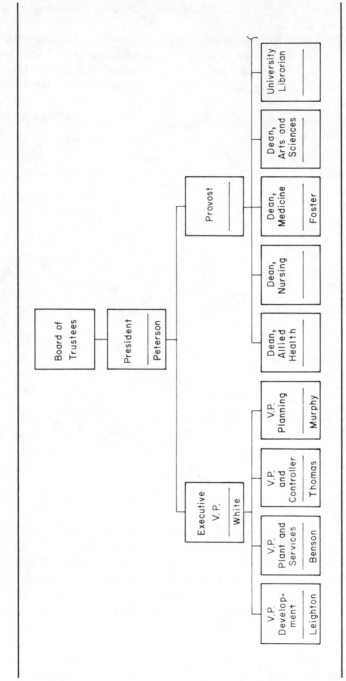

Figure 10.1 Administrative Organization Chart—Jefferson University

with faculty members and administrators in clarifying specifically what the building should consist of. Schematic designs had been prepared. Fund-raising staff had been hired and paid; lots of proposals had been written, brochures prepared, prospects identified and solicited, trips made. The net result was that the expenses of the campaign had eaten up a great deal of what had been raised; about a million was still due to be collected in the future.

Mike Thomas, vice-president and controller, did not let Evelyn forget the cash flow problem either. The bills had to be paid as they were incurred; much of the fund-raising progress was in pledges; payments were dribbling in over a number of years. That meant that Mike had to use other money to pay the bills, to be refunded when and if the pledges were paid. The payment record was good; these were major donors, who honored their commitments. Mike could be pretty sure of his repayments. There remained a related problem, however. Time was going by, and inflation was a major factor. He was paying bills in current dollars; the pledges, when they were paid, would be worth less, but the costs of the building would be going up—potentially leaving a gap in the financing.

There didn't seem to be much doubt about the need for the building. The present library conditions were less than marginal. The accreditation team for the American Medical Association gave the school its accreditation, to be sure, but only on the clear understanding that the new facility would be complete by the time of their next visit. The accreditation teams for the nursing and allied health schools had also criticized the inadequacy of the facility and scope of the collection. Working with expert consultants, the university librarian had developed a detailed program for the needed facility.

The medical school also had an image problem. The allied health school had its own new building, constructed about ten years ago. The nursing school was building superb new facilities. The medical school, the "flagship" of the complex, had never in its 80 years of existence had a new building. It was housed in converted manufacturing buildings. These made good laboratories, because they were constructed to support sizable machinery; but the close columns and relatively low ceilings make for terrible classrooms. The recent advent of the nursing school had required shoehorning additional faculty members into already crowded quarters. In an era when all three schools were trying to increase research activity, there was a critical shortage of research lab space. Some of the functions that

*could be moved from present quarters into the new building would
free space that could be converted to lab use (at some additional
capital cost, of course).*

*So the needs were clear, but the financing wasn't. Early cost
estimates ranged from $9,000,000 to $15,000,000, depending on
the size of the building and the mix of components proposed for it. A
site was acquired in a good central location. Cost estimates kept
rising as people got more and more enthusiastic about the possibilities, and as construction costs rose with inflation. Evelyn Leighton
took over the development division after the campaign had started,
reviewed the discouraging progress to date, changed the fund-
raising staff, and set to work. Not much happened. There was an
acting dean of the medical school at the time who, despite his best
efforts, could not be as effective as a permanent dean could be; and
there was still some general skepticism about the university's
ability to raise that kind of money. Some of the alumni remembered
the strenuous efforts that had been made to raise funds for the new
allied health tower, and the disappointment when the campaign fell
far short. The building plans had to be cut back; and for years the
allied health students have had to carry an extra $800 per student
per year on their tuition to pay the mortgages on the building.*

*This year, Dr. Peter Q. Foster was appointed dean of the medical
school. He had been the director of a major medically oriented
foundation. A nationally known researcher, he also brought strong
administrative skills and high aspirations to the city campus. He
quickly realized the need for the new facility, but added an even
more urgent dimension to its importance. He and many of his
health science colleagues realized that the ways in which future
health practitioners and others needed to have access to information was radically different from the past. They should not be
looking through card indices or thumbing through past issues of
periodicals; they should be inquiring directly from data bases by
computer. Nothing of that sort existed at the university, though
there were of course computer terminals in the library for accessing
Medlines and other search services.*

*For the health schools, such developments had particular
urgency. Each of the schools is linked for educational purposes with
many associated institutions. The medical school has over a dozen
major teaching hospitals and an additional thirty hospitals with
specialized programs. The health sciences schools could and
should provide core information access services to all these*

institutions, tying them together into an even more effective teaching and patient care network. The development of the new library would provide that possibility. Unfortunately, however, money doesn't come just because you need it.

Dr. Foster promptly undertook serious study of the possibilities. An outside consulting group worked with a core group of medical school and central administration people on a financial feasibility study. Cost estimates for various building sizes and configurations were prepared, starting at about $20,000,000 and going on up to $35,000,000. Estimates of the incremental costs of operating the building were worked out; the added costs would raise the tuitions of all three of the health sciences schools from $800 to $1300 per student per year. The consultant, acknowledging the importance of the project, recommended down-sizing the building as much as possible, so as to bring it within the capacity of Jefferson University to afford.

Then came an almost incredible break. President Peterson and Evelyn Leighton had over the course of two years been working quietly in Mexico with an elderly very wealthy medical school alumna. And indeed, with long and patient work, she was persuaded to grant the school a total of $15,000,000 through a private foundation. Suddenly, everyone's mood brightened.

It was now clearly possible to build the building. The question of total size remained. The huge grant was not enough. Would $23,000,000 be adequate? $25,000,000? $30,000,000? How much more could the university raise? What would the operating costs be, and who was going to pay them?

"Damn it, Evelyn, I think we ought to get going," said Al, after reviewing the fact sheets White had distributed. "The old gal gave us enough to get started; but we have to go through a formal application process to her foundation, and the deadline for that is a month from now. It will take my people that long to get the application done, once we've made our decision to go ahead. Our present estimate is $23,000,000. There's some room for slack in that, because we can always leave a couple of administrative office floors unfinished if we have to, and we can save the cost of the furnishings on those floors. Can't we raise the $8,000,000?

"What about the operating costs of the new building?" asked Ralph White.

"They are going to be high," said Jerry Murphy, the vice-president for planning. "That building will add about $1,500,000

to the budgets of the schools every year. With 600 medical students, 600 allied health students, and 200 nursing students; that means over $1000 per student per year. Maybe the medical students can stand it. The tuition is very high there, but there are still a lot of people who want to get into medical school; and the earning potential of the graduates is high. But interest in allied health is slowing down, and their earnings aren't as high; I don't want to see us sock another $1000 on top of the $800 they are already paying for their own building. And as for the nursing school, those tuitions are already incredibly high; I'd hate to see us load anything more there. It's going to be hard enough to get the nursing school onto a balanced budget under the best of circumstances."

Mike Thomas took out his calculator. "Since we can only count on about 5% or 6% as a long-run payout rate on endowment, it would take an endowment of $30,000,000 to generate that $1,500,000 annual income, if the students aren't going to pay it. Can you raise $38,000,000, Evelyn?"

"Come on, you guys," replied Leighton. "We got you the $15,000,000. Give us a little time and I think we can probably raise at least enough to cover the balance of the cost of the building. Psychologically, having the grant money in hand helps us, because it gives a sense of reality to the whole project. This is the biggest project we're going to have on the health sciences campus for many years. We can do it. It may take some time, that's all."

"Let me add one complexity" said Murphy. "If all we were doing was to build a conventional library building, we'd know how to do it. The building itself will not be that complicated; Al and his crew have a good handle on those costs. What about the new technology? We're going to be trying communications and computer linkages that haven't been tried anywhere else. That means that there's going to be added systems development expense, and some rather unusual equipment costs, right? And we can pretty well bet that there are going to be some mistakes made; we're not perfect; we don't have all the answers going in. My own guess is that we could easily add $1,000,000 to $1,500,000 in unanticipated systems development costs to the project. When can we have any better handle on those costs?"

"Dr. Foster has several committees working on the program right now," said Al. "The problem is that they may take some months thinking through all the pieces of this puzzle, and we have to make a decision very quickly. I can pretty well specify the cash payment schedule for the building right now, though. Figure about $100,000 per month starting in April when the project gets board approval, and then after a year, figure $1,000,000 per month for the 23 months of construction."

Evelyn piped in: "Some of my staff has been working with the National Library of Medicine to see if we can get systems development support. They don't have any money right now, but it's possible that something may come through on that in the future. We may also be able to get some support from computer manufacturers who'd like to be involved in the development so they could use the technology elsewhere."

"Evelyn let's come back to the fund raising for a minute," said White. "How sure are you?"

"My best guess is as follows: I can be 90% sure of raising $4,000,000; for $6,000,000, I guess about 70% sure; for $8,000,000, about 50% sure. I think there is a chance we can go even higher— maybe $10,000,000, but that's very risky. We should be able to get those pledges in the next three years; most of those pledges will be payable over three years. And just to anticipate Mike's next question, you should deduct about 8% to 15% from the total for fund-raising costs."

"You guys are all forgetting the problem of how we get from here to there," added Mike. "Al, you're going to be spending money on the building design and then on the construction. We can draw down on the foundation grant pretty quickly, but what do we do for the rest of the money? Evelyn can't guarantee that she can raise it. And even if she does, you heard how long it's going to take. That means I may not get some of my cash for six or seven years. We're awfully tight for working capital now. We financed the classroom renovation project out of working capital, and the hockey rink as well. And we haven't yet raised the funds to pay for those. There's just so far I can stretch. I can borrow some from the banks, of course, but that will cost us at least one point over prime. Who's going to be paying those interest charges? They should be charged to the project, but that just raises the total cost; the medical school operating budget is already tight and probably can't afford to absorb them."

"Look, we're not getting anywhere" said Murphy. "Al, you want to build the building, and you've got time constraints. We need a decision now. Mike, you've got real cash flow problems, and you're worried about whether or not we'll ever raise the construction *money. I'm concerned about the operating costs and the unknowns in the systems development. Evelyn's a born optimist, but even she can't guarantee how much she and the president and Dr. Foster can raise, or when."*

Al boomed in: "Come on. I say we go ask the board for approval of the $23,000,000 project. That's what Dr. Foster wants. We've got some flexibility within that total to cut back if we need to—maybe $2,000,000. That gives Evelyn her fund-raising target. And it gets us the building we've all been talking about, the best thing that's happened to this place in years."

"Okay," said Ralph White. "You've brought out the important factors. I think we've chewed on this enough. I understand the various concerns around the table. Now here's what I think I'll recommend to the president and the board: can you all support a recommendation to . . ."

Elements in the Organizational Decision-Making Context

Using the new library case as an example, we will look at various aspects of organizational decision making. First, we need to define more precisely what is meant by "group" decision making in organizations. That will lead us into an examination of organizational structure.

With that background, we can look more closely at the "responsible individual" (Ralph White in the case), at the group involved in the decision process, and at the relationship between them.

We also need to look at the nature of the decision to be made—its urgency and complexity—since that also will affect the way decisions are made. Finally, we can sketch out some prescriptions and cautions for organizational group decision making, for both the responsible individual and the group members.

GROUP VERSUS INDIVIDUAL DECISIONS IN ORGANIZATIONS

Throughout this chapter, the "group" will include those people whom the responsible individual involves in the decision process, formally or informally, usually collectively. Ultimately, it is one person, the responsible individual, who actually makes the decision. However, because group members are actively involved in the decision process, that process is consistent with our definition of group decision making discussed in Chapter 1.

Ralph White needed and wanted to involve his staff—the people who worked for him. Each of them brought expertise to some dimension of the problem: fund-raising for the project, designing and building it, managing the university's finances so as to support the project, thinking through the ways the project would affect tuition rates, and so forth. Each of the staff members would be responsible for implementing part of whatever decision was made. It was important that they all be engaged in the process so that they could contribute to, and understand, the final decision.

Note, however, that the group was a limited one. White did not bring Dr. Foster to the meeting, or the president. He did not include any board members, even though their approval would eventually be needed. Nor did he include medical school students, who would be concerned about tuition increases. Or the university librarian, who would be the principal official responsible for operation of the new facility. Does this mean that their views were not considered?

It is generally not possible in large organizations to include everyone in major decision groups. White knew quite well how anxious the librarian and Dr. Foster and the president were to get the project started; he knew what the librarian's professional program entailed; he knew what the rise in tuition would mean to the students; but White had to decide on his own recommendation to the board, balancing the need for the facility against the institution's and students' ability to support it financially.

The line between individual decision making and organizational group decision making is hard to draw clearly. White's staff group, meeting together with him and chewing over a specific decision, falls neatly into the group decision-making model we have been talking about, where a responsible individual makes his or her decisions in consultation with an actively engaged group. Stretching the definition a bit, we might consider that there was a group decision process even if White had only arranged a conference telephone call among his staff. If he consulted each of them individually, letting each of them know where the others stood, one might still argue that his staff, as a group, was involved in his decision. The stretching of the definition snaps, however, if all that White did was to sample the views of various constituencies; then we would have to say that White was making an individual decision, taking into account to some degree the view of others.

THEORIES OF ORGANIZATIONAL BEHAVIOR

Theory X and Theory Y

Traditional texts on organization describe most firms or institutions as having some sort of hierarchical structure, such as that shown in Figure 10.2. The people in each layer carry out the orders of the individuals to whom they report. Straight-line direct reporting relationships are pictured and prescribed. Each person reports to a single boss and performs a single function. The number of individuals whom a supervisor can effectively manage (the individual's "span of control") is an issue of some interest. And little attention is paid to the needs, wants, or interests of the individuals involved. The organization chart of Jefferson University would, if taken at face value, indicate this type of organization.

This form of organization evolved from the military model. The general gives orders to the colonel who in turn directs the major, who directs the captain, who directs the lieutenant, and so on. Orders flow directly down the line of authority. The general and the colonel may also have "staff" officers, specialists in military intelligence or in logistics. These staff specialists are out of the chain of command but but gain their influence by providing information or service. Military organizations are necessarily authoritarian. The private ordered by his sergeant to attack is not supposed to engage in a debate about the tactics.

Not all organizations require or profit from this sort of strictly hierarchical management. In Chapter 9 on corporate decision making is a discussion of "Theory X" and "Theory Y" motivation, reviewed in abbreviated form here. Traditional organizational theory, and the military organization in particular, tend to be based on Theory X concepts. In these views, people are basically lazy (and/or scared, in the military context). They must be coerced, controlled, directed, threatened with punishment. Effective leadership must recognize these traits and behave accordingly.

Theory Y takes a different view. Work is as natural as sleep; people will exercise self-control and self-direction in pursuit of objectives to which they are committed; most individuals can be creative and ingenious and constructive in their work. And here again, effective management should recognize these human traits and utilize them.

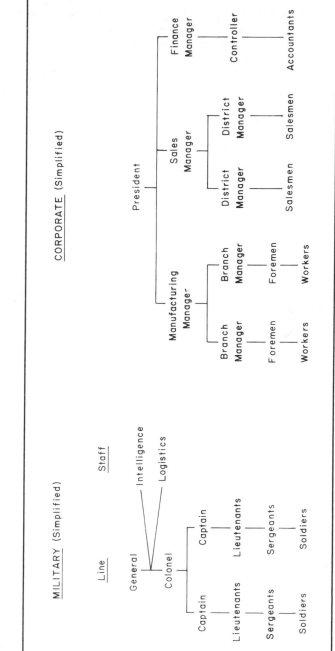

Figure 10.2 Traditional Organization Structures

291

If Theory X reigns in the military, Theory Y has to be recognized and followed in most volunteer groups and most organizations of professionals. Coercive, authoritarian behavior toward members of the League of Women Voters or the local school board or members of a law firm is apt to be counter productive. Under Theory X, decisions, are made unilaterally by those in charge; under Theory Y, decisions are more likely to participatory.

A Mixed Model

Most modern organizations cannot be simply characterized. They tend to be elaborate blends of staff and line structures. Within them, managers tend to behave somewhere between Theory X and Theory Y. There are few decisions in a major institution that are made solely and unilaterally by one individual. Most major decisions must at least be weighed in the responsible individual's head for their acceptability to the group. Many are in fact talked through extensively. Other major group decisions evolve over time by accretion of numerous small decisions; without stretching the point too far, one might even say that some institutional decisions arise from the ecology of the organization. Organization charts that purport to show how decisions are made will have as many dotted as straight lines, with individuals reporting directly to one supervisor, but following the procedural guidelines of another office, and involved in a number of decision groups. The chief accountant in a branch factory, for instance, reports to the plant manager, but must follow the accounting rules set up by corporate headquarters; and he or she will be involved in decisions about new products and equipment purchases as well as accounting. Union organizations and other formal or informal groupings of employees express their views on acceptable administrative behavior and institutional values as well as on their own working conditions. Direct orders are given, of course, through more often on the factory floor than in the engineering department. The further up the organizational hierarchy one goes, and the more technical or professional the skill of the people involved, the more likely the responsible individual's orders are to be couched politely, and the more often they are the product of discussion rather than of administrative fiat. Consultation and persuasion become the typical modes of communication. Persons at all levels involved with a particular product of service may be brought together in "quality circles" to share their thoughts on improvements.

What Harvey Brooks (1983) says about the relationships between boards of trustees and university administrators holds equally true for responsible individuals and groups:

> While it is true that ultimate authority lies with the Board, the effective exercise of that authority must be based on a series of informal understandings that can best be summarized the word "trust." If and when authority has to be exercised explicitly at the level of the Board, it is a symptom that trust has been undermined, and the institution is in serious trouble until and unless trust among the various levels of authority. This is in contrast to a model in which the Board makes policy more or less autonomously, and the officers of the organization implement the policy, or a model in which proposals and initiatives float up through the various levels of the organizational hierarchy, and are selectively weeded out until they reach the level of the Board. Of course, both sorts of behavior occur in organizations, and the problem of organizational effectiveness depends on the proper blending of "top-down" and "bottom-up" activity. As a practical matter, the question of ultimate authority should be beside the point; if it is not, the organization is in serious trouble.

Authority and Power

Authority may be defined as "the power to make decisions which guide the behavior of subordinates." (Simon, 1961, p. 125) In the military, that authority is of paramount importance; disobeying a superior is of the utmost seriousness, and military justice is constructed on that principle. But in other organizations, an individual's authority is limited to the area in which his or her orders will be accepted by subordinates. That area varies widely. In a small manufacturing company, the foreman's authority may be extensive in work assignments, tools to be used, and so forth, but may be limited by union agreement on wage rates and certain working conditions. The managing partner in a law firm may, by consent of the partners, exercise authority over supporting staff and recruitment of juniors, but may have little or nothing whatever to say about the way the partners conduct their cases.

Job mobility also imposes limits on authority. While there are real constraints on the movement of individuals from one organization to another, the arbitrary power of the manager is limited by his need to retain the contributions of those who carry on the function for which he is held accountable.

If the strict hierarchical concept of organizational structure seems overly authoritarian and simplistic; if most managers conform wholly neither to Theory X nor to Theory Y; and if most decisions in modern organizations involve a number of individuals; then we are dealing with group decision making of a special sort. To be efficient, organizations need leadership, direction, administration, and management. They appoint individuals in charge of specific areas and hold them accountable for getting results. These individuals in turn have to earn and retain the support of the people on whom they count to achieve those results.

It is the decision-making relationship between these responsible individuals and the people with whom they work that is the focus of this chapter.

One should not infer from the attention given in this chapter to that relationship that all organizational decision making is based on personal and power relationships. The chapter on corporate decision making outline several techniques used by groups to arrive at sound fact-based conclusions. Organizational decision making does, however, differ significantly from the rational decision-making model used in traditional economic theory. Herbert A. Simon (1961), who won a Nobel prize for his work on administrative behavior, describes what he calls "administrative man," as distinct from the "economic man." In the firm, "economic man" pursues a single goal—maximization of profits—and has perfect information on all alternatives and their consequences. "Administrative man," on the other hand, pursues many goals simultaneously, and has only partial information on which to base decisions. He cannot maximize. He must "satisfice," doing the best he can with the information he can get within the time in which he has to make the decision. But he is not "Freudian man" either, all affect and instinct. "Administrative man" if of course not wholly rational; but he is *intendedly* rational. His decisions will be rational once we understand the premises on which they were based.

In his theory of human choice, Simon points out that

the decision is too gross a unit of analysis and must be dissected into its component premises . . . [An individual's] role is a specification [for instance] of some but not all of the premises that enter into an individual's decisions . . . Many other premises also enter into the same decisions, including information premises and idiosyncratic premises that are expressive of personality. Behavior can be predicted, then, when the premises of the decision are known [or can be predicted] in sufficient detail" [Simon, 1961, p. xxx].

An individual brings both factual premises and value premises to a decision. While the factual premises may be conscious and rational, the value premises may be unconscious and emotional.

An organization's leaders attempt to bring many of these premises into coherence with each other by striving to develop organizational objectives. An organizational objective is not some sort of "group mind" but is ":a personal objective of all the participants. It is the means whereby their organizational activity is bound together to achieve a personal satisfaction of their own diverse motives" (Simon, 1961, p. 17). The behavior of an institution may be made more "rational" in terms of the organization's goals, by influencing the premises that the individual brings to each decision. The individual can be "rational,,only to the extent that he is *able* to pursue a particular course of action, he has a correct conception of the *goal* of the action, and he is correctly *informed* about the conditions of the action" (Simon, 1961, p. 241). In each of these areas, the manager—the responsible individual—can take actions to influence factual and value premises.

The Responsible Individual

The protaganist is our organizational group decision-making drama is referred to here as the "responsible individual." He or she is the person in the organization assigned decision responsibility and authority in a particular area—the department head, construction supervisor, foreman, president, treasurer, personnel manager, or head nurse. Ralph White has the responsibility for decisions on new buildings, among other things, subject to approval by the president and the board.

In volunteer organizations, the responsible individual might be elected by other group members instead of being appointed, or may simply be the individual who emerges as leader by taking active responsibility.

It is important to distinguish among responsibility and authority and power. This discussion refers to the *responsible* individual—that is, the person who is held accountable for the results. That individual may have *authority* to make decisions legitimated by his or her superiors in formal job description and, more importantly, by his or her superiors' acceptance and support of those decisions. *Power,* on the other hand, is exerted. On the television drama *Dallas*, Bobby Ewing once complained to Jock that although Jock had given him the power to run Ewing Oil, Jock kept interfering in company actions. Jock had to point out that he gave Bobby the title; no one can give "power"; power is something you have to take, to earn. Ralph White has been given the authority to make decisions about new buildings, and is held responsible for the results of those decisions. But he has to make decisions. If he delays or is indecisive, the medical dean or librarian or president will press for and get a decision on their own, in effect taking the decision power away from White. In the long run, designated authority must reflect power, and responsibility for the quality of decisions must be assigned where the decisions are made.

The actions of others will reveal whether the designated responsible individual has authority and power; indeed, the behavior of the responsible individual may be influenced by whether or not he or she feels in possession of sufficient authority, and, if not, by a desire to gain it.

Several factors in the responsible individual's position are important in understanding her or his relationship to the group:

(1) His or her "attitude" on the administrative hierarchy. Typically, the further up the organizational ladder an individual is, the more influence the responsible individual has—the more levers the individual has in his or her hands to assure that the decisions are carried out. Typically also, the higher up the individual is, the further removed he or she is from detailed information about the nature of the situation. One of the skills in administrative organization is to locate responsibility for specific decisions at the proper levels, where the responsible individual is high enough to see the whole of the problem and to have the levers of control in his or her hand, but low enough to have a good feel for the problem. White is the "right" person to make decisions about new construction, because it is only at his level that information about building costs, facility needs, fund raising, tuition impacts, and overall finance all come together. The responsible individual's relationships with a group will be influenced by this hierarchical position. If the individual is too high, he or she may tend to use the group only to get the facts and understand the issues; from the group's point of view, they may feel they are not participating. If the individual is too low and has no decision power of his or her own, he or she may tend to use the group only to gain support for her own proposed decisions.

(2) The "line" of "staff" character of the responsible individual's position is also important. While there may not such clear distinctions between these elements as there used to be, still, the line officer typically has more more authority and can be more directly held responsible for success or failure. This dimension of the individual's situation is referred to in the chapter on social psychology of group decision making (Chapter 2) as position power. In the "line" relationship, the individual usually can more directly reward or punish group members for success or failure; in "staff" relationships, the position power is diminished.

(3) The manner in which the responsible individual got the position is also of concern. In corporations and similar institutions, the individual is almost invariably appointed. The power of the appointing authority, the reasons for the appointment, the term of appointment and similar factors may all influence the way the group relates to the responsible individual. In some volunteer or professional partnership organizations, the individual may have been elected to the position; if so, the nature of the group electing him or her needs to be understood. Is there a clear term of office, or can the individual be promoted or fired at will? How does the particular decision to be made relate to the individual's continuing in a position of responsibility? The concept of "position power" outlined in Chapter 2 relates to this factor and also to the ability of the individual to influence group members, which will be discussed in a later section.

(4) The role the individual has been asked to assume (or has assumed for him or herself) in the organization is also important. Often, an individual is given responsibility for a function in a company or institution, but clearly understands that his or her responsibility goes beyond simply carrying out that particular duty. A mayor may be elected on a platform of doing something about crime in the streets; his or her mandate, then, goes beyond simply doing the mayor's normal job. A new plant manager may be appointed with the specific additional task of phasing out one product line and starting another. Ralph White views his job not only in terms of making correct facility decisions, but also of creating an effective team to manage the affairs of the institution. This additional agenda will influence the individual's relationship to the group.

(5) The personality and management style of the responsible individual is also important in understanding his or her relationship with a decision group. The individual may be democratic or autocratic. His or her willingness to consult, to involve others in the process, even to delegate decision making in certain areas, may well vary. Even though it is said that there is no limit to what a person can do if he or she is willing to give the credit to others, some individuals want to be

lone rangers. As was seen in Chapter 2, each of the styles can be effective, depending on the nature of the group situation.

(6) Finally, the degree of support and loyalty that the individual can command among the members of the group can be important. The cohesiveness of leader-member relationships was discussed in Chapters 2 and 3. An individual who was just elected by an enthusiastic group can usually ask a great deal of them. In a corporation or university or agency, the responsible individual can usually count on greater cohesiveness and support from persons he or she appointed or hired his or herself than the individual can from those who are holdovers from prior administrations. A group that has won significant accomplishments under an individual will tend to stick with him or her closely, whereas the unproven individual may have only tentative support.

Characteristics of the Group

Just as the responsible individual's style can influence his or her behavior toward the group, the group's size, composition, and internal relationships can affect its decision-making role.

The size of the group assembled for a decision is typically rather small, as it was in our own case study, ranging perhaps from three or four individuals to a maximum of ten to fifteen. This group may, of course, be one of a whole series of other groups which together compose the New England Telephone Company or the U.S. Postal Service or Stanford University. Few decisions actively involve all such groups, however; we will be paying special attention to the group of individuals working closely together on some task or aspect of the total institution's mission. The group may be quite heterogeneous in background and skills; the task to be done is what brings it together. The group's membership is intentionally limited, though there may be no formal restriction on size. Ralph could have brought in others if he had so chosen or omitted some of those whom he did invite. By and large, the membership size is understood and some degree of cohesiveness and feeling of belonging results from membership.

The association of the individuals in this group is at least to some extent voluntary. Evelyn and Al work here because they need the paycheck, to be sure; and they may have objected to being assigned to this task; but they can usually quit or transfer if they wish to. If the enterprise is a volunteer organization, such as a Big Brother service club, or a hospital board of trustees, the individuals are fully voluntary. People may belong to an organization because of the extrinsic rewards it offers—salary, benefits and the like. They may be fully as much attracted by intrinsic values, such as the character of the people they work with, and the mission of the institution. Dedication to the objectives of the organization can be an important source of the willingness of individuals to work together, especially in nonprofit institutions. A further distinction needs to be made, however. There is a difference between the individuals loyal "to the *objectives* of the organization, who will resist modification of those objectives . . . and the individual who is loyal to the *organization* and who will support opportunistic changes in its objectives that are calculated to promote its survival and growth" (Simon, 1961, p. 118).

The members of White's "group" have structured relationships. They are "officers," not simply individuals with private opinions. They have organizationally determined roles to play and responsibilities to carry out with reference to whatever decision is brought before them. Thomas, for example, is responsible for the university's finances, and won't let anyone forget it. Each individual carries a title denoting his or her responsibility. This degree of formality is more often found among business and institutional groups than among volunteer groups, but structured roles tend to evolve even among volunteers. The group may consist, as it did in this case, of the members of the responsible individual's department or office. In a complex organization, there may be a variety of duly constituted groups—the president's cabinet, the heads of the various departments in the division, and so forth. These may, as in the examples given, be constitutionally defined in terms of their hierarchical position. Other types of duly constituted groups include preselected grievance committees, or functional groups, such as the financial officers of each division, or faculty committees on tenure and promotion. Members of the latter set of groups are often appointed, but may sometimes be elected. The responsible individual may thus have to deal not only with those individuals he or she appointed (or in whose appointment he or she concurred or was involved), but also with groups that were not of his or her choosing.

Relationships between group members not only tend to be structured, but they may also have to be durable. Ralph, Evelyn, Al, and the others, have worked together for some time, and presumably will continue to do so. That long-term relationship influences the way they act toward each other; no one can afford to alienate another, because each may need the others at some point in the future. This means that each must be willing to compromise, to accomplish what is best for the institution. In contrast, members of one time aggregations such as lobbying groups, can single-mindedly pursue one objective in a complex situation (such as air quality in an argument over proposed industrial development) without having to participate in reaching compromise solutions.

The group members (other than the responsible individual) may be equal among themselves—as social workers each with their own case loads, for instance, or the group of vice-presidents in the library case—or there may be a range of skill levels and elaborate pecking orders based on seniority of job assignment. The issue of whether this group has greater or lesser power than another group in the institution may be of great concern to the group members them-selves, but is not an issue for purposes of this analysis.

The frequency and kinds of decisions required by the task the group is performing will also affect the way the group functions. Ralph's staff group is typical of most in that the same group and is assembled regularly for managerial decisions in many areas. Usually the group in question is involved in a task or series of tasks—in building a house or winning an election or teaching the set of romance language courses. These tasks require a series of decisions along the way. By way of contrast, process-oriented groups (e.g., therapy groups) may make relatively few decisions. Almost invariably, the work of the group is divisible; each person carries on some aspect of the total. The group may be charged with maximizing its output, as when volunteers endeavor to raise an extraordinary sum of donations for a public television station in a short time; or it may wish to optimize a broader institutional goal by coordinating its work with those of other groups, as college fund raisers may do in working closely with admissions and public relations officers. Rewards are typically collective: everyone gets paid when the job is done, or feels satisfaction together from the group accomplishment. An important dimension of the group's task, discussed in more detail in Chapter 2, is whether it is additive (where individual strengths are pooled, as in a tug of war), or conjunctive (where the group can move only at the pace of the least proficient), or disjunctive (where the group's success depends on the most proficient), or discretionary (where the group must coordinate the contributions of its members). Although organizational group taks may fall in any of these areas, they are usually conjunctive and discretionary at least to some degree. The library decision isn't satisfactory unless each of the group members can accept and support it, both personally and in their structured roles. As the group members work together over time, they and the responsible individual come to understand any decision elements that are apt to take longer or require more attention, and the team and the process can be altered accordingly.

The personalities and backgrounds of the members of the group affect the decision process. Attitudes, biases, degrees of authoritarianism, self-centeredness—all are present in each member. The responsible individual needs to bear these in mind in choosing the group and in leading the group toward decision.

When thinking about whether or how to involve a group in a decision, the responsible individual should carefully consider the extent to which the group accurately reflects the views of the community that the decision will affect. It doesn't help a hospital administrator much to discuss possible changes in hospital nursing policy with the duly elected representatives of the hospital's doctors, for instance, if the physicians and the nurses do not agree.

The responsible individual may not find ready-made groups to involve in the decision process, particularly in volunteer organizations or in new situations in existing organizations. Perhaps no group exists. Or perhaps there is a group that might be asked to be involved, but that the responsible individual feels may not be responsive to his wishes or to the situation, like the group of doctors. The responsible individual can then appoint or otherwise form an ad hoc group, chosen specifically for its appropriateness to the task at hand, perhaps asking the nurses to elect representatives to talk with him or her.

The responsible individual may prefer to discuss a decision with a variety of individuals rather than with a group. While the decision dynamics are obviously different under this arrangement, this interaction can still be viewed as group decision making; most of the same observations apply. If, for instance, the chairman of a board of selectmen discusses a pet idea separately with each of his two colleagues, and finds no support, he will not need to bring it up for formal vote. This "pseudo-group" concept was discussed in Chapter 1.

Characteristics of Organizational Decisions

Thus far, we have looked at organizational decision making in the context of theories of organizational behavior, with attention to the roles of the responsible individual and the group. To complete the theoretical review, some understanding of certain characteristics of decisions in organizations is useful.

The first and most important step in organizational group decision making is for someone, usually the responsible individual, to recognize that a decision is needed and to articulate what it is. The recognition of the need or opportunity for a decision is critical; control of the definition of the decision to be made and of its timing are extremely important.

Sometimes there are clear decision points. More frequently, a decision emerges from a process. White had been thinking about the library problem for some time, consulting, talking with people. Each of the other participants had been involved for months. A decision point had been reached, but the decision itself had been evolving over a period of time. White had a deadline thrust upon him, in effect, by the approaching application deadline to the foundation and an upcoming board meeting.

The decision that White and the group had to make could have been defined in many ways. To go ahead or not? How much risk the university could stand? What size to go ahead with? How much faith to have in the fund raisers? The trade-off between tuition impact and building size? The responsible individual must seize the opportunity to define the question in the way he or she thinks will yield the most fruitful results. An all-or-nothing ("go-or-no-go") approach in the library case may be emotionally satisfying, but unproductive of intelligent debate.

Most organizational decisions are complex. Building the new library affects physical plant, curriculum, student tuitions, fund raising, public image, university financial strength, future staffing needs, and other matters. White needed to bring his staff together to deal with those complexities.

One seldom has all the information that would be needed for a perfect decision analysis. What other fund-raising prospects are there and how likely are they to give? What will the costs be for the information-systems development? What will inflation do to building costs if we wait? What would be sacrificed if we cut the size a bit? And so forth. The decision, as noted previously, must be aimed to "satisfice," since rational maximization is not possible.

Organizational group decisions are almost always political, at least to some extent. There is often a range of possible answers; the optimal solution will be the one that gains people's support, not necessarily the one with a mathematical solution that is fractionally superior. Who pushes the hardest, and what can be gained by supporting or modifying some decision? What does the president want? What will the board accept? Clearly Dr. Foster (the dean) was influential in the decision process without even being there. Who has the initiative? Decisions should always be made as logically as possible. Every available analytic tool should be used. White had asked each of his people to provide analyses of the fact, and shared these fact sheets with everyone. Alternatives had been studied. The decision, however, will be informed by the consensus of the group and guided by what will be acceptable to the president and the board.

To repeat a point touched on earlier, a critical consideration for organizational decision making concerns the level at which a decision is best made. There is a trade-off between organizational power and breadth on the one hand, and time and information on the other. The lower one is in the organizational hierarchy, the closer one is to the specific details, the better one's information and "feel" is for a situation. Al Benson, the vice-president for plant and services, knew much more about the proposed building design than anyone else there. He knew less about the fund-raising details, however, than Evelyn Leighton did. White knew less than either about their respective areas, but had a better overview of the whole. The president was out of town, busy on another fund-raising mission. He has an even better overview of the needs of the university as a whole than White does, but has so many other things to accomplish that he cannot dig into the detailed implications of alternative decisions. Thus, White is the logical person in the organization to make the decision. He is high enough to have the necessary overview, but not so high as to be loaded with other responsibilities or unable to because of time to get at the needed information.

Decisions have various degrees of complexity and urgency that influence the way they must be handled. Consider the following:

— How urgent is it? The fire chief usually doesn't have time for group decisions.

— Who is affected by it, and in what ways? If the decision affects the functioning of the group (what time to hold the next meeting, which projects to tackle next, etc.), the responsible individual may well choose to involve the group members, and may even delegate the decision to them. If the decision is one that does not involve them or their expertise at all (such as a decision on some other group's functioning in which the opinion of the responsible individual was asked), or if it involves the group members in a personal way (which group member to lay off), the individual may choose not to bring the group into his decision process.

— Is it complex or straightforward? Does it have a heavy technological or professional component? In a complex working environment, the individual responsible for decisions may well not have all the technical or professional expertise needed. He will need to cnsult with the experts in the group to make the decision.

— How uniform are the values and assumptions of the responsible individual and the group likely to be with respect to the problem? Is it a situation in which they will have widely divergent points of view? An automotive executive sensing that there is a fundamental mismatch between his company's product and the desires of the market should do more than simply ask the advertising managers for advice.

Decision rules are often unclear in administrative groups. The responsible individual is held accountable for the decision and for its execution by superiors and by the group itself; he or she will want and need freedom and authority to made decisions. The decisions, as noted earlier, have to be acceptable both to the superiors and to the group that will help the individual carry them out. Are decisions made by the group as a whole? or by a cluster of members? Must they be unanimous, or can a plurality decide? The answers will depend on the nature of the group and of the leader and on the task to be performed. As is pointed out in Chapter 9 on corporate decision making, there are advantages and disadvantages to group decisions; the represent commitments by the group; but for that very reason, they tend to be irreversible.

The ease with which a group can make or concur with decisions can be one measure of the effectiveness of those decisions. High group morale can indicate satisfaction with the decision process. Implementation can also be a key. A decision is probably reasonable, if the group members can agree with only a minimum of discussion on the division of responsibility for implementation. Reluctance to tackle implementation can signal unspoken disagreement with the decision. Gauging the "quality" of decisions can be very difficult in some administrative situations where criteria are vague. One measure of quality is that the decision permits the group to continue as a working unit. Just as it can be said that the primary motive of a corporation is to make enough profit to continue to exist in the long run (and not enough to attract many competitors into the field), so one implicit aim of most organizational groups is to continue to function together effectively over time.

Understanding and Using the Group Decision Process: The Practical Side

Thus far, we have dealt with a rather theoretical discussion of the elements of organizational group decision making—theories of organization, and characteristics of the responsible individual, the group, and the decisions themselves. The balance of this chapter reviews some of the practical considerations a responsible individual should have in mind in deciding whether to involve a group in the decision and in structuring that decision.

Confronted with a decision to be made, the first question the responsible individual should think through is whether to involve a group, and how. Ralph White, having thought about the building problem for some time, could simply have made the decision himself rather than consulting his group. He felt it important, however, to involve the group for two reasons: to be sure that he had their input; and, by involving them, to be sure that they understood and would support the decision. Some uses of a group may seem to place the responsible individual in a dubious moral or ethical position (see Chapter 5 on ethical decision making). Most readers who have spent any substantial time involved with the workings of an organization will, however, recognize the necessity for administrative leadership that can distinguish satisfactorily between the alternatives presented below, and can use a group to help deal with difficult situations. A group can be used, with relationship to a decision, in at least the following ways;

— to help the responsible individual gain an understanding of the problem or situation by talking it through. The director of an engineering design group may simply need to be educated about the details of a particular manufacturing problem.

— to identify where the group feeling is with respect to a particular issue or circumstance. The responsible individual may be in the position of the senator asking where his or her constituents are so that he or she can go out and lead them.

— to give him or her advice on the solution or the range of possible solutions to the situation. It is rare that any responsible individual has the corner on ideas, and it is useful for her or him to listen.

— to avoid having to make an unpopular decision or to soften its impact by sharing the blame. The individual can refer it to the group. Any

responsible individual knows that his or her leadership and authority—
that is, the ability to influence people's behavior—can only sustain so
many unpopular decisions. It is not illogical to want to share the
burden with the group.

— to gain support for a decision, either a positive or a negative one. The
responsible individual may find group support for a decision helpful in
selling that decision to his or her superiors, as testimony to its
soundness or acceptability. She or he may also find group support (or
at least group acquiescence) helpful in putting across a negative or
unpopular decision.

— to gain advocates for a point of view. She or he may be able to educate
the group to see the problem or situation from his or her perspective, or
at least gain sufficient understanding of the need for the steps proposed
to withhold opposition. Where you stand depends on where you sit, as
they say. The responsible individual can in effect get the group to set in
his or her chair for a while.

— to help him or her implement a decision. If the membership of the
group is carefully chosen, its members will be opinion leaders in the
larger community, and can help to defend and explain the steps or
decision taken. Under some circumstances, the responsible individual
can even use the group selection process to enlist those who will, in the
future, be given administrative or managerial responsibilities, and can
use the group process to help educate those individuals.

— to confront individuals with the view of others. In Chapter 3, the
effects of the group on the individual were discussed at length. The
responsible individual can use a group to bring pressure on the
members toward consensus, as well as using it to present a strong front
to outsiders. Group consensus can constitute a "social reality" with
respect to which the individuals both in the group and affected by it
must orient themselves.

— to rationalize a decision already made. Neither an individual's
decision nor a group's decision is necessarily "rational" in the sense
that it optimizes the possible outcomes. It may only be rational when
the ego needs (the value premises) of the persons involved are
understood and factored in. But the decisions need to be rationaliz-
able; that is, one has to be able to give plausible explanations for them.
A group can help the responsible individual both by reaching
conclusions it knows he wants, and by finding such plausible
explanations for that decision, for their own benefit and that of the
affected community. In Chapter 6 on social risk assessment, the
legitimating function of committees was discussed at some length.

The responsible individual may, if he or she is astute, be able to
structure the group dynamics so as to make better decisions. For his
decision, White brought together individuals representing all the

important points of view, and let the discussion bring critical issues to the surface. See the discussion in Chapter 3 on the use of "devil's advocates" to force the group to confront unpopular scenarios and to consider all possible options. In deciding whether to involve a group, the responsible individual should keep in mind some of the strengths and weaknesses of group action.

In general, a group (or more specifically, the individuals in a group) can:

— discuss a problem or situation and illumine its causes, complexities, and consequences.

— edit or at least react to a document or draft or series of suggestions.

— eliminate possible actions by their reactions to the suggestions, thus narrowing the field of possible decision alternatives.

— help the responsible individual implement whatever course of action is eventually decided upon, in their individual capacities as members of the community involved.

— create a climate of involvement, symbolically involving the whole community.

— represent the community affected by the decision at least to some extent. This ability is clearly dependent on the manner in which the group was picked and on the perception of the rest of the community about the members of the group and of the process of selection. The minority students on campus may not feel well represented if the dean of students handpicks one minority student to be spokesman; they might feel better if they elected someone.

— can, if well led, come to understand the problem of task from the point of view of the responsible individual. In this way, the individual can use the group as a way of disseminating a broader understanding of the reasons or background for some decision.

— can, with astute and persuasive leadership, reach conclusions that are in the interests of the group as a whole or of the community or institution as a whole, but that may not be in the best interests of the individuals involved. A committee dedicated to the overall task of reducing taxes may be able to come to agreement on service cuts that individuals on the committee would not favor if asked separately.

There are, of course, corresponding tasks that a committee or group is less apt to be successful at:

— writing. It usually works better if some individual, either the responsible individual or a member of the group, drafts and the group edits or comments.

— deciding quickly. In most cases of individual-group interaction, the group is in fact not asked to decide. The individual makes the decision, having heard the views of the group. Sometimes, the individual may delegate decision responsibility to a group, of course; when he or she does so, he or she needs to allow the group time for the decision process. Usually, the group structure requires that the members hear each other out before any decision is made.

— taking initiative. The group can respond to tasks that are given to it, perhaps in imaginative ways; but it usually is constrained by (as well as inspired by) the identities and premises of the individuals who make it up.

The "responsible individual" is just that—responsible. White can and will be fired if he makes too may bad decisions, even if the ideas for those decisions originated in the group and if they had the support of the group. In general, one cannot or does not fire a group. As with a baseball team, one fires the manager if the team does not do well. It would be very serious for Jefferson University to have to remove at one blow all its top administrative managers; the university could, however, get along for a while without any one of them. The responsible individual must remember in dealing with the group, however they are involved, that he or she is accountable for the results.

In selecting a group and in guiding its deliberations, the responsible individual has a variety of options open to him or her to influence the decision processes of the group:

— He or she exerts a basic influence by the selection of the members of the group. Each of those members brings his or her own values and preferences to the decision task; to the extent the responsible individual is aware of these, he or she can influence the outcome of the decision.

— He or she can use assignment to the group as a reward or as a punishment. No one wants to serve on the committee that adjudicates traffic fines. But most people want to serve on those committees they think are important.

— To the extent that he or she in involved in the group himself, the responsible individual can use assignment of particular tasks within the group as rewards or punishments.

— She or he can assure that the group members are given whatever support they need to do the job, in staff, information, or budget.

— She or he can obviously reward or threaten individual members to sway their opinions.

— He or she can act on the advice of the group, which increases its prestige, or he or she can ignore its advice, which decreases that prestige but makes it harder to recruit smaller groups in the future.

— He or she can publicize the work and results of the group process, or can suppress such publication.

Finally, with respect to the particular decision in question, there are several tips the responsible individual can keep in mind:

(1) control the timing and the nature of the decision to be made, to the extent possible. As noted earlier, it is often unclear when a decision is needed, or even that one is needed at all, and equally unclear as to just what that should be. The responsible individual should define the decision to be made in the way in which answers are apt to be most productive.

(2) constitute the group carefully. The importance of group composition is stressed throughout the book, and is especially important in the context of organizational decision making. Be sure that each important point of view has an effective advocate. Collect for the "group" the individuals whose expertise is relevant to that decision, keeping in mind the possible desirability of including people affected by the decision, or people responsible for carrying it out, or those whose political role is important in getting support or approval for the eventual decision.

(3) don't make unnecessary decisions. As with good practice for judges, make the minimum decision needed. White will not now ask for approval to proceed with construction; he will more likely decide to authorize the application to the foundation at the full amount, and to proceed with a design that permits the later deletion of one or two floors if fund raising is unsuccessful or if construction bids come in too high.

It should be clear that tips on effective group decision making for group members are very closely related. First and most obvious: be sure you understand the decision to be made. If it is not from your point of view the proper definition of the question, see if it can be more productively focused. Second, be aware of minority opinions. The dissenters may in fact turn out to be right; and even if they are not, the influence of minority opinions on the group is a factor to be respected (see Chapter 2). Third, seek to understand what the responsible individual wants from the group, how he or she is using the group in the decision process. Understand, if possible, why you were included. With this backgroud, you will be able to participate more sensitively and knowledgeably in the specific decision to be made.

Postlude and Prescription

The last several pages of this chapter read like Machiavelli. Their purpose is to help those who may be given responsibility for decisions in an organization to understand some of the dynamics in their relationships with the groups they need to carry out their tasks. And for those who will be members of such groups, the message is carried on the other side of the same coin: observe how you may contribute to the decisions, but also be conscious of how you may be used in that process.

In an administrative setting, the involvement of groups in the decision-making process is both desirable and inevitable; everyone involved will be well served by having the process as open and well understood as possible.

References

Brooks, H. Personal correspondence, January 24, 1983.

Chaffee, E. E. *Rational budgeting? The Stanford case.* Program report No. 82-B3. Institute for Research on Educational Finance and Governance, School of Education, Stanford University, 1982.

Guzzo, R. A. (Ed.) *Improving group decision making in organizations: Approaches from theory and practice.* New York: Academic Press, 1982.

Simon, H. A. *Administrative behavior.* New York: MacMillan, 1961.

INDEX

Arrow's Impossibility Theorem, 110-114

Blackball rule, 144-145
Borda weighting scheme, 101, 106-110
Brainstorming, 271-272; disadvantages of, 272

Coalition formation, 206-211; bandwagon effect and, 210-211; minimum winning coalitions and, 207-210; ritual of unanimity and, 211
Cohesiveness, 51-54, 83-84; advantages of, 53; disadvantages of, 54, 83-84; sources of, 52-53
Communication, channels of, 55-58
Condorcet principle, 109-110
Corporate decision making, 251-279; commercialization and, 277-279; creative problem-solving techniques of, 270-274; decision matrix as aid in, 275-276; examples of, 251-252; role of corporate manager in, 253-257; theories of management and, 253-255

Decision: and extent of agreement required, 38; definition of, 17; reversibility of, 39
Decision matrix, 275-276
Decision rules and processes, 38-41, 142-146

Deindividuation, 71-75; examples of, 74
Deviates, 88-94; minority influence by, 92-94; negative reactions to, 88-91
Diffusion of responsibility, 70-71
Downs's theory of political nomination, 185-192

Ethical group decision making, 115-149; black ball and, 144-145; case study of, 126-142; definition of, 115; group goals and, 116; majority rule and, 144-146; policies and rules in, 117-120; practical reasoning in, 122-126; public advisory committees and, 169-172; role of participation and responsibility in, 116-117; utilitarianism and, 139-140
Ethical norm, 115, 125-126

Fairness, importance of, 19, 211-212
Foreign policy group decision making, 215-249; by Departments of State and Defense, 226-229; availability of information and, 238-239; by executive branch groups, 222-232; Cabinet and, 225-226; crisis and, 232-249; examples of, 80, 82-83, 85, 87, 216-219; importance of actors in, 235-237; National Security Council and, 224-225; outside input in, 239-241; preplanning and, 242-243; role of time in, 237-238; role of White

House in, 223-224; standard scenario of, 243-246; uniqueness of United States in, 219-221; variety of issues in, 232-247

Foreign policy decision-making issues, 232-247; direct security, 232-247; protracted security, 232-247; routine, 232-247

Group: definition of, 16; destructive effects on individual of, 69-94

Group composition: importance of, 24-29; policy decisions and, 165-167

Group consensus: functions of, 75-79; guidelines for avoiding, 259-260; pressures toward, 75-81; social reality and, 77-79

Group decision making: coalition formation and, 206-211; compared to individual decision making, 21-24, 146-148, 260-261, 288-289, 306-309; corporate environment and, 251-279; creative problem-solving techniques for, 270-274; decision matrix as aid in, 275-276; ethical aspects of, 115-150; establishing an effective group and, 258; experimental studies of, 45-46; factors that influence the quality of, 24-41, 46-68; foreign policy and, 215-249; illustrations of, 15-17; increasing the effectiveness of, 66-67, 111-113, 148, 178-179, 212-213, 247-249, 305-310; legal analogy to, 158-160; organizational behavior and, 280-310; political process and, 181-214; preliminary distinctions in, 16-18; program evaluation (PERT) of, 262-270; public policy and, 165-167; quality of, 18-21; sequential process of, 261-262; social psychological perspectives on, 45-68; social risk assessment and, 151-180; step-wise analysis of, 41-44; varieties of foreign policy issues and, 232-241

Group decision: definition of, 17; implications of definition of, 17-18

Group members: foreign policy decision making and, 235-237; influence among, 167-169; openness of, 27-28; personality characteristics of, 25-26, 47-50, 257; power among, 28-29, 300; similarity among, 26-27

Group norms, appropriateness of, 84-86

Group size, 25-26, 54-55, 298

Group tasks, 33-38; and interdependence, 35-37, 50-51; structure of, 34-35; timing of, 37

Groupthink, 79-88, 94; characteristics of, 88, 94; definition of, 80; examples of, 51, 80, 82-83, 85, 87; group size and, 55; leadership and, 86-88; prevention of, 82, 84, 86-87

Implementation, importance of, 44

Juries: composition of, 47-49; experimental study of, 45-46; unanimity rule in, 144

Leadership, 30-33, 58-66; centrality of, 32, 55-57; contingency model of, 62-64; determinants of, 59-61; emergence of, 30-31; idiosyncrasy credit and, 65; risk taking and, 64-66

Leadership style, 32-33, 61-64, 86-88

Minority rule, 146

Organizational decision making, 280-310; characteristics of, 301-304; example of, 281-288; group characteristics and, 298-301; responsible individual and, 295-298, 305, 309; role of authority and power in, 293-295; theories of, 289-294

Pareto principle, 103
PERT/CPM technique of project management, 262-270
Political conventions, 192-213; coalition formation at, 206-211; communication and, 205-206; decision rules and processes of, 204-205; group composition at, 200-202; group leadership and, 202; group tasks and, 202-204
Practical reasoning, 122-126; ethical reasoning differentiated from, 124-125
Presidential nominations, 181-214; caucus method of, 192-193; Downs' theory and, 185-192; methods of, 192-200; political conventions and, 192-213; spatial model of, 182-192
Programmed invention, 272-273

Rationality, acceptable risk and, 173-179
Recombinant DNA controversy, group decision making in, 153-154
Responsible individual, 295-298, 305, 309
Retail location theory, 182-185

Satisfaction and morale, importance of, 20
Social loafing, 70-71
Social risk: acceptability and, 177-179; calculation of, 174-176
Social risk assessment: advisory groups and, 165-169; case study of, 153-154; competing models of, 152, 156-158; decision modalities for, 160-164; definition of, 154-155; dualistic model of, 156-157; functions of, 155-156; group decision making and, 151-180; integrative model of, 157-158; intramural model and, 161; public advisory bodies and, 163-164; role of rationality in, 152, 173-179; special commissions and, 161-162; technical panels and, 162-163
Social risk assessment theory, desiderata of, 177-179
Synectics, 273-274

Theory X, 254, 290-294
Theory Y, 254, 290-294
Theory Z, 254-255

Utilitarianism, ethical decision making and, 139-140
Utility, definition of, 42, 98

Voting: analysis of preferences and, 101-102; Arrow's Impossibility Theorem and, 110-114; Borda weighting scheme in, 101, 106-110; Condorcet principle and, 109-110; criteria for rationality in, 103-109; definition of, 97; group transitivity and, 105; illustrations of, 99-101; independence of irrelevant alternatives and, 106-109; Pareto principle and, 103; positive association and, 106; rational method of, 97-114

ABOUT THE AUTHORS

Hugo Bedau holds a bachelor's degree from the University of Redlands, master's degrees from Boston University and Harvard University, and a doctorate from Harvard. He has taught at Dartmouth College, Princeton University, and Reed College. Since 1966, he has been on the faculty at Tufts University, where he holds the title of Austin Fletcher Professor of Philosophy. He is the author of *The Courts, the Constitution, and Capital Punishment,* coauthor of *Victimless Crimes: Two Views,* and the editor of several other volumes. He is also the author of numerous articles and reviews in philosophical, legal, and political journals and magazines. Bedau has received research grants from the Russell Sage Foundation, the Social Science Research Council, and the National Endowment for the Humanities, travel grants from the Foundation for Research in Philosophy of Science and the American Council of Learned Societies, and fellowships from Harvard Law School and the Danforth Foundation. He is member of the American Philosophical Association, the American Society for Political and Legal Philosophy, the Society for Philosophy and Public Affairs, the American Association of University Professors, and the American Civil Liberties Union, and is listed in Who's Who.

Richard A. Chechile holds a B.S. and M.S. in physics from Case-Western Reserve University and an M.S. and Ph.D. in experimental psychology from the University of Pittsburgh. Chechile has worked in research and development for the General Electric Company, Rockwell International, and Philco Ford. Since 1973, he has been on the faculty of the Psychology Department of Tufts University where he is currently an Associate Professor. The author of many publications in physics and psychology, Chechile is a member of the American Psychological Association, the American Statistical

Association, the Mathematical Psychological Association, the Psychonomic Society, the Scientific Research Society of North America, and Sigma Xi. Currently, he is doing research in the areas of decision theory, mathematical psychology, cognitive psychology, and human factors.

John A. Dunn, Jr., is currently Vice-President for Planning at Tufts University, with responsibility for institutional research and for coordination of program, facilities, and financial plans. He previously held the titles of Board Secretary and Special Assistant to the President. He hold a B.A. from Wesleyan University and an Ed.M. from Harvard University, and came to Tufts after ten years of manufacturing and general management experience.

John S. Gibson is Director, International Relations Program, Tufts University, and is also Professor of Political Science. he received his Ph.D. in international law and comparative jurisprudence at Columbia University and served as director of the World Affairs Council of Rhode Island and also of Boston until he came to Tufts in 1956. He returned in 1963 to become director of the Lincoln Filene Center until 1973 when he assumed leadership in the development of the Tufts International Relations Program. He has authored or coauthored a number of books international affairs and race relations and has been directly involved in the United States Information Agency's International Visitor Program for over thirty years.

Percy H. Hill, holds a B.S. degree in Mechanical Engineering from Rensselaer Polytechnic Institute and a S.M. degree from Harvard University. He is president of two companies, one dealing with the innovation of new products and the other concerned with consulting in the human factors area. Since 1948, he has been on the faculty at Tufts University, where he holds the title of Professor of Engineering Design. Hill is a registered professional engineer in Massachusetts and New Hampshire and holds patents on Johnson & Johnson's Reach toothbrush. The author of many publications involving engineering, mathematics, and design, Hill is a member of the American Association of University Professors, the American Society for Engineering Education, the American Society of Mechanical Engineers, the national honor societies Tau Beta Pi and Sigma Xi, and the Human Factors Society. The recipient of the

Frank Oppenheimer Award for 1968, the Distinguished Service Award in 1977, and the Fred Merryfield Design Award in 1982 from the American Society for Engineering Education, Hill is listed in Who's Who in American Education, Engineers of Distinction, Who's Who is Technology Today, Who's Who in Engineering, and Who's Who in Consulting.

Sheldon Krimsky, Associate Professor of Urban and Environmental Policy at Tufts, received his B.S. and M.S. in physics and his doctorate in philosophy from Boston University. He completed a year of post-doctoral studies in economics and environmental policy and has taught at Boston University, the University of South Florida, SUNY at Stony Brook, and Wesleyan University. Dr. Krimsky served on the NIH Recombinant DNA Advisory Committee and the Cambridge, Massachusetts Experimentation Review Board, which drafted the first legislation regulating recombinant DNA research in the United States. Currently engaged in a study for the Science Council of Canada on regulatory and policy issues in biotechnology, he recently started the International Network on the Social Impacts of Biotechnology. He has written widely on policy and regulatory issues of biotechnology. *Genetic Alchemy: The Social History of the Recombinant DNA Controvery* was published by the MIT press in 1982.

Jeffrey Z. Rubin holds a B.A. in biology from Antioch College and a doctorate in psychology from Teachers College, Columbia University. Since 1969, he has been on the faculty at Tufts University, where he is professor of psychology and director of the Tufts Center for Decision Making. He received the American Psychological Association's Young Psychologists Award of 1969, the John Simon Guggenheim Memorial Foundation Fellowship in 1977-78, and numerous research grants. He is author of many scholarly articles in the areas of third-party negotiation and entrapment, and has authored and edited numerous books, most recently *Dynamics of Third-Party Intervention* (Praeger) and *Social Psychology, Second Edition* with Bertram Raven (Wiley).

Bradbury Seasholes is Associate Professor of Political Science at Tufts University. A graduate of Oberlin College and the University of North Carolina, he has authored and edited works on black politics, political socialization, voting, campaign finance, state government, and urban issues. While Director of Political Studies at the University's Lincoln Filene Center for Citizenship and Public Affairs, Seasholes was selected by the U.S. State Department's American Specialist Program to lecture in Asia on American Presidential elections. He has served as campaign and policy consultant to several congressional and local candidates and officeholders. Since 1970, he has been the Massachusetts elections analyst for ABC News.

Walter C. Swap received his B.A. from Harvard and Ph.D. in Social Psychology from the University of Michigan. He has been on the Tufts faculty since 1971, where he currently is Associate Professor and Chairman of the Department of Psychology. He has published in the areas of attitude change, interpersonal attraction, and personality theory. In 1983, he was the recipient of the Lillian Leibner award for excellence in teaching.